THE
ANTIQUE
COLLECTOR'S
HANDBOOK

THE ANTIQUE COLLECTOR'S HANDBOOK

HOW TO RECOGNISE, COLLECT AND ENJOY ANTIQUES

Anne Stone

in association with
ANTIQUE COLLECTOR

EBURY PRESS
LONDON

First published 1981 by Ebury Press
National Magazine House
72 Broadwick Street
London W I V 2BP

ISBN 0 85223 199 7

Designed by Harry Green
Drawings by Chris Evans

Filmset and printed in
Great Britain by
BAS Printers Limited, Over Wallop, Hampshire
and bound by
Cambridge University Press

Contents

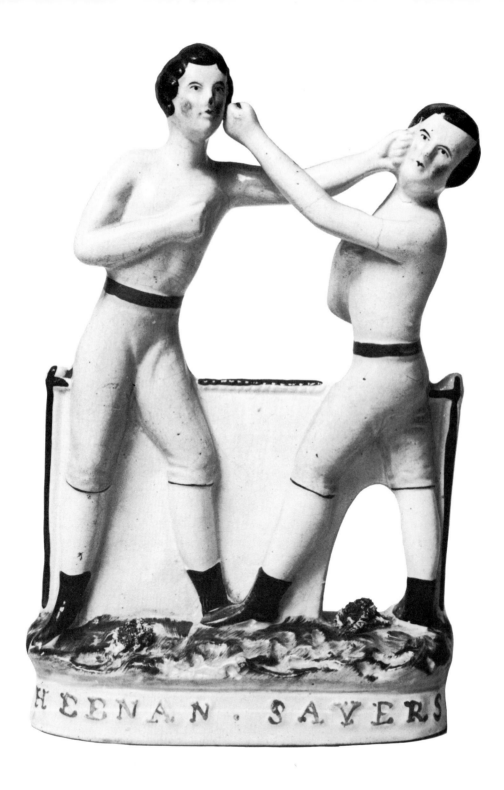

HEENAN · SAYERS

Introduction

Staffordshire portrait group of champion boxers, John Heenan of America and fighting Tom Sayers of Britain. The contest took place in April 1860, at Farnborough, Hampshire, in characteristic attire and without the aid of modern boxing gloves. *c* 1860.

This book was prompted by the difficulty of finding a general work on antiques suitable for the many interested, but often bemused, beginners who attend my classes. The spectrum of antiques is vast, and over the years a corresponding body of literature has built up so that now, faced with the shelves devoted to antiques in a bookshop or library, the choice can be overwhelming. Many of these books, however, are highly specialised – usually dealing with a specific category, such as furniture or silver – while others provide a more scholarly examination of a particular class or example of antique, perhaps the work of an individual designer or factory. For the newcomer to the history of decorative arts, often undecided about what he likes most and unsure about where to begin, the task of ploughing through a lengthy reading list can appear daunting and thus becomes set aside as a future task. This book endeavours to shorten that reading list by squeezing a large amount of information into one volume, in the hope that the beginner won't be discouraged in his attempt to start what is, even for the experts, the never-ending process of learning about antiques.

To aid our purpose, the book is divided into four chapters, each dealing with one of four centuries, from the 17th to the 20th. Each chapter is sub-divided into three sections. The first section serves as an introduction to the period; it provides a brief glimpse at the people who made and the society who used the various objects which, with the passage of time, have become today's antiques. It is interesting and amusing to notice the number of 'antiques' – originally sold as cheap, inconsequential frivolities – which now enjoy a considerably elevated social and financial status. We also look at the houses they lived in, both inside and out. For two hundred years ago, people structured their homes and interiors in quite a different way to that which is commonly assumed to be comfortable today. The middle section of each chapter – these four middle sections form the principal part of the book – looks at the stylistic changes which occurred in the five main areas of the decorative arts during the century under consideration. Finally, there is a brief section providing useful tips for the aspiring purchaser – whether he is buying from an auction room, a dealer, or a market stall – and for those happy people, the explorers of attics and rescuers of rubbish, who find booty in old tiles and bottles and match boxes.

My thanks are gratefully extended to the many people involved in the writing and production of this book. I am particularly indebted to Brian Coultas, my editor Susie Ward, Dr Heidelberger and Maureen Ashman, who have given invaluable advice, criticism and encouragement over many points which required clarification. And finally to my students, without whose questions and curiosity my own knowledge of, and interest in, antiques would cease to expand so quickly.

PART ONE

The Seventeenth Century

The Seventeenth Century
Historical and Social Background

The death of Elizabeth I in 1603 brought an end to the Tudor dynasty and an end to the last truly English monarch to sit upon the English throne. The accession of James I saw the establishment of the house of Stuart for the rest of the 17th century and unified forever Scotland, England and Wales into the Britain that we know today. After the long harmonious period of stability under 'that Bright Occidental Star, Queen Elizabeth' life under the early Stuarts saw a marked decline. Deepening recession, hardly aided by James I's carefree and lavish gifts to both favourites and foreigners, and the gradual but continuous abrogation by the monarch of affairs of state – long held to be the concern of Parliament – could only bring about a state of crises. The succession of Charles I on the death of his father in 1625 did nothing to improve the sense of impending strife. Furthermore the growing religious divisions between Puritan and Catholic were only worsened by the sympathies of the court, headed by a Catholic Queen, Henrietta Maria. The early Stuarts' sincere belief in the Divine Right of Kings to govern unimpeded was shattered by the outbreak of Civil War in 1642, with traditional royalists fighting new parliamentarians.

The Civil War and after

The Parliamentary forces, headed by Oliver Cromwell, emerged successful after the battle of Naseby in 1645, displacing the legal sovereign, Charles I. The King, believing to the last in his own absolute authority and in the rightness of his cause, was executed on a chill January day in 1649. His beheading took place under the shadow of the recently-completed Banqueting House (finished 1622), which ironically had been conceived as a magnificent focus of the new royal palace intended to glorify the power of the crown.

Life under Cromwell and his generals was dour. Factions of extreme Puritans brought about the closure of theatres, fairs, and the outlawing of any sort of festivity. For a time even the doors of churches were closed, sending the Anglican church into exile. Superstition and hysteria instigated appalling witchhunts, which reached their peak during the years 1645–47. Many fled the country to join the royal family in exile, though some like the diarist John Evelyn, returned to the country intermittently in order to administer their own estates – if they had not been sequestered – and perhaps watch over the affairs of others unable to return. For those who did travel abroad, many chose to live in centres such as Paris, or at Versailles where the brilliant court of Louis XIV offered a base to the homeless English court. Holland, with its tolerant background and bourgeois affluence, was another haven for English exiles. But others filled these restless years in travelling extensively to countries hitherto little known, such as Spain and Italy.

The Restoration—a return to beauty

The death of Cromwell in 1658 heralded the return of the King from exile. On May 29th 1660 John Evelyn wrote in his diary 'this day, his Majesty, Charles the Second, came to London after a sad and long exile and calamitous suffering both of the King and of the Church . . . This was also his birthday and with a triumph of above 20,000 horse and foot, brandishing their swords, and shouting with inexpressible joy; the ways strewed with flowers, the bells ringing, the streets hung with tapestry; fountains running with wine . . . the windows and balconies, all set with ladies; trumpets, music and myriads of people flocking, even so far as from Rochester, so as they were seven hours in passing the city . . . I stood in the Strand and beheld it, and blessed God.'

Charles II reigned from 1660 to 1685, presiding over a gay, loose-living court which seemed to do its best to dispel forever the awful realities of the Civil War and its aftermath. Gifts from abroad, celebrating the king's restoration, were showered upon the new monarch. Among them was the famed Queen's bed, which according to Evelyn was 'an embroidery of silver on crimson velvet, and cost £8,000 being a present made by the States of Holland, when his Majesty returned.'

The political dilemmas which had brought about the Civil War had not been solved either by Cromwell or by Charles II and on the latter's death in 1685 were once again brought to a head on the accession of his younger brother James II. Charles had always remained ambivalent on the question of his religious affiliation. So long as he appeared to support the English Protestant Church his position seemed secure. But James II openly professed himself a Catholic and within three years of his accession this proved to be his downfall. A return to the Catholic faith was assured for future generations of Stuarts, following the birth of a son to Mary of Modena, James's young second wife.

The Glorious Revolution

The Glorious Revolution of 1688 brought no bloodshed in its wake. The crown was offered jointly to James's Protestant elder daughter, Mary (born to his first wife, Anne Hyde) and her Dutch prince, William of Orange. But the condition of acceptance was that the new monarchs should rule by and through Parliament, banishing forever the possibility of absolute monarchy and of the tyrannical despotism which the kingship of Charles I had threatened. It was the beginning of the kind of constitutional monarchy still practised today. The reign was stable and successful and under William III's outstanding military leadership. England became once more a real power in Europe. Queen Mary, William's wife, had tragically died of smallpox in 1694, illustrating the very real dangers of disease

Dark red earthenware jug with white slip decoration applied to the body. It is glazed with a thick treacle-like lead glaze. Wrotham, dated 1674.

and sickness in the 17th century. The problem had reached critical proportions during the Great Plague of 1665. Evelyn speaks of '10,000 poor creatures perishing weekly' in London. 'I went all along the city and suburbs from Kent Street to St James's, a dismal passage, and dangerous to see so many coffins exposed in the streets, now thin of people; the shops shut up and all in mournful silence, not knowing whose turn might be next.'

Silvered mirror carved with fruit, flowers and cherubs. Silvering was as fashionable as gilding in the second half of the 17th century. c 1670.

The death of William in 1702 brought the ascent of Queen Anne, Mary's younger sister, to the throne. The military successes on the Continent begun by William continued under his niece. Such victories as Blenheim (1704), Ramillies, Oudenarde and Malplacquet were gained under the brilliant generalship of John Churchill who was elevated to the peerage and created Duke of Marlborough in 1702. A grateful nation poured thousands of pounds into the building of the Marlborough home, Blenheim Palace, one of the finest examples of English baroque architecture, conceived more as a 'monument for the Queen's glory than a private habitation for the Duke'.

Seventeenth-Century Interiors and Furnishings

One of the most important architects in the 17th century was Inigo Jones, architect to both the early Stuart monarchs. His buildings were the first true expression of Italian Renaissance architectural principles to be seen in England and reflected a total sense of harmony, balance and order, both internally and externally. Hitherto, a symmetrically arranged façade had borne no real relationship to the disposition of the rooms behind it, which rambled in a muddled way through the interior of the building. Despite the achievement of his masterpieces, such as the Banqueting Hall and the Queen's House at Greenwich (1617–35) – the one a public building, the other domestic – a number of houses based on earlier Jacobean models continued to be built. Great houses such as Hatfield (begun 1607), and Blickling Hall – contemporary with the Queen's House – were designed and built well into the first half of the century. Both contained a number, if not all, of the conventional, old-fashioned, features in the form of Hall, High Great Chamber and Long Gallery. In contrast, the new model, begun by Jones and developed after the Civil War, showed great novelty and imagination of treatment.

Scattered influences from a returning court

The Italianate influence – seen principally in the regular, carefully-controlled proportion and symmetry of the entire building – dominated the new models of architecture during the first half of the century. But with the Restoration of King Charles II in 1660 a number of other influences became immediately visible, most of them brought back by returning exiles from countries such as France and Holland. In particular the Dutch influence was to be seen in the slightly curved, slanted roof, dominant central pediments, and the introduction of the sash window which replaced the old-fashioned casement type. Houses which had been built along the lines of earlier traditional designs were modernised, especially during the aftermath of the Restoration in 1660, a period of national confidence and optimism. Rebuilding and redecorating programmes were widespread, and the vocation of architect took on an added dimension.

One such 'revitalised' house was Ham House in Surrey, first begun by Sir Thomas Vavasour in 1610. In the 1670's the Countess of Dysart began to alter what was a straightforward early Jacobean house. Originally based on an H-plan, distinguished by the addition of a pair of turrets rising above the roof line, it became a house displaying much more classical lines. Oval niches placed above symmetrically arranged ground-floor windows were filled with classical busts. The roof was altered to a much more fashionable straight slant roof with a bold cornice.

Page 14: The Entrance Hall, Nether Lypiatt,
Gloucestershire. Although the house was built by
Judge Cox in about 1705, it owes much in its design
to the architecture of the mid-17th century, and in
particular to the work of Sir Roger Pratt. The
Entrance Hall is lavishly fitted with costly panelling
in chestnut, and centres on a finely carved
mantelpiece made from local greystone. The
furniture was added in the early 1900s, but
principally consists of 17th-century pieces.
(Courtesy of Country Life)

Wainscot, or panel back, chair with elaborately
carved cresting and ears (lugs), with stretchers
running typically close to the ground. First quarter
17th century.

The legacy of Wren and Vanbrugh

The most distinguished architect working at the end of the 17th century was Sir
Christopher Wren, closely followed by two equally-prominent figures, Sir John
Vanbrugh and Nicholas Hawksmoor. All three made significant contributions
to the baroque style of architecture which developed late in the 17th century.
But the crowning achievements of Vanbrugh were not realised until the grand
designs of Blenheim and Castle Howard in Yorkshire were built during the early
years of the 18th century.

Baroque was a variant of the classical style in use since the second quarter of
the century. But instead of imparting a sense of harmony and tranquility it
cultivated a sense 'of dynamic movement through composition in mass, the use
of curvaceous forms and exuberant decoration, and a bold contrasted stress on
light and shade.' Such drama was highly visual in its appeal, designed to impress
the beholder through powerful forms.

Inner harmony – the 17th-century ideal

But if the exterior of buildings at the close of the century appeared dramatic –
with their broken skylines, focusing on a central block and richly rusticated
surface treatment – interiors were no less so. The 17th century saw a general
but perceptible increase in comfort combined with an ostentious display of
formal luxury. Life amongst the aristocracy, and to a lesser extent the
increasingly influential gentry, was relatively formal, particularly for those at
court. This formality extended beyond the sphere of the court to the country
house, which was intended to provide domestic accommodation for the family
and servants as well as suitable rooms for lavish entertainment. In many houses
the lord and lady of the manor were housed in separate but equal state and
accorded their own suite of rooms, for marriages in the 17th century were often
made for social and material conveniences rather than for love. Individuals were
accorded a number of rooms, linked together by interconnecting doors rather
than a passage, an idea that was greatly developed in France in the middle of the
17th century.

The number of rooms varied, depending on the wealth and social status of the
owner, but at the very least there would have been an initial chamber which
might be used as a dressing room or a withdrawing room. This would be
followed by a bedchamber and beyond that a small, luxuriously-appointed but
cosy room referred to as the closet. The closet was of all the rooms the most
private, and was the one room in which the occupier might pursue his or her
own interests – writing letters, reading or studying undisturbed.

In a palace, the number of rooms increased and several withdrawing rooms

Late 17th-century oak trestle table joined by a central stretcher. The trestle table was the forerunner of the joined table popular during the 17th century. About 1685.

might precede the bedchamber, which was generally called a State Bedchamber or the Grand Bedchamber in anticipation of an important occupant. The withdrawing room was more like an antechamber. It doubled up as a waiting room or reception in which foreign ambassadors were received, and it was sometimes dignified by the presence of a throne.

The bedchamber was the most important room and was decorated accordingly. It had little of the private connotation it has today, and was frequently used for meetings and friendly appointments. It was, for example, quite acceptable for the lady of a house to receive visitors while still in bed.

Furnishings to furniture

Architectural features, such as doors, windows and fireplaces were given elaborate treatment in the 17th-century interior. Doors placed in corresponding positions in each room emphasised the feeling of parading through the apartment as the visitor progressed from one room to the next. Fireplaces, though somewhat lighter in treatment than the massive architectural edifices found in early Jacobean houses, nevertheless continued to rise from floor to ceiling. A mirror or painted panels were sometimes used to decorate the space over the mantel in much the same way as they were used above doors. To complete the effect, they were surrounded by festoons and swags of finely carved flowers, fruit and trophies of game. Most famous among the artisans who produced such carvings was Grinling Gibbons, but the comparable skills of the London carver Edward Pierce can be found in the decoration of the great staircase at Sudbury Hall, Derbyshire, one of the finest of its type executed in the 17th century.

There was no shortage of luxury materials for use in the 17th-century interior. Walnut, kingwood and ebony were the most prestigious timbers used in furniture-making, but large areas of cheap panelled wood were frequently 'grained' in imitation of the more expensive woods. Floors were commonly of cedar or oak and were left unpolished to facilitate ease of cleaning (scrubbing with damp sand), although in a few rooms geometric parquetry floors were laid. Scagliola, a type of imitation marble, was used for fireplace surrounds and marble brought in at great cost was used for flooring. Ceilings were divided into compartments, the ribs of which were decorated in stucco with classical bay leaves after the style introduced by Inigo Jones, and grandiose allegorical schemes were painted on walls and ceilings. In minor rooms the treatment was less elaborate. Walls and floors were often left plain or continued to exhibit the type of wainscoting familiar since the previous century.

Unlike the earlier part of the 17th century, furniture was arranged in an increasingly formal way following the Restoration. Chairs and stools deployed in rigid lines along the wall were upholstered in fabrics designed to match the wall hangings and the rich brocades or velvets on the bed. Suites of matched furniture, including a table, mirror and pair of candlestands, were placed against the pier wall. Mirror plate was both expensive and necessary in the 17th century. Its cost made its display ostentatious, but its presence increased the light in dark corners of the room, while at night it threw back the soft glimmer of the candles placed on top of the shoulder-high stands.

Seventeenth-Century Furniture

Single chair made during the second quarter of the 17th century and called a back stool. It is sometimes described now as a farthingale chair.

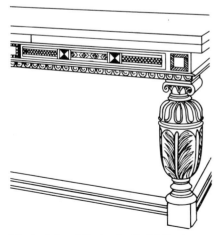

Joined oak draw-table showing English Renaissance ornament in the legs (cup and cover motif, surmounted by Ionic capitals), and an inlaid chequer pattern along the frieze. *c* 1600.

The evolution of 17th-century furniture styles can be broken into two distinct categories: the first developed in the early Stuart period from 1603 and continued up to the middle of the century, and the second began with the Restoration of Charles II in 1660.

Woods and decoration

In the early part of the 17th century there is little to distinguish between the forms and styles of Jacobean furniture and the preceding Elizabethan forms. This is particularly so with middle class furniture; while furniture made for the aristocracy signposts prevailing fashions, middle class furniture tended to lag behind and reflected – in the greater simplicity of form and ornamentation – the smaller pocket of the purchaser.

The most widely-used timber was oak, or wainscot (imported oak), although other indigenous woods such as ash, elm, beech, holly, fruitwoods and even walnut were used. Carved decoration – in the form of split turnings and columnar mouldings – was often applied to the surface of the furniture, but the cup and cover motif developed in Elizabethan times continued as a popular device. This gradually became less bulbous in the early 17th century but was still widely used to decorate the end posts on four-poster beds, massive dining tables or the newly introduced draw leaf table, and court cupboards. Other sculptural motifs included highly carved figures taken from heraldry or mythology, although these were generally reserved for finer pieces. There was also a tendency to cover flat surfaces of furniture with a type of low relief carving. Panels on chairbacks, chests, doors and even friezes on tables

were often decorated in this way. Repeat patterns were used for this type of carving, and often took the form of rather curiously translated Renaissance ornament such as gadrooning, guilloche

Carved and turned oak chair characteristic of Yorkshire-Derbyshire. It is sometimes called a mortuary chair when a motif commemorating Charles I appears on the cresting.

patterns and acanthus leaves. Another form widely used during this early half of the 17th century, although it was to fall gradually out of favour in the second half, was a type of shallow carving in the form of strapwork – literally the curling forms of cut leather straps – arcading and floral motifs.

Colour played an important part in decoration. It was achieved by a variety of means, including the use of paint, gilding and silvering; but inlay woods such as ebony, holly, boxwood, bog oak and fruitwood are found on contemporary pieces from both London and the provincial towns. The pattern which commonly adorned the back panels of armchairs and

Three-tiered sideboard called a court cupboard, used to display family silver in the Great Hall or Great Chamber and often elaborately carved and decorated. c 1600–25.

Oak joined stool made in about 1630. 17th-century examples are expensive and rare. Many good copies were made in the 19th century and are much cheaper.

Early domestic bookcase in oak of similar form to the first recorded example made for Samuel Pepys, the diarist, in 1666. Such pieces of this period are rare.

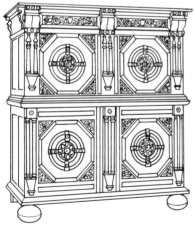

Chest of drawers with a shallow drawer in the frieze, a deep drawer in the middle section and three shallow drawers concealed behind doors in the bottom. Dated 1653.

bedheads varied – from trailing foliage and flowers to a variety of boldly executed geometric patterns. Even pictorial and heraldic representations were not unknown.

Households were still sparsely furnished in the 17th century, but would have included a variety of chairs, stools, benches (settles were also found in more humble homes) and tables, as well as a more prized and expensive piece like a court cupboard, press cupboard or, costliest item of all, the great four-poster bed. But seat furniture was certainly the largest single category and the joined stool the most common form of seating in the 17th century.

Restoration furniture

Following the restoration of Charles II, furniture became lighter in appearance and a greater variety was quickly introduced. While oak continued to be used for the more humble pieces made by the joiner and country craftsmen, walnut imported from France and the American colonies rapidly became the fashionable timber. However, it was the introduction from the Continent of new cabinet-making skills which revolutionised furniture-making techniques in the second half of the 17th century. Even so, the influence of the joiner in middle class furniture-making continued to dominate the production of vernacular styles, despite the emergence of the cabinet maker. The speciality of the cabinet maker was the production of flat surfaces capable of taking veneers. Decorative patterns were achieved by the use of marquetry and parquetry. Early examples of marquetry are characterised by a large open sort of pattern but by the close of the 17th-century decoration had become noticeably refined. An abstract style called arabesque, seaweed or endive marquetry was popular.

The adoption of a more luxurious and comfortable way of life in the post-restoration period saw the introduction of several new types of furniture. Daybeds,

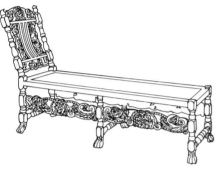

Walnut daybed with carved decoration and a caned seat. This would be covered with a cushion, fixed by tapes tied beneath the caning. *c* 1675.

often made *en suite* with chairs and stools, and winged armchairs sometimes equipped with adjustable backs by the addition of iron ratchets – referred to in inventories as 'sleeping chayres' – were among these innovations. Personal items such as dressing mirrors supported on rectangular-shaped box stands, equipped with a drawer underneath, reflected a gradual increase in a range of smaller, more feminine pieces. Elaborately veneered and carved wall mirrors were made in increasing numbers despite the high cost of buying mirror plate. Less flamboyant examples made immediately after the return of the king boasted discreet ripple moulding. Furniture designed for letter writing came in the form of small gate-leg writing tables with elaborately spiral turned legs, as well as scriptoires and writing cabinets equipped with pigeon holes and drawers, supported on waist-high stands.

The range of so-called 'India wares'

imported from the Orient by the East India Company led to the widespread use of woven cane in the second half of the 17th century. This technique was generally used on chair seats and back panels but was also to be found on table tops and even candlestands. Carved decoration was still widely used in the second half of the 17th century – although it began to take on a different form – exhibiting a preference for turning, both bobbin and spiral (barley twist), as well as the more sculptural scrolling shapes of the S form. Chairs too were carved in an increasingly elaborate way but while early examples in the reign of Charles II appear rather square and crude in execution, those made at the end of the century are distinguished by refinement in the carving and an elegance brought about by the greatly increased height of the chair backs. Other modish imports were lacquer panels, often later made up into cabinets, but the

Oak-topped double gate leg table capable of seating six people. The base is of walnut and shows the characteristic turned legs and stretchers popular during the Restoration.

Walnut armchair with spiral-turned supports and caned back and seat. This style was introduced shortly after the restoration of Charles II. *c* 1665.

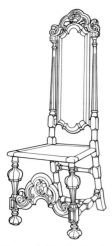

A carved and painted chair showing the increased height of back and narrower proportions favoured in the late 17th century. c 1695.

Walnut chair with elaborately carved and pierced back in a style associated with Daniel Marot, court architect/designer to William III. c 1695.

More elaborate candlestands began to appear following the Restoration and this late 17th-century example, carved and gilded, is very French in taste. Torcheres are usually about 4 ft in height. c 1695.

Cabinet on stand with marquetry decoration in differently coloured woods. These were luxury items intended to hold valuable curiosities. About 1675.

prohibitive cost of the process meant that it was soon imitated by a cheaper technique known as English japanning. For more practical wear, chests of drawers were made in increasing numbers. These were often made along traditional lines established earlier in the century. Decoration in the form of applied mouldings, giving such pieces an architectural appearance, was used up to the end of the century. Large numbers were made by joiners working in simple oak but more elaborate pieces were also made, either veneered or decorated in fashionable woods such as walnut and ebony.

Continental influences

During the final decade of the 17th century furniture design reflected Continental trends, with special influence exerted by work of the court designer Daniel Marot. Upholstery played an increasingly important part in much seat furniture and particularly in bed designs. This emphasis away from the carved surface of wood was also to be seen in the replacement of spiral and scrolling shapes with the introduction of straight forms. This was particularly noticeable on the legs of chairs and tables, where a simple mushroom capping at the top of the leg would often provide the only form of decoration. Such simplicity was to anticipate the styles of Queen Anne's reign at the beginning of the 18th century.

Seventeenth-Century Pottery

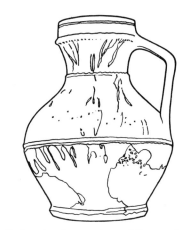

Buff-coloured earthenware jug partially covered with a green lead-glaze. Lead-based glazes were in use from the 9th to the 19th century. 16th century.

Prior to the 17th century, English earthenware production was restricted to a very simple, even crude, form of pottery. Decoration was correspondingly simple and was largely confined to the use of lead glazes. These came by their haphazard colour through the addition of oxidised metals – for example copper filings, which resulted in a green tint. Designs were restricted either to removing the clay by scratching or cutting the surface or by adding clay to the surface in the form of applied slipware decoration.

Peasant pottery

The latter form of decoration was widely used throughout the 17th century by a number of pottery centres in Kent, London and Staffordshire. These wares, made of red and white clays, are sometimes also described as 'peasant pottery' or peasant wares. A slip is a finely ground clay, often of a contrasting colour to the base ware. It is watered down to a thick liquid consistency and applied to the object in much the same way as icing is piped onto a cake, through the end of a spout or a nozzle. Although this method of decoration was familiar from Medieval times onwards, the earliest identified centre for this type of 17th-century peasant ware was at the Wrotham potteries situated between Maidstone and Sevenoaks, Kent. On the site a piece has been found dating back to 1612. The last known item to be confidently dated is from 1739. Many of the pieces made at the Wrotham potteries are marked with the name of the pottery, together with the name or initials of either the potter or person for whom the piece was intended. A number of pieces were intended not for ordinary domestic use but to celebrate an important oc-

Earthenware tyg, or three-handled mug, with applied slip decoration. The cottage loaves used as finials on the handles are typical of Wrotham wares. Dated 1621.

casion such as a betrothal, a wedding or even a christening. Although it is known that a number of ordinary wares, such as bricks, tiles and plain-glazed plates, cups and breadpans, were in general production, only a few hundred of the more fanciful examples remain. These double-handled mugs, jugs, candlesticks and dishes are now generally beyond the pocket of the average purchaser.

The type of lead-glazed clays used at Wrotham were of a rich red-brown on dark brown colour. Early examples of slip-ware decoration were less elaborate than those pieces made in the middle of the 17th century. The slip was often applied in the form of impressed blobs depicting rosettes, flowers, stars and raspberries. Later, plaited ropes of slip were twined round elaborately looped handles, and dashes of slip applied to the rims of plates and the edges of handles gave the appearance of being stitched on.

After Wrotham, the next pottery centre making similarly-decorated slip wares was situated in the London area. These

Miniature cradle in lead-glazed earthenware, decorated with slip-trailed patterns. It was either given as a gift on the birth of a child or used to help fecundity. c 1700 (L 10¾ in.).

products, often described as Metropolitan wares, are known to have been made over a period roughly contemporary with the

23

Commonwealth – from about 1640 to 1660. Made of a lighter coloured red-brown clay than that found at Wrotham and decorated with a contrasting white slip, these pieces reflect the sober attitudes of many Puritans with deeply held religious convictions. Although dashes are less vigorous than those on contemporary Wrotham wares, Metropolitan pieces frequently carried exhortations of a pious nature: 'Of earth I am et tes most tru. Destain me not for so are you' is the inscription on one chamber pot. Other articles included jugs, mugs and bowls bearing reminders of man's own frailty such as 'Remember thy end truly' and 'Watch and Pray'. Like the wares from Wrotham, Metropolitan pieces are sought after today – and perhaps because of their scarcity rather than through any aesthetic considerations, they command high prices.

The rise of Staffordshire

Whilst the London potteries may have been brought to an abrupt end by the fire of London in 1666, after which little mention of them is made, the production of slipwares was carried on further north in Staffordshire. The rise of Staffordshire as the leading centre of English pottery production from the 17th century coincided with the increasing use of coal-fired furnaces to overcome the dwindling supplies of timber.

Several names are particularly associated with these Staffordshire slipwares from the middle of the century onwards, such as William and Ralph Simpson, Richard Meer (Meir), the Glass family and Thomas and Ralph Toft. Of special interest is the appearance of the Toft family name, which has caused these slipwares

Large ornamental earthenware dish, decorated with red slip-trailed patterns on a yellow lead-glazed ground. Made and signed by Thomas Toft, a famous Staffordshire potter. c 1675 (D 17¼ in.).

Blue-dash charger, so-called because of the border decoration. It displays a favourite biblical subject, Adam and Eve, painted in polychrome colours. c. 1650–75.

to be known sometimes as Toftware. As with other slipwares, only the more elaborate decorative pieces survive today, such as the large decorated dishes or chargers. However, unlike Wrotham wares these Staffordshire pieces are rarely datable. The chargers are frequently decorated with a delicately trailed trellis-work pattern on the broad, flat rim. Bold designs are portrayed in the middle, or well, of the dish and include a wide variety of subjects: formal bird and plant designs, mermaids, and important national figures such as the King and Queen.

Tin-glazed earthenware and stoneware

Tin-glazed earthenware, or delftware, was introduced to England during the second half of the 16th century. It did not become well established, however, until the early years of the 17th century. By the end of the first quarter (c 1625–30), an identifiable English style had developed. London was to dominate the production of tin-glazed earthenware throughout the

17th century, although other centres sprang up from the time of the Restoration onwards. It was noted in 1698 that there were '7 white Earthenware houses about London, two at Bristoll – and one at Norwich, which is since broke'. Tin-glazed pottery, also described as tin-enamelled pottery, is characterised by a dense white body colour which chips

Tin-glazed earthenware dish decorated with the newly introduced tulip as a central motif in polychrome, high-temperature, colours. Probably made in Bristol. c 1675–1700.

Blue-dash charger in tin-glazed earthenware, showing equestrian portrait of William III, a keen horseman. *c* 1690.

Tin-glazed earthenware blue dash charger, commonly called English delftware. This example painted in blue, green and yellow has a portrait of William III. *c* 1700.

easily, revealing the red-brown clay underneath. This opaque background is achieved by adding oxide of tin to a glaze and provides a good background for painting. It is still in use today, and is found particularly on the traditional tin-glaze wares made in Italy called Maiolica. But even there the rising cost of tin has led some potters to use other less-expensive substitutes. Typical of the large decorative chargers are the floral motifs – including the newly introduced tulip – and portraits of later Stuart Monarchs, especially William III mounted on a spirited rearing horse. Both these designs were typical of the last three decades of the century. Earlier ones included fruit painted with a background of leaves, biblical scenes – the Fall was a particular favourite – and a number of boldly-drawn geometric designs.

Stoneware is a distinctive form of pottery still produced today for domestic use. Many modern oven-to-table pieces are stoneware. It is made from a highly refractory clay which can be fired at a high temperature (1200° – 1400°), without danger of the pot collapsing in the kiln. It is much more versatile and resilient than pottery fired at a lower temperature. In addition to being impervious to liquids, it is capable of being cut and turned on a lapidary wheel, although its slightly rough and abrasive surface tends to be a drawback. This roughness is commonly overcome by giving the stoneware a thin glassy surface by throwing salt into the kiln during the firing. At high temperatures salt vitrifies and coats the object with a thin glassy surface.

Stoneware had been known in England since the 16th century, when quantities began to be imported from Germany. Although at least two partnerships received patents to manufacture stoneware during the early part of the 17th century, then often described as Cologne ware, nothing survives of these early factories. It was not until the appearance of John Dwight in 1671 that English stoneware production finally developed.

Dwight and the Fulham pottery

Dwight (*c* 1633 – 1703) was an Oxford-educated man who, like many of his contemporaries, brought a scientific approach to his chosen field of interest. Although he trained as an ecclesiastical lawyer, in which capacity he served the Bishop of Chester, he soon made clear his avowed intention of improving quality by both producing stoneware and by imitating the then-fashionable Chinese porcelain which was being imported. This is reflected in the patent he obtained on 14th April, 1671, which gave him the exclusive right to manufacture a 'transparent ware commonly known by the names of Porcellaine or China Persian ware'. The patent also notes his right to make 'stoneware, vulgarly called cologne ware'.

Dwight established his Fulham factory in 1672, but few of its products which can be attributed with any certainty remain.

Salt-glazed stoneware wine bottle of a characteristic everyday type, found on the site of John Dwight's pottery in Fulham. The applied decoration may refer to a named inn. *c* 1680.

Red, unglazed, stoneware mug with applied relief decoration in the form of sprigs of flowers. The high quality of this piece suggest it may have been made at the Elers factory. *c* 1695.

It is probable that he believed himself to have discovered the art of making true porcelain, since some pieces – notably mugs – made of a whitish-coloured salt-glazed stoneware (an imitation of *blanc de Chine*) were so finely potted that the thin walls are almost transparent. At the same time he was experimenting with kneading together different coloured clays to produce a 'marbled' or 'agate' effect. Similar agatewares were to become fashionable around the middle of the next century.

Despite Dwight's success in renewing his original patent when it expired in 1684, it was not long before others were imitating his products. In 1693–4 he fought a number of actions against potters infringing his rights, among whom were the Netherland-born brothers David and John Elers. The Elers were silversmiths turned potters, who arrived in England in about 1688 and initially worked in Fulham before at least one of them moved north to Staffordshire in 1693. They are noteworthy for making a type of unglazed rich red-brown stoneware of a standard never before seen. The majority of items were small straight-sided tea caddies in the shape of tea bottles, tea pots, cups and saucers, and globular-shaped mugs decorated with finely proportioned and well-spaced sprigs of flowers. Although the brothers were known to be in London by about 1700, it is probable that the very high standard of their work – particularly of that made in Staffordshire – inspired later potters. Certainly by the the 18th century the Staffordshire potteries were famous for the quality of their products.

Seventeenth-Century Silver

Since the Middle Ages, the brilliant artistic and technical expertise of the silversmith had made his work more highly prized than that of almost any other craftsman. Coveted for its intrinsic beauty, it was – perhaps more importantly–also valued as a vehicle of wealth and power; a very visible form of wealth which could be displayed in all its dazzling magnificence as it gleamed on groaning boards.

Scarcity of an important heritage

But examples of silverplate made before and during the first half of the 17th century are now increasingly rare and very little is to be found outside private collections and museums. The reasons for the disappearance of what was once a prodigious amount of important and historic items are manifold. The impact of the Civil War (1642–49), when quantities of silver plate was either forcibly sequestered or voluntarily given up in support of either side, is the reason usually cited. But the drain on silver actually had begun much earlier. A large amount disappeared following the dissolution of the monasteries, the wars of the late 16th century, and the extravagant handouts of James I.

The waywardness and lavish disposals of King James I (1603–25) from the Royal

Small two-handled dish with repoussé (embossed) decoration in the shape of flower heads. These dishes are sometimes called wine tasters. 1674.

James I seal top spoon showing the characteristic flat, slightly tapering stem introduced during the 16th century and slightly more oval shape of the bowl. Late 17th-century spoons are more common. London 1606.

Jewel House are well documented. Such was the extent of his generosity that on one occasion alone he presented a feted Spanish envoy with little short of 30,000 ounces of priceless royal plate. Other reasons, more down to earth, were closely linked to the vagaries of fashion. Because of its ability to be re-worked silver was, and still is, in constant danger of being melted down and made up into something else a little more fashionable.

A court commodity

Stylistically, early Stuart plate differs little from the pieces made in the closing years of Elizabeth's reign. However, there was a tendency away from the massive rich effects achieved through heavily embossed decoration to a lighter style, using engraved decoration and flat chasing. Motifs also reflected this trend and instead of the earlier ornate semi-naturalistic floral designs simpler, more stylised, flower arrangements were trained in graceful curves and circles. These stylised flower patterns were set within plain reserves of variously-shaped panels, usually circular or rectangular. These in turn were offset by a textured background dimpled with tiny pounce marks. This Dutch influence which superceded the earlier Renaissance forms was particularly evident in the work of the silversmith van Viannen, who for a time enjoyed the patronage of Charles I. Other motifs included whale-like sea monsters and the cartilagenous forms of the auricular style – arabesques and embossed diapers – or trellis patterns. The acanthus leaf, one of the most consistent motifs to appear from the 17th to the 20th centuries, was also used.

Plate for eating and drinking formed part of the lavish ceremonial accorded to these activities, and was generally subject to elaborate decoration. Gold and gilding continued to be used quite heavily on important plate. This included the formal and still costly salt, which had played a significant, if lingering, part in courtly custom since medieval times. To be above or below the salt was a reflection of a person's social position and is a term still used today. This large and symbolic piece gradually went out of fashion during the first half of the century, though a fine example was made during the Restoration period. Known as the Seymour salt, it was made in 1662 and presented to Queen Catherine of Braganza. But it was one of the last to be made on such a magnificent scale. By the time of King Charles I's reign (1625–49) salts were generally much smaller and a square, circular or polygonal hour-glass shape, standing on small feet, was more characteristic.

Drinking vessels, in the form of flagons, tankards, wine cups and beakers were both plain and decorated, but few were as lavishly treated as the costly and imposing standing cups. In particular obelisk-shaped steeple cups must have been made in considerable numbers, since 149 of them have weathered the years to remain with us. The obelisk was held to be a symbol of authority and, when kings ruled as if by divine right, the design was appropriate. Other items of plate treated in a decorative manner were the ewer and basin. In an age when the fork was not in daily use – indeed it was hardly known before the end of the 17th century – the washing of hands before, during and after a meal had become ritualised into a formal ceremony and the appurtenances of the ceremony were given due importance. Furthermore these items were amongst the largest pieces to be made and were thus well fitted for the purpose of display.

The Puritan interlude

During the years of uneasy peace following the end of the Civil War and the beginning of the Restoration, England was ruled by Oliver Cromwell. The puritan spirit of the time disapproved of the frivolities of earlier days and the legendary Stuart extravagances. Thus silversmiths suffered from the decline of their former patrons, many of whom had fled overseas, as well as from a terrible shortage of silver, the result of melting down and dispersal during the Civil War. Those pieces that were made tended to be much plainer, and many items were left completely undecorated. Although this 'puritan' silver was made throughout the rest of the century, it contrasted sharply with the styles and techniques re-introduced at the time of Charles II's restoration in 1660. Not only was there a new vitality in decoration but also an increase in the forms and types of items made, many in accordance with newly-introduced fashions brought back by exiles from overseas.

The return of splendour

The second half of the century saw the introduction and development of a number of different styles. The strength of the Dutch tradition, popular during the time of Charles I, was continued and revitalised by the Dutch influence brought back by the English court which, immediately prior to the Restoration, had been residing

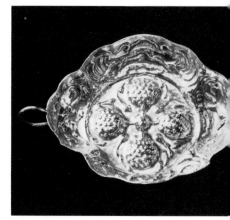

Small Charles I sweetmeat dish with wire work handles with repoussé decoration in the auricular style then fashionable. 1641. (w 3½in).

in Holland. Dutch taste was again revived during the reign of William and Mary in the closing decade of the century. French tastes were also of importance during these years, since many exiles returned from the dazzling court of Louis XIV. A notable number of French silversmiths were of Huguenot extraction, and when the Edict of Nantes protecting their religion was revoked in 1685, these artisans fled to England in order to escape religious persecution. Their influence re-

Charles I wine goblet of a very popular shape. Silver made before 1650 is increasingly difficult to find and it is correspondingly expensive.

mained well into the 18th century. Other fashions which prevailed included the keen interest taken in the wonderful and priceless objects brought back from the Orient by the re-established East India Company. Chinoiserie decoration, which had already had such a widespread influence on contemporary furniture and pottery, was also characteristic of silver during the second part of the 17th century.

Large formal pieces continued in use

Toilet set box engraved with chinoiseries. Such sets enjoyed considerable popularity during the Restoration, due to the East India Company. 1685.

Porringer, London 1679. Engraved initials between 'plumed mantling' usually indicate the family surname by the top letter and christian names by the bottom ones.

Silver saucer with makers mark 'I.P'. Decorated with engraved motifs showing a running acanthus leaf pattern and arabesques of flowers and birds. 1680.

during the latter part of the century. The copious ewer and basin remained popular as a decorative embellishment despite the fact that they were really redundant by about 1700, following the introduction of the fork. Many were redeployed as part of newly fashionable toilet services, equipped with a range of boxes for patches, and partnered with some fine table mirrors. Silversmiths continued to produce ewers and basins well into the 18th century and a fine example by Paul de Lamarie was

assayed in 1742. The distinctive helmet-shaped ewer, based on classical Roman forms, was popular by the late 1680's and was also used for much smaller jugs. But the most extravagant examples of silver plate were the rare and immensely costly items of furniture which were made at this time. Both Charles II and William were presented with suites of silver furniture, and priceless pairs of silver andirons adorned the hearths of the nobility.

The emergence of the bourgeoisie

By the second half of the century, silver was increasingly used for more ordinary tablewares. Tea, coffee and chocolate beverages, available in London since the middle of the century, led to the introduction of various pots in which to serve these hot drinks. Early tea pots varied widely, but were sometimes pear-shaped and had small silver spout caps attached to the lid by a fine chain. Shapes used for coffee and chocolate pots at this time make them indistinguishable but for the small covered hole situated in the lid of the chocolate pot. Into this a long, thin swizzle stick, or *molionet*, could be inserted

A large tumbler cup with armorial engraving. London 1683.

Very early dinner plate made in 1688 by T. S., London. Silver plates had been in use for about 125 years and gradually replaced the wooden trencher.

29

for the purpose of stirring the thick steaming chocolate.

Individual table salts began to appear at the Restoration in keeping with the more relaxed atmosphere and comfortable surroundings. Though the introduction of flint glass by George Ravenscroft in the 1670's signalled the end of the silver wine goblet, at the close of the 17th century tankards still remained widespread. In the second half of the century they had straight tapering sides and were fitted

Late 17th-century tankard with slightly domed lid and an erect thumb rest. The marks are clearly shown on the plain undecorated side. 1693.

A tankard without a lid but decorated with reeding and gadrooned motifs round the base. This variety is often considerably less expensive than the lidded version. 1695.

Late 17th-century spoon shaft engraved with 'Die to live', a constant reminder from the Puritan times of man's fragile mortality.

Single-handled dish, often described as a bleeding bowl. These may also have been used as porringers or simply as a shallow dish. 1682. (D 4½ in).

with a hinged, slightly raised, flat lid. The S-scrolled handles were fitted with elaborate thumb pieces sometimes cast in the form of an animal.

Decoration was much more vigorous than it had been during the Commonwealth period. Embossing was widely practiced, echoing plants and floral devices like the tulip and carnation, both popular motifs in contemporary marquetry and on delftware. Decoration took the form of borders or encircled entire beakers or tankards. Other motifs included rope mouldings, cut-card decoration and acanthus leaves. Engraving was used particularly for armorial devices but chinoiserie and floral designs provided occasional relief.

Large, very rare, goblet of a type attributed to the late 16th-century glass maker Jacopo Verzelini with diamond point engraved decoration. Dated 1581.

Wine glass made in the Venetian style probably in the Netherlands or England, usually called *façon de Venise*. 17th century.

English glass production made rapid strides during the 17th century. Like much of Europe, England had been dominated by Venetian glassmaking techniques and styles; this domination was to continue in the first half of the century. But it was to be seriously challenged immediately following the Restoration in 1660. The fruits of this period, which led to the development of lead glass, had far reaching effects on the industry in the closing decade of the the 17th century and throughout the 18th century.

The continental pacesetters

Our knowledge of the development of English glass making in the first half of the 17th century is largely based on contemporary documentary evidence, as there are too few remaining examples to provide a coherent and representative picture. Glass makers at this time continued to produce the type of Anglo-Venetian or 'cristallo' glass which had been introduced via the Netherlands during the reign of Elizabeth I. Cristallo – a type of soda glass – was developed by the Venetians before the 15th century. A fragile metal which suffered from colour imperfections, it was, however, prized for its ductile qualities. These enabled glass makers to blow the metal very thinly, which gave the appearance of great clarity and allowed glass makers to create highly fanciful designs. Stems, invariably the strongest part of a drinking vessel, could be created in the form of twisting serpents, and carefully wrought and coiled wings were attached to the sides and bowls. Fashionable filigree patterns were created by trailing milky threads of glass (lattino) across the surface. A main drawback of this delicate metal, however, was its unsuitability for

carving and cutting, although exceptionally careful use of a diamond stylus could allow engraving without shattering the glass.

The glass industry, like many others in the early 17th century, was largely controlled by a system of monopolies headed by financiers and industrialists rather than craftsmen. But, despite the entrepreneurial efforts of men who sought to impose such monopolies on the English glass industry, it is probable that much glass continued to be imported from the Continent throughout the 17th century.

The first glass industrialist

The most colourful and important figure in the first half of the 17th century (1615–42) was a retired vice-admiral, Sir Robert Mansell, whose rise to power coincided with an important edict affecting the English glass industry. In 1615 the use of wood was banned as a fuel for glass making. At the time Mansell was a partner in a company which was to pioneer

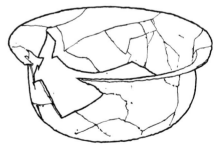

Bowl in black glass, a colour not widely popular but known to be made at Haughton Green near Manchester in the first half of the 17th century.

the development of coal-fired furnaces, with the building of a new glass house at Broad Street, London, in 1617. By the following year Mansell was in control of the company and shortly after held the monopoly for all sorts of glassware made by the use of coal. Much of the product was table glass, in the form of drinking vessels and bottles, but the glasshouses also made flat glass for use in mirrors and even in spectacles. Mansell died in 1656 but his control of the English glass industry had never seriously been threatened until the Civil War in 1642.

Although the monopolistic system, typified by Mansell in the first half of the century, was continued after the Restoration in 1660, a new spirit of enquiry and vigour entered the glassmaking industry. This renaissance extended into other disciplines and is best reflected in the setting up of the Royal Society in 1662; an important body of men who were themselves responsible for voicing the need for good, clear glass to be used in their scientific and optical experiments. This preoccupation coincided with a general increase in public demand for more glassware as

'Royal Oak Goblet' commemorating the safe escape of Charles II from Puritan soldiers while hiding in an oak tree. 1663.

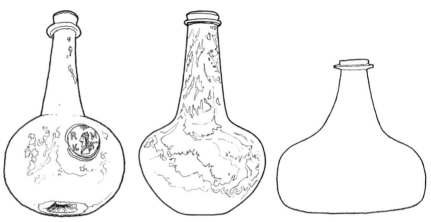

The earliest intact example of a sealed bottle, dated 1657, though others are known to have been made earlier. Note the kick in the base for stability.

Bottle in yellow-green glass without seal. c 1670.

Simple free-blown bottle in green glass with a more 'shouldered' body and shorter neck. The trailed string rim was to keep tops in tightly. c 1690.

well as a demand for better quality glass of a 'very Bright cleer and whit sound mettall'. The search was spearheaded by the increasingly powerful Glass Sellers Company which had been reincorporated in 1664. It was the Company's aim, not only to improve the quality of metal used in glassmaking, but also to make English glassmakers less dependent on Continental materials.

Ravenscroft and white glass

The man who was to transform the English glass industry was George Ravenscroft (1632–83), himself a glass merchant familiar with the Venetian trade. In 1673 Ravenscroft opened a glasshouse in the Savoy, London, and it was here that early experiments into discovering a new type of metal were conducted. It is clear that a new 'cristalline glass' had

been discovered within a year of opening the glasshouse, since Ravenscroft applied in 1674 for a patent exclusively to make and sell his new glassware for a period of 7 years. In the same year he came to an agreement with the Glass Sellers Company, who agreed to buy and sell his entire production of glasswares.

But the new crystalline glass which Ravenscroft had developed was marred by a basic defect. Due to an excess of alkali in the initial batch – the 'aggregate of the various ingredients' prior to fusion by heat – the glassware suffered from 'crizzeling'. Crizzeling was a progressive disease caused by the appearance of fine hairline cracks in the body of the glass and was often accompanied by a roughened and moist surface which led the glass to crumble. Despite this drawback the Glass Sellers Company continued to accept Ravenscroft's wares and went further by authorising the setting up of a new glasshouse at Henley-on-Thames, some 30 miles west of the City of London. The distance between this glasshouse and London provided the secrecy necessary to shroud any experiments and it was here,

A *façon de Venise* wine glass, of a straightforward nature. Its conical bowl is supported on a hollow knop surmounting a classical baluster stem. 17th century.

An imported Venetian wine glass, its waisted bowl culminating in a bulbous base. The cigar-shaped stem is hollow and the conical foot is folded. 17th century.

A *façon de Venise* wine glass with a round funnel bowl on a ribbed knopped stem. The latter is almost disguised by the applied turquoise scrolls and cristallo trails. 17th century.

Glass jug probably made by George Ravenscroft at the Savoy Glasshouse with mould-blown, ribbed body and foot. *c* 1675.

Jug in clear, colourless lead glass with a slight raised decoration, called by Ravenscroft 'nipt diamond waies'. Last quarter of 17th century.

with the aid of a Venetian called Da Costa, that Ravenscroft was to develop the full lead glass of a type still in use today.

By 1676 after further experimentation, Ravenscroft resolved the problems caused by crizzeling. This was achieved by introducing a farily high percentage of lead oxide into the batch. The resultant metal proved revolutionary. Its clarity and fine clear 'white' colour were quickly noted. The new metal was much heavier than the earlier type and did not need to be blown so thinly or with the same speed. When in a glyptic (cooled) state it was not as brittle as cristallo, a factor which when combined with its excellent refractory qualities made it a desirable medium for cutting. In order to distinguish the new lead glass, or flint glass as it was called for a time, the Glass Sellers Company agreed in 1677 that it should be impressed with a Raven's head. Today only about 20 pieces impressed in such a way are known to have survived.

Although the fact is unrecorded, Ravenscroft died in about 1683. The legacy of his influence insured, however, that refinements and experiments continued to be made throughout the 1680's, notably by Ravenscroft's successor Hawley Bishopp, who took over from Ravenscroft in 1678. The Italianate type of pre-Restoration glass did not disappear immediately and early examples often displayed short, hollow-blown stems. But as awareness of the new metal grew, so gradually did the forms and style of ornament.

By the end of the century glassware was noticeably more solid and simple with little or no decoration. Stems of this period usually show a variety of solid bulbous or baluster shapes. Straight-sided

Early example of a lead glass tazza exhibiting a moulded bowl. The stem is knopped and the foot folded under at the edge for strength. About 1680.

Deep bowl, one of a pair, probably made at the Savoy Glass house known as 'the Buggins Bowls'. The engraved decoration was better suited to the thinner-walled soda lime glass. *c* 1680.

bowls were generally wide brimmed, exceeded only by the width of the deeply folded foot. Decoration of the surface, when it was used, was often in the form of raspberry prunts, a popular motif on contemporary rummers, and a bowl pattern approved by the Glass Sellers Company was described as 'nipt diamond waies' (raised trellis pattern). All these features went towards a monumental style in glassmaking which was to find its finest expression during the earliest years of the 18th century in what has since become known as the Queen Anne style.

Crewelwork

Embroidery which uses a fine two-ply woollen-based thread on a linen and cotton twill is called crewelwork. Some of the finest examples were produced during the 17th century, particularly during the second half, and are sometimes collectively known as 'Jacobean embroidery'.

During the 16th century the increasing stability and growing economic prosperity of England under the Tudors were reflected in the greater comfort and in-

life, especially on plants with herbal associations. Another source were the gaily coloured 'palampores' or printed cottons imported by the East India Company, though these in turn may well have been influenced by English patterns sent out for copying.

The East Indian chintz hangings were enthusiastically copied by well-to-do ladies up and down the country, on textiles put to every conceivable use. The most common pattern was the 'Tree of

Late 17th-century/early 18th century crewelwork bedhanging in various shades of red.

creasing use of luxurious items in the home. The use of embroidery to adorn the homes of the merchant and upper classes, rather than for the decoration of palaces or religious institutions, became more widespread. It was further encouraged by the introduction of the steel needle. Early designs were based on plant and animal

Life', but others show a colourful array of stylised and exotic plant, flower, animal and bird life, often depicted standing on a hillock. Other important sources during the later 16th- and 17th-centuries were the Bible – natural enough at a time when religious observance was closely adhered to – and heraldic and emblematic devices.

35

By the 17th century the growing stylization and the large range of stitches were giving crewelwork distinctive characteristics, such as the use of detached flowers within larger expanses of open space and richly coiling plant stems.

The Restoration of Charles II in 1660 brought a revived interest in crewelwork after a slight decline in its popularity during the middle of the century, when stumpwork was fashionable. Colours became more subtle due to the improved use of shading, and stitches – though fewer in number – were more cunningly used. The range of stitches increased to include coral, herringbone and stem stitch. Single colours – using the long and short stitch which allowed for the greatest subtlety of shading – on entire monochrome patterns, achieved complexities of design unknown earlier in the century. Greens and reds were especially popular. In addition to the exotic variations based on the Tree of Life pattern, were plants of English inspiration – a special case was the acorn and oak leaf which symbolized Charles II's daring escape while a fugitive from the soldiers of Cromwell's army. Exceptionally fine examples were made for bed-hangings as well as for upholstery and clothing panels.

Andirons and Firebacks

An andiron is a metal frame on which burning logs are supported. They had been used since Roman times, but after the introduction of the grate in the late 17th century, the andiron gradually went out of use.

Early hearths, rising up from the middle of the room, had necessitated simple and functional andirons. But the removal of these open fires to a position against the wall freed the andiron from its purely functional constraints, and decoration became more feasible. Stylistically the 17th-century andiron changed little from its 16th-century predecessor. It continued classical decoration of Renaissance derivation, such as columns, strapwork patterns and nude half-figures or caryatids. By the middle of the century, during

Pair of silver andirons decorated with lion masks, putti and with melon-top finials. 2nd quarter 17th century.

the sombre days of the Commonwealth, decoration was minimal, often showing only the family coat of arms or a personal monogram.

After the Restoration a greater degree of lavishness affected the decoration of andirons, which were cast and pierced. The newly-introduced flat iron bars could be worked into delicate scrolling patterns and had the added benefit of being lighter in weight. The use of solid silver andirons, in place of bronze, brass, or wrought and cast iron examples, was a mark of extreme wealth, but even in Charles I's reign bronze andirons plated with silver had not been unknown. As andirons became more expensive many people introduced 'creepers', which were similar but smaller and less elaborate.

Like andirons the fireback was an essential part of the equipment used in a fireplace. Made of cast iron these weighty slabs stood at the back of the fireplace to protect the wall from the heat of the fire and are sometimes called iron chimneys. Decoration was simple and rather crudely formed. Coats of arms accompanied by dates were fashionable throughout the 16th and 17th centuries. From the Restoration onward decoration became more elaborate. Pictorial themes, particularly taken from the bible and mythology, were commonplace. Popular topical events were a secondary theme. The larger fireplaces common at the beginning of the 17th century encouraged firebacks of a massive size, but the increasing use of coal led to smaller fireplaces, and instead of the large square-shaped slabs typical of the early years, the fireback gradually became narrower and taller. By the close of the century a number of these now almost elegant pieces were decorated with arched tops.

Pewter

The production of pewter for domestic articles reached its zenith during the 17th and early 18th centuries, when virtually every item used in the home was made of this metal. The majority of common utensils included plates, bowls, dishes and hollow ware such as flagons, tankards,

Rare and costly pewter charger commemorating the wedding of Charles II to Catherine of Braganza in 1662. Floral, heraldic and sun motifs show wriggle work decoration.

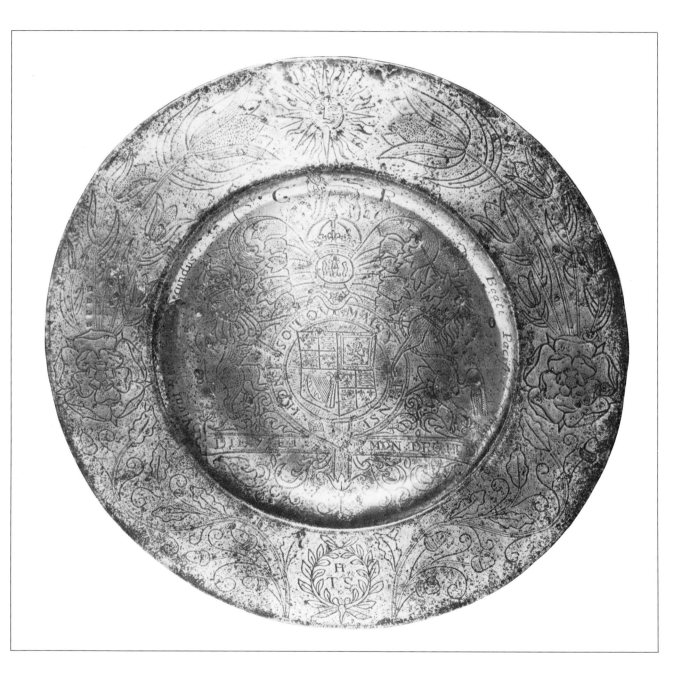

beakers and measures. Fashions tended to follow those already established in silver design so that, for example, flagons followed the characteristic silver drum shape, completed by a cover fitted with a scrolling thumbpiece. Pewter was also used for candlesticks, salt cellars, shoe buckles, inkstands and snuffboxes.

Pewter is a metal alloy made up principally of tin, but with the addition of

Pewter flagon with a lid of the 'beefeater' type, so-called because it resembles a beefeater's 'squashed hat'. The type is characteristic of 1650–80.

copper, zinc and lead. Its production was carefully controlled by the Guild of Pewterers, set up in 1438. The Guild sought to control the quality of the items supplied by their registered master craftsmen. The Guild also had certain rights to the principal constituent of this metal, Cornish tin, with the profits being put towards the costs of the Guild itself. Like the Gold and Silversmiths Guild, the Pewterers established their own series of 'touchmarks' and only an acknowledged master craftsman who had already 'made his mark' was entitled to have his wares thus digni-

fied. The Fire of London in 1666 destroyed the Pewterers' Hall and the long-established touchplates, but within three years the Guild was revived and continued unimpeded until the 19th century.

Single-handled pewter dish called a 'porringer' – used for porridge, possets or caudle. Less commonly called a bleeding bowl. Late 17th century.

Tobacco boxes

The weed tobacco had become the centre of a fashionable habit by the beginning of the 17th century, some forty years after its introduction during the reign of Elizabeth I. The principal method of smoking at this time was the pipe, as cigars and cigarettes were unknown before the 18th century. Snuff, however, was a popular alternative. As well as the pipe, or set of pipes, which were commonly of the white clay-bodied 'church-warden' type, other implements used for tobacco smoking included a rack or case to support the long-

stemmed pipes, ember tongs to light the tobacco and the tobacco box or jar in which was kept the precious leaf.

The tobacco box was characterised by a tightly fitting lid, which differed from its near companion the snuff box with its hinged lid. Shapes and sizes varied but oval boxes of between three and four inches in length were typical. Materials varied according to the tastes of the time and the user, but everything from precious gold and silver to tortoiseshell, leather, wood, horn and pewter were used. The very plainest were generally made of undecorated leather or wood, but personal tokens and gifts were often subject to some form of patterning or surface ornamentation. Tortoiseshell and horn, which can be laminated to provide any thickness desired, are also capable of moulding and offered ideal surfaces for carving and appliqué. Popular subjects included portraits of well-known national figures or of loved ones. Abstract and realistic carved decoration was used on wooden and mother-of-pearl boxes. A favourite theme for boxes made of oak was the massive oak tree, the 'boscobel' oak, in which Charles II was said to have hidden after escaping from his army's rout at the Battle of Worcester in 1645. Many of the examples bearing this carving actually claim to have derived from the wood of this famous tree.

Seventeenth-Century Antiques
What To Look For

Viewing and Buying
Museums, special exhibitions, specialist dealers and leading auction houses.

Furniture
Predominant woods: walnut and oak
Repairs are inevitable to furniture of this age. It is the extent of these repairs that might have bearing on the price and value.

Points to Watch
Common alterations include many minor repairs such as feet replacements – especially bun feet – usually subject to damp and worm; handles, small moulding and veneer replacements (called patches).

Major alterations include large moulding and veneer replacements or substantial carcase restorations. The former can be detected by slight colour changes in the wood, unnatural breaks in moulding, lines and wood grains following different directions.

Many reproductions of 17th-century furniture were made in the 19th century, some using original carved timber. This can make them difficult to distinguish from genuine 17th-century pieces.

When in doubt obtain a second opinion.
Mirror plate: a good 17th-century mirror – typically of the cushion-frame form, often with elaborate marquetry decoration and complete with pierced cresting – may well lose at least a third of its value by the replacement of the original plate with a new one.

Pottery
17th-century pottery, both earthenwares and stonewares, has been *the* subject for collectors for many years. Items now tend to be increasingly difficult to find and relatively expensive. For this reason many collectors include damaged pieces in their collections which, despite being marred, can give great pleasure and interest while being less costly.

Silver
17th-century silver is becoming increasingly rare and expensive. Spoons are the only remaining area which is still within reach of the average collector's pocket. Prices otherwise are generally much in excess of £100.

Glass
The relatively small amount of glass extant from the 17th century precludes all but the most dedicated from pursuing this field. Very early examples of English lead glass are even fewer in number. The largest category of glass surviving from before 1700 includes decorative cups with covers, and bowls mainly used for ceremonial rather than domestic purposes.

PART TWO **The Eighteenth Century**

The Eighteenth Century
Historical and Social Background

The cultural aspirations held during the reign of Queen Anne did not differ significantly from those held in the closing years of the reign of William III. But at the time of Queen Anne's death it was evident that the great exponents of English baroque taste – Wren and Vanbrugh – were old and in decline. In their place, younger men, such as the Scottish lawyer turned architect Colen Campbell, and rich powerful patrons like Robert Walpole and the aristocratic Earl of Burlington, sought a fresh approach to the arts. They wanted to break with the dramatic theatricality of the baroque and return to the cool, harmonious intellectualism of Roman classicism. William Kent provided the artistic genius and Andrea Palladio – the 16th-century architect from whom they took their name – the source of inspiration. He, in turn, had been influenced by the writings of the ancient Roman, Vitruvius.

Foreign influences and The Grand Tour

A number of books appeared in support of these new Palladian ideas. Among them were Colen Campbell's seminal work 'Vitruvius Brittannicus' (1715–25) and the newly-translated work of Palladio, 'Quattro Libri del Architectura'. Both works were dedicated to the newly-crowned George I (1715–27). In so doing, the authors expressed their affiliation with the political faction – the Whig aristocracy – surrounding the new Hanoverian monarch. The Palladians' search for a purer form of classicism was to dominate the artistic direction in England for much of the 18th century. This, the golden age of classicism, gave way only briefly in the middle of the century to a brief flirtation with rococo styles. Even the classicism of the second half of the 1700's retained many of those aspects established by the Palladians early in the century, such as the sense of proportion and the forms and motifs of the ancients. This continued despite the fact that its main exponent, Robert Adam, interpreted these forms in new and vigorous ways.

The opening years of George I's reign marked the rapid spread of the Grand Tour. This type of extended cultural field trip had been popular during the 17th century, but by the 1720's it was considered an essential educational ingredient for the young man of taste. Such a trip encompassed those countries considered to be the 'politer parts of Europe', and concentrated particularly on France and Italian centres such as Florence, Venice and Rome. The fact that some people thought the grand tour was 'carried a great deal too far' was evidence not only of how many young men were continent-bound, but also of how long these sojourns sometimes took. Not content with one grand tour, the Earl of Burlington in the second decade of the 18th century followed it up soon after with a second tour, concentrating on those aspects which he realised he had

Salt-glazed stoneware teapot painted in enamel colours over the glaze. The portrait is of Frederick the Great, King of Prussia, who achieved widespread popularity in this country in the middle of the century. *c* 1760.

Cricket table in pearwood. Usually made in elm, ash, oak or other local timber rather than fruitwood. This type of country furniture is still inexpensive.

missed the first time round; principally the architectural works of Palladio. Later in the century the aspiring young architect Robert Adam (1728–1792) rounded off his education with a grand tour lasting nearly four years. Even at the close of the century the architect Henry Holland sent the young Charles Heathcote Tatham to Rome to study the works of the Ancients and to make copies of these venerable artefacts to send home to his employer. But the broadening experience of the Grand Tour was brought abruptly to a close at the turn of the century with the cataclysm of the French Revolution and the advent of Napoleon's campaigns. Travel abroad became both difficult and dangerous.

However it was only natural that on completion of a classical education the discerning young scholar should seek to build for himself a house which reflected the fruit of his travels. For the aspirations and ideals of classical antiquity had become those of a new generation, and throughout the 18th century these attitudes were expressed in a number of different and sometimes curious ways. Garden settings were turned into Arcadian vistas – laid out with classical statues, grottoes, temples and cold bathing pools despite the unsuitability of the latter for the English climate. Political and aristocratic celebrities of the day were immortalised forever in statuary, wearing the toga of Imperial Rome. Eccentrics like Mrs Carter of Tunbridge Wells – whose reputed ability to speak Latin faster than anyone else in the realm made her famous – were courted and fêted.

Not only were the landed gentry and the aristocracy preoccupied with improving their country seats or laying out parkland settings, but many interested themselves in agricultural improvements. During the 18th century it became the habit for the followers of the London – and even the provincial – social season to decamp during the month of June and return to their country seats to a round of house parties and country pursuits. Such country migrations became part of the social calendar. Travel had been greatly facilitated by the rapid improvements made during the century in both road surfacing and carriage-making. But while agricultural innovations and legislation did much to improve the life of the English landowner, it also brought hardships for the small yeoman farmer and estate tenant in the form of land enclosure acts and higher rents.

The urban dominance

Many sought work in the burgeoning cities and towns springing up, particularly those in the Midlands: among them Sheffield, Wolverhampton and Birmingham. All had been small villages at the start of the century, but with growing industrialisation such villages had developed into sizeable urban centres with a

Small jug, typical of the wide range of useful wares made by the Worcester factory, which had a very large output. The black enamel transfer-printed decoration is over-glaze. Many of the scenes shown are miniature portrayals of idealised 18th-century life. *c* 1760.

manufacturing power sufficient to threaten that of London. But London remained the largest and most important city during the 18th century. Its population amounted to a little over ten per cent of the nation's inhabitants and by the close of the century reached nearly a million – almost twice what it had been fifty years before.

The capital continued to be the financial, political and legal centre of the country but it was also the heart of the elite society, catering to the whims and fancies of the rich and famous. Shopping centres arose in Oxford Street and Bond Street to meet the demands of the new residential areas which sprang up throughout the 18th century. But while the golden age brought increasing material comforts for the rich, many of whom had made their fortunes overseas through cotton and sugar plantations, life for the very poor was one of degradation and misery. 'One poor man was just creeping out of his sick bed to his ragged wife and the little children who were half naked, and the very picture of famine,' ran one first hand account of a slum in the East end of London, 'when, one bringing in a loaf of bread, they all ran, seized upon it and tore it to pieces in an instant.' As well as famine and poverty, disease too was rife. However, the nation's health altered for the better by the end of the century, following an overall improvement in diet and discoveries such as Edward Jenner's vaccination against smallpox, one of the worst scourges affecting both rich and poor.

If life for the very poor was harsh – some of the best illustrations of low life can be found in the work of the artist William Hogarth – it tended to be a continuous round of social events and entertainments for the upper classes. But the members of this elite were not drawn exclusively from the aristocratic families of England as happened on the Continent. By the 18th century there was evidence of increased social mobility, aided by the traditional easygoing relationship between classes bonded together by common values and a common interest – of which many examples were to be found in small local communities. It is of note that in the middle of the 18th century (1746), Lord Sackville of Knole was ready to accept his head gardener as captain in the same cricket side which played a match under the careful scrutiny of the cream of English nobility, including the Prince of Wales. Nor is it surprising that one of the finest and most successful furniture makers of the century, John Gumley, who was widely patronised by both royalty and nobility, achieved social distinction by marrying his daughter to the Earl of Bath. Some of the best accounts of social life in the 18th century can be found in the diaries of women such as Caroline Girle and Fanny Burney, both daughters of prosperous middle class professional families. These two blue stockings rubbed shoulders with nobility *and* royalty in the

Assembly rooms of Bath and for a time Fanny Burney was herself a lady in waiting to Queen Charlotte, wife of George III (1760 – 1820).

Bath – second capital of fashion

The elegant spa of Bath was second only to London in social importance during the 18th century and was pre-eminent among the spa towns of England – Clifton, Buxton, Harrowgate, Tunbridge Wells and York. It was the place to which many people decamped at the end of the London season to take the waters or simply to continue the round of parties and social calls. In any event few people would have owned their own property in the town; instead lodgings were taken. A fashionable address in the Royal Crescent, only finished in 1774, could cost up to £140 per annum, a considerable sum. But to some – such as Dorothy Yorke, widow of a prosperous Welsh landowner – everything in Bath seemed 'excessive high'. The town provided a wide range of facilities including the baths. Pump rooms were, literally, the watering place of those who wished to see and be seen, dispensing tea, spa water and other beverages. The Assembly rooms were another lodestone.

A comfortably-off landowner would hardly have had difficulty in adding the season at Bath to his social calendar. Not only was it fun but was useful for those in need of a marriage market, or on the lookout for a position in the influential world of politics. From early in the day the round of social calls began, culminating in an evening entertainment such as a ball. The main meal of the day was dinner, taken during the course of the afternoon. Gradually, however, this meal came later and later and, by the end of the century, to the discomfiture of many traditional folk, dinner was being taken as late as 6 or 7 o'clock in the evening.

In the country however, the fewer people within easy reach made the long leisure hours more difficult to fill. House parties and group entertainments were one way of occupying the day. When the weather was bad, family and guests gathered together and while someone read aloud, or played the piano, others would immerse themselves in card-playing or in some more productive activity such as japanning. That these attempts were usually of poor quality was rather sourly alluded to by Horace Walpole, younger son of the Whig Prime Minister, Robert Walpole, when he referred to 'two vile china jars that look like the modern japanning by ladies'. But country matters remained the primary source of entertainment for the landed gentry. Quite apart from horticultural and agricultural pursuits, hunting, horse-racing and even archaeological excavations were all indulged in. There were parties, balls, and routs during the evenings, and although numbers at such gatherings varied enormously they

Pearlware figure of Isaac Newton made at the Leeds pottery. Pearlware was a very refined creamware with a slightly blued glaze. This gave it the appearance of being as white as porcelain. About 1790.

Typical scene used for transfer-printed decoration on creamware and soft paste porcelain. About 1770.

tended to become more sophisticated and larger as the century wore on. In particular balls were popular; some were held in private houses and some in the exclusive but public Assembly rooms, presided over by society figures. Chief among them was Beau Nash, who was widely accepted despite his humble background.

Eighteenth-Century Interiors and Furnishings

The pursuit of the arts was a particular preoccupation of the 18th-century gentry. Standards of good taste governed all their activities, and in particular their attitudes to architecture. A distinctive feature of many large country houses built during the 1720's and 1730's, some of which were palatial, was the importance placed on the first floor or *piano nobile*. The rusticated ground floor was designed to act as a podium to emphasise the main reception rooms usually situated on the floor above. Many of the external features of the house called attention to the importance of the main rooms on the piano nobile. Fenestration, for example, continued to be executed in a symmetrical fashion, but windows on the first floor received exceptional detailing in the form of pediments and columns. Staircases and other approaches to the interior stressed the dominance of the first floor. At Wanstead (now demolished), one of the most ambitious house schemes of the early Georgian period, the piano nobile was reached via a grand double external staircase. This led up to a noble portico behind which was ranged a huge columned hall. Another grand staircase was that designed by William Kent for the Earl of Leicester at Holkham Hall, Norfolk (1730–60). The unpretentious entrance leads the visitor to the almost bleak austerity of the palatial frontal exterior. It provides no hint of the grandeur of the marble hall inside, which recalls Palladio's earlier designs for a Temple of Justice. Inside, a magnificent staircase leads up to some of the finest piano nobile reception rooms conceived at this time. In this first half of the 18th century, whether in a magnificent palace such as Holkham Hall or in a relatively modest house, this floor was the focus of the most sumptuous treatment available to the owner's means.

A dream of marble halls

In especially fine houses an antique gallery was invariably a feature of the interior, calculated to display the classical statuary and artefacts lovingly brought back after a Grand Tour of Europe, with the most prized spoils those from Italy. Many owners, if they did not manage to get away themselves, despatched agents to do the work for them. Niches – embellished with carefully selected classical statues – decorated elegant galleries, whose antecedents lay in the old-fashioned Long Gallery. The library, too, had developed and its occurrence multiplied noticeably, although it was not found in more modest houses until later in the century. Other rooms on the first floor of a large and important country house might include a salon, a drawing room, a dining room and a suite of state apartments. The latter was a feature of the grand style fashionable in the previous century, which continued in use in many of the great houses of England throughout the 18th century.

49

Turn of the century stool that converts to form library steps. This type of mechanical furniture was very popular by the end of the 18th century and in the early 19th century. Libraries were generally found in most late 18th-century houses.

Page 48: The Salon, Clandon Park, Surrey. Situated immediately beyond the hall, this four-walled reception room was intended as the second room of entry and is flanked on one side by the State Bedroom and on the other by the formal Green Drawing Room. The blue-and-white colour scheme illustrates Palladian theories of colour and provides a striking contrast to all the other rooms, especially to the cool white marble hall. The limited use of furniture is characteristic of the period and serves to underline the Salon's principal use as a room of assembly.

A decorative theme fashionable in dwellings large and small, was the light-coloured entrance hall – one with real or imitation marble walls, columns in pale buffs and off-white tones, and black-and-white flagged floors. This provided a striking contrast to the spectacularly rich effects conjured up in the main reception rooms leading out of the hall. Rooms of cube-like proportions were hung with rich velvets and silk damasks in dark greens and strong crimson. The textiles contrasted vividly with the white-and-gold woodwork and plasterwork decoration of the coffered ceilings, windows and door frames. Occasionally even the glazing bars in the windows were gilded – as they were at Holkham Hall – but this was not typical. Strong colour schemes were fashionable and even in less opulent homes wood-panelled walls were painted in buffs, blues and greens.

The era of the town house

Town houses built shortly after the accession of George II (1727–1760) complied with the general principles laid down by Palladian architects and tended to remain faithful to this pattern throughout the 18th century. Internally the houses reflected the architectural evidence already available externally and special emphasis continued to be given to the first floor rooms. Series of town houses, such as those designed by John Wood for the development of Queen Square, Bath (begun 1729), were treated as a single unit, giving the whole a palatial aspect. One way of enhancing the unity of these streets of houses was to treat the central houses more emphatically by giving them porticos.

Inside a fairly modest three- or four-storey building, the externally rusticated ground floor would be given over to a small, narrow entrance hall and back and front room. There would also be access to the basement in which the domestic rooms – kitchens, larders, pantries and most menial of all, the scullery – were located. Behind the house was a small garden, access to which was usually through the back parlour. Beside the front door – which set the classical tone of the house by means of its imposing columned and pedimented frame – a link extinguisher often would be fitted to the railing, shaped like an angel's trumpet. This was for putting out the torches normally carried by a link boy during the hours of darkness.

On the first floor, the main drawing room was situated above the hall and front parlour and looked out over the street through elegant sash windows. The smaller room behind would be used as an extension to this room or to provide a dressing room for the lady of the house. In either case visitors would be received in both rooms, although in the latter case the dressing room probably would have the more personal stamp of its erstwhile occupant. On the second floor were situated several bedrooms designed for the use of the family, while servants had beds in a series of much smaller and sometimes rather cramped attic rooms above. There were few bathrooms, as they are known today, in use in the 18th century. But people became increasingly aware of the benefits of cleanliness and hygiene during the course of the century, and made use of bowls or receptacles which could be carried into the bedroom filled with hot water brought up from downstairs. Public baths were a feature of the age and during the 18th century many people praised the benefits afforded by 'taking the waters' in the burgeoning spa towns up and down the country.

The character of Palladian furnishings

Furniture and furnishings in the 18th century were designed to last considerably longer than they are today. Furniture – particularly large costly pieces such as a bed or a bureau bookcase – was passed down for generations. Many an 18th-century drawing room or parlour not at the peak of fashion might resemble that of at least a decade earlier. It was not incongruous to find a set of elderly chairs or a comfortable old wing chair used in conjunction with more recent purchases. In the country it was customary for large householders, wishing to modernise their homes, to throw out perfectly serviceable if rather outmoded pieces to tenants or servants living on the estate. Thus alongside rustic pieces of country furniture might stand an item of evident superiority. The one law to which interior decoration did conform was the deployment of furniture. Chairs, when not in use, continued to be set out in a formal, symmetrical fashion around the walls of the room. Pictures and mirrors were placed in carefully structured settings – often within a panelled scheme – and fireplaces, the only form of heating available, were given prominent positions. The use of dummy doors – which led nowhere but were intended to enhance the careful design of the room – was typical of the concern for symmetry and proportion in 18th-century design.

By the middle of the 18th century social and economic changes effected an evolution in interior decoration, although architecture was a great deal less affected. The ponderous, rich Palladian schemes of the second quarter of the 18th century gave way to much lighter, brighter – even garish – colour schemes with the onslaught of the rococo fashion in the 1750's. Rococo emanated from France where it had developed during the second decade of the 18th century. In Britain its expression was a reaction against the formal splendour of the Palladian style and represented a serious challenge to the pre-eminence of classicism. Many of its forms were derived from nature, such as flowers and foliage, and characteristic motifs included shells, rockwork and C and S scrolls.

Part of a design for a pier glass frame in the full rococo style showing ho-ho birds, icicles, chinoiserie figures, and C- and S-scrolls. This type of decoration gave full scope to the carver's work, which was frequently gilt. Design plate *CLXIX* from Chippendale's *Director* (1762).

The earlier cool, solemn halls with their symmetrically arranged columns were enlivened with applied plasterwork decoration – swirling shapes and cartouches picked out in white and gold against a range of much lighter pastel colours including salmon pink and lemon yellow. Lighter colours were favoured too for drawing rooms, in place of the heavier red and green velvets and damasks. Panelled decoration with applied plaster flowers, scrolls, and trailing plant forms became the rage, although it rarely reached the opulence of fashionable French interiors. Doors and fireplaces, which had previously been emphasised, were now merged more discreetly with the background. Expanses of gold and white, a common decorative combination for drawing rooms, glittered in reflections from hanging and inset mirrors, lit by myriad candles. A compliment to the increasingly lighter and more frivolous interiors was the perceptible tendency for informal gatherings. Entertainments were more varied. People were able to do what they wanted when they wanted, rather than being governed by convention and a rigidly defined sense of etiquette. But the debunking of society's long-revered tenets took time, and the informality inspired by rococo taste did not reach its apex until the opening years of the next century.

The mandarins of fashion

While classical Palladianism continued to provide the source of inspiration for a great majority of people, the leaders of the *beau monde* strove to find new and decorative ideas and themes. The fascination for the Orient had prevailed intermittently in England since the previous century. By the middle of the 18th century it was again taken up and enjoyed a considerable revival. Not only was furniture, silver, and even porcelain made in imitation of Chinese goods, but whole rooms – especially bedrooms – were decorated with chinoiseries. Imported, hand-painted wall papers were used to set off furniture designed in a complementary fashion. Ornamental chinamen and pagoda-shaped rooftops glittering with gold leaf adorned wall sconces and mirrors. Rooms set aside for drinking tea displayed the same exuberant spirit. The exotic Chinese Room at Claydon House, Buckinghamshire, was one example, as were the picturesque oriental temples which now dotted the garden landscape.

Chinoiserie was not the only style to enjoy success in the middle decades of the 18th century. The Gothic revival, regarded by its high priest Horace Walpole as a return to 'venerable barbarism', was another source of inspiration. Interiors were transformed into medieval Cathedral transepts with ribbed arches and delicate tracery; windows and doors were gothicised with cusps and pointed arches. In common with the Chinoiserie style it was fun, fanciful and relatively short-lived. Although few could afford the expense of decorating their entire house in such an exotic and extravagant way, it is probable that many houses displayed at least an item of furniture or silver *à la mode* in order to proclaim awareness of the fashionable currents of the time.

Adam and his influence

The advent of neo-classicism during the last forty years of the 18th century was to have a more wide-reaching and longer-lasting effect than any of the mid-century styles. In a sense it was a continuation of the earlier form of neo-classicism under the Palladians, only the rules were different. The early exponents of the old school were dead and gone; in their place the Scottish architect Robert Adam reigned. Adam had the experience of a traditional classical education and had finished it with a Grand Tour of Europe, culminating in Italy, during the years 1756–1760. Though this was very much in the best tradition of Grand Tours undertaken by arch-Palladians such as Kent, Burlington and Leicester, a number of events had taken place in the intervening thirty years. The great archaeological sites of Herculaneum and Pompeii had been excavated and for the first time knowledge about the domestic architecture and habits of the ancient Romans was available. At the same time Greece was being rediscovered, although the effects of this much more austere form of classicism was not properly felt until the very last years of the century.

Under the lead given by Robert Adam, Neo-classical motifs replaced rococo ones although light colours remained popular. While tapestries and textiles were favoured for some reception and drawing rooms, Adam recommended that no textiles be used in eating rooms as the fabric would retain the smell of the food. Instead he suggested that plaster panels with stucco decoration and inset painted panels, depicting suitable classical themes, would be appropriate. Although considerable attention to detail had been paid to the earlier Palladian interiors, it was not until the advent of Robert Adam that the smallest details in a room became the subject of careful design. Whereas Kent preferred the monumental, Adam favoured the delicate. A special theme – such as an anthemion or urn – was often picked out on the furniture as well as on door handles and in the complex ceiling designs. Elements derived from Greek pottery (misidentified as Etruscan) were common decorative fodder, as were the so-called grotesques derived from Raphael's 16th-century Vatican decorations. Furniture continued to be treated formally, as it has been throughout the 18th century, and was arranged in lines along the walls. Elaborate side tables played an increasingly important part in the architectural treatment of the room.

On the whole, however, there was a turn toward greater informality which led to the gradual restructuring of the internal layout of rooms and their

The new neo-classical style which was introduced in about 1760 was typified by the classical shape of the urn. It was much used between 1760–90.

Robert Adam, the great arbiter of neo-classic taste, particularly admired Roman art. This griffin is typical of the ornament used by the ancients.

Key pattern, derived from ancient Greek
architectural ornamentation, was widely used to
decorate silver, glass, ceramics and furniture in the
neo-classic taste. Here it is used on a dark blue glass
wine cooler, picked out in gilt.

furnishings. The most significant development was the re-positioning of the main reception rooms on the ground floor and their gradual separation from the dressing room or bedchamber. Only in the grandest houses were state apartments – complete with state bedchamber – retained, but even these were on the way out. Instead communal rooms were taking their place. A number of new rooms began to cater for special social gatherings: music rooms, billiard rooms, dining rooms and boudoirs. The shock waves engendered by the French Revolution in 1789 played their part in breaking down barriers. Although important occasions were still marked by a degree of ceremony and formality, interior decoration during the closing years of the century makes plain the difference. Items of furniture, particularly large numbers of small tables, were moving into the middle of the room. At the turn of the century this fashion was acknowledged by the introduction of the sofa table, which was intended to be free-standing and was usually placed in front of a sofa. People began to lounge on sofas rather than sit bolt upright. All these factors looked forward to the 'proper air of confusion' and the search for comfort which were to characterise interiors in the 19th century.

Eighteenth-Century Furniture

Red japanned beech chair with green and gold decoration, showing the simple, elegant, curved lines of much earlier 18th-century furniture. The splat is curved to suit the sitter's back in keeping with the growing demand for comfort at this time. It amply demonstrates the influence of oriental furniture in the form. *c* 1710.

Small chest of drawers sometimes called a batchelor's chest. The top unfolds and is supported on extending rails. Bracket feet have replaced the old-fashioned bun type. *c* 1710.

The 18th century witnessed an increasing number of swiftly changing styles; the most dominant of these can be described briefly as Queen Anne (1700–25), Palladian (1725–45), Rococo (1745–60), and Neo-classicism, inspired by Robert Adam (1728–92), and pursued by his followers George Hepplewhite (d. 1786) and Thomas Sheraton (1751–1806).

Restraint and quality

A notable reticence in furniture design marked the first quarter of the century, in sharp contrast to the general flamboyance of the latter part of the 17th century. Although many of the more expensive techniques of the earlier period, such as japanning, gilding and marquetry work, continued to be used – particularly on more formal pieces – plain veneered surfaces were increasingly preferred by both the aristocracy and the growing middle classes. Walnut remained the most fashionable wood throughout this period, to be finally superseded by mahogany which began to be imported in about 1725. Supplies of walnut were readily available from Virginia in the United States and from the continent. The American source was particularly valuable after 1709, when much of Europe suffered from a severe winter which destroyed many of the walnut plantations. Yew was another wood used at this time, but oak remained the timber favoured by country joiners, estate carpenters and even the provincial cabinet makers who sought to imitate the fashions of London.

The introduction of the cabriole leg in about 1700 is one of the most distinctive features of early 18th-century furniture. It was widely used on tables, chairs and stands for chests (more commonly known

This chest on chest is also known as a tallboy and like most good quality furniture of the early 18th century is veneered in fine walnut. Due to their large size these pieces are not as 'desirable' as many other examples of furniture and are often relatively inexpensive. *c* 1725.

This chest on stand differs only slightly from the above by having a stand consisting of one long and two short drawers. The shaped apron and claw-and-ball feet were popular decorative motifs at this time. *c* 1720.

as tallboys or highboys). It varied from a simple cabriole outline to decoration in the form of motifs such as scallop shells carved at the top or 'knee' of the leg. Feet generally took the form of a simple pad, but the more elaborate claw-and-ball design became popular after about 1710. The shape of chair backs developed from the more linear style of late 17th-century examples to the subtle curvature of the hoopback. The graceful serpentine-shaped back splat complemented for the first time the outline of the sitter's back.

Many of the new pieces of furniture which made their appearance in the late 17th century now became fully developed, reflecting the increasing prosperity of the nation. Writing tables assumed the form of the bureau, still fashionable today, and bookcases were added on top to form bureau bookcases. Cabinets and chests

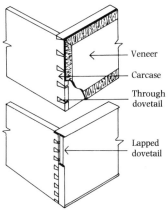

Veneer

Carcase

Through dovetail

Lapped dovetail

The ability to make flat surfaces join together smoothly at right angles by the use of a dovetail joint was the skill of the cabinet maker. It superseded the traditional joiner's mortice and tenon construction for more fashionable work.

Walnut-veneered kneehole writing desk with narrow lines of feather banding around the drawer fronts and top. The bracket feet have been given an ogee outline. c 1725.

were now raised on stands supported by cabriole legs. Card-playing, a favourite pastime of the leisured classes, dictated that a large number of card tables were made. Elaborate examples equipped with money wells, candle stands and carved decoration in the form of shells, were opened up by cunningly contrived hinged 'concertina' supports, although the simpler gateleg was more common, if less stable.

Kent and the English Baroque

Many of the pieces fashionable in the Queen Anne period continued well into the second quarter of the century, executed in the newly popular mahogany. But, whereas the majority of early 18th-century English furniture was characterised by a simple graceful elegance, these later examples became more elaborately carved and heavier in appearance and a marked architectural style became evident. This style, based on the classical principles of the 16th-century architect Andrea Palladio, found particular demand in contemporary Whig households. Its greatest exponent was the designer William Kent, its most indulgent patron the Earl of Burlington. Bureau bookcases, clothes presses (wardrobes), cabinets, chests-on-stand and even beds were treated in this architectural manner and were decorated with a variety of classical pilasters, columns and broken pediments.

To augment this rather narrow repertoire, Kent borrowed freely from contemporary Italian baroque furniture. Lion or human masks were finely carved on friezes and legs, often complimented by the introduction of well-carved hairy lion paw feet. These proved a popular alternative to the well liked claw-and-ball design

Very elaborate, formal side table with intricate surface patterns, usually gilded but sometimes silvered. This type of furniture is often attributed to James Moore. c 1715.

introduced earlier in the century. Other motifs of classical origin included Vitruvian scrolling, Greek key pattern and scallop shells, the latter a particular favourite of Kent's. Much Palladian furniture was designed specifically for individual Palladian houses of the day and was correspondingly grand. The lavish style and monumental scale of these houses provided a magnificent backdrop to the rich furnishings which adorned them. Fabulous textiles did service as upholstery and quantities of gold leaf covered many of the finest pieces. But whilst such furniture was beyond the means of most people, many of stylistic forms and motifs were adapted by both London and provincial cabinet makers for more humble pieces.

The influential publications

By the middle of the 18th century most of the styles current in London had found their way into provincial workshops. The rapid spread of urban styles, which now

seem to follow in quick succession, came about through the increasing number of published pattern books, some of which had already been in circulation since the 1740's. (e.g. Thomas and Batty Langley's *City and Country Builder's and Workman's Treasury of Designs*, 1740.) The most extensive pattern book of the period, Thomas Chippendale's *The Gentleman and Cabinet Maker's Director*, published in 1754, was so popular that the book was reprinted twice, with only minor amendments, in 1755 and 1762.

The publication of 'The Director' coincided with a corresponding taste for chinoiserie, pseudo-Gothic fashions, and the rising rococo style recently introduced to England from France. Chinoiserie was a

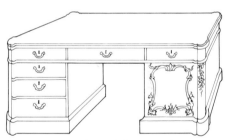

Design plate from Chippendale's *Director* showing choice of two patterns for a library table. 1754.

style loosely based on the forms and ornaments found on actual Chinese furniture. For the most part they were highly fanciful (conjectural) and included Chinese figures, bells, birds – particularly cranes – dragons, and even adaptations of Chinese buildings such as temples. (One famous fourposter bed was made up in the form of an open-sided Chinese temple.) Fretwork and lattice work was also used for the friezes of tables or chairs and for the newly-introduced china cabinet designed to display fashionable porcelain pieces.

The Gothic taste, which enjoyed a considerable revival in the middle of the 18th century, had never really disappeared from the vernacular English repertoire. Established in the middle ages, its 18th century expression was entirely superficial, making use of cusps, pinnacles and pointed arches associated with medieval

Hoop back 'Windsor' chair in yew with decoration in the revived Gothick taste greatly popularised by Horace Walpole. Mid-18th century.

architecture. Gothic motifs are often found on relatively simple articles of country-made furniture, such as chairs, as well as on the fine pieces favoured by the eccentric Horace Walpole.

The flowering of rococo

Rococo was a frivolous, gay style which broke with the serious, intellectual approach espoused by the Palladians. It provided a mode of decoration which was a radical departure from classical forms, although some motifs – such as the acanthus leaf – remained very popular. Instead

furniture was characterised by a much lighter design, often combined with chinoiseries or with Gothic extravagances. Carved decorations appeared in the form of C and S scrolls, serpentine shapes, shells, abstract flame designs and other motifs drawn from nature. As a style it was best suited to pieces which were not hampered by functional considerations

Design for a girandole from Thomas Johnson's *Twelve Girandoles* published in 1755. They are among the best expressions of mid-century rococo tastes.

and which gave the carver unlimited scope for his skills. Mirrors, girandoles (wall lights) and certain types of side or console tables are among the best examples. But it did have an effect on the appearance of more ordinary pieces. Chair backs became more open, with pierced and carved decoration replacing the earlier solid splat back. An elaborate example of this was the well-known Ribband-back chair design in the *Director*. Variations of this type of pierced decoration appear in more humble pieces like 18th-century Windsor chairs, some-

times described as Chippendale Windsors. These chairs were made right up to the middle of the 19th century and they, along with many 18th century designs, are enjoying a revival in the 20th century.

A number of pieces of furniture were popularised in the mid-eighteenth century, many of them intended to comple-

Mahogany chair showing the widespread influence of Chippendale's style on this type of furniture, particularly in the design of the back splat. *c* 1760.

ment a particular activity or ceremony. Tea drinking, fashionable since the Restoration, led to the tea table becoming widespread at this time. These small tables generally either had a rectangular top, supported on legs at each corner, or a circular one, supported on a central pedestal. Both were fitted with a rim, gallery or pie crust trim to prevent the tea things from falling off. They were usually made in mahogany, although similar tables with turned pedestals and circular tops, generally without the raised edge, were made in less expensive timbers such as oak, yew and fruitwood. These pedestal tables were made in very large quantities but were rarely as finely carved and decorated as the superior mahogany models. Other pieces of furniture which began to be widely used included the commode – a formal version of the chest of drawers, designed for display in the drawing room. Small breakfast tables, with

decorations such as round and oval patera, anthemions, ram's heads, urns, sphinxes, and delicate swags of flowers, all of which had been familiar to ancient Rome. The curved line – a keynote of the rococo style – was gradually eliminated and straight lines became prominent on table fronts, chair backs and most types of case furniture. Straight legs on chairs and

was so popular during the 1770's and 80's.

Hepplewhite and Sheraton

Although Adam espoused a very grand formal style of decoration, his taste was popularised by later designers, notably George Hepplewhite and Thomas Sheraton. Both men have given their name to

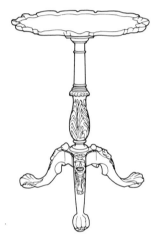

Finely carved mahogany tripod table. Plainer examples, often in oak, beech, elm or fruitwoods, were made well into the 19th century and are inexpensive. *c* 1760.

The formal commode, for display rather than use, often has doors enclosing a series of drawers. Despite its rococo outline the marquetry decoration is neo-classical. *c* 1770.

Satinwood Pembroke table with some marquetry decoration. Commonly oval in shape, they can also be rectangular and even butterfly-shaped in outline. *c* 1780.

enclosed shelves under the frieze drawer, were used for light meals in the quiet of a bedroom. These were later to develop into the so-called Pembroke table.

The revival of marquetry decoration in the 1760's corresponded to the appearance of a new neo-classical style. Marquetry had not been fashionable since the end of the 17th century, but now it provided decorative relief to the linear style favoured by architects and designers such as Robert Adam. Rococo motifs, many of which had been based on natural forms, were discarded in favour of classical

tables often finished in elegant tapering spade feet and were often fitted fitted with brass or leather casters.

There was a demand for small items of furniture throughout the latter part of the century, and the Pembroke table, which developed from the earlier breakfast table of the mid-century, now became widespread. The delicate linear treatment of furniture was complemented by the introduction of lighter-coloured timbers such as satinwood and harewood. These woods provided a perfect foil to the rich effect of both floral and pictorial marquetry which

entire ranges of furniture, although not a piece exists which can be absolutely attributed to either. Their fame rests on their collected drawings, which served as models for major and minor studios and craftsmen of the period. Hepplewhite's book of drawings, *The Cabinet Maker and Upholsterer's Guide*, published two years after he died in 1786, popularized many of Adam's designs. However, the book was aimed at a middle class society who could never have afforded the enormous accounts which Adam presented to many of his wealthy clients. Forms were simplified, expensive techniques such as gilding and marquetry were no longer used or were imitated by cheaper methods such as painted decoration. Although Adam must be credited with developing the oval and shield motifs used so successfully on chairbacks and mirrors-on-stands, these designs were popularised by Hepplewhite and are today very sought after.

Sheraton, who published his book *Cabinet Maker and Upholsterer's Drawing Book* in serial form over the period 1791–94, made fashionable a much more rectangular style than his predecessors, and this is particulary noticeable in his designs for chair backs which are more square in form. Thin stringing lines emphasise the angularity of much of Sheraton's furniture and were often used along the borders of tables, case furniture and seat rails.

A number of pieces of furniture were developed in the last quarter of the 18th century, notably the sideboard. This was generally fitted with lateral wine drawers (cellarettes) and cupboards, and a central drawer. An example designed by Sheraton is fitted with a brass gallery at the back. Both Hepplewhite's and Sheraton's plans exhibit a simple feminine elegance, although many of the designs in Sheraton's later book, published in the opening years of the 19th century, give way to the latent exoticism of some Regency fashions and to a fussiness of detail not apparent in the furniture of the late 18th century.

Mahogany settee with serpentine-shaped back. Relatively plain examples, such as this one, can be inexpensive and compare favourably to the cost of a modern settee. About 1770.

Wardrobe design featured in George Hepplewhite's *The Cabinet Maker and Upholsterer's Guide*, first published in 1788. They are usually made in mahogany.

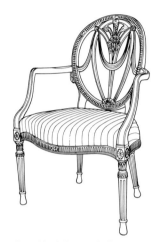

Chair with oval back design which was very popular during the last quarter of the 18th century. It displays the Prince of Wales's motif in centre top. *c* 1775.

Design from Sheraton's *Drawing Book*, 1791–94, intended as formal seating in the drawing room. Notice the rounded front which sets it apart from straight examples.

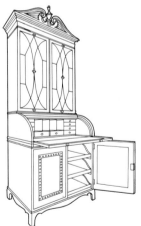

Another design from Sheraton's *Drawing Book*, showing the newly fashionable cylinder-topped desk with bookcase above.

Secretary desk with bookcase which displaced the earlier type of slope-top bureau. Design from Hepplewhite's *Guide*, first published 1788.

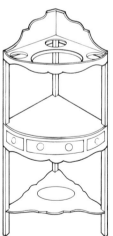

Corner basin washstands are now often used to hold plants. They make an attractive display piece. *c* 1794.

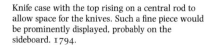

Knife case with the top rising on a central rod to allow space for the knives. Such a fine piece would be prominently displayed, probably on the sideboard. 1794.

Eighteenth-Century Pottery and Porcelain

Four tin-glazed earthenware tiles showing a ship printed in black enamel (Liverpool, c 1760); flowers painted in blue on a manganese (purple) ground (Lambeth about 1760); Chinoiserie figures painted in manganese (purple) and a shield also manganese (both Liverpool about 1760). The tin glaze provided a crisp white background colour on which to paint other colours. All 5 in. square.

Tin-glazed English 'delftware' tile painted in underglaze blue. Single tiles are still very inexpensive and are a charming representative of their period. About 1760.

Earthenwares

There were a number of technical and material improvements made in earthenware production during the course of the 18th century. In particular the introduction and refinement of a whiter-bodied pottery, known as creamware, was to become widespread during the second half of the century and was finally to oust the more traditional delft and stonewares.

The refinement of delftware

Many of the delftware patterns popular in the previous century continued to be made and decorated in established blue and white colours. But during the century there was an increasing use of polychrome decoration and by 1756 transfer printing was also occasionally used on delftware made at Liverpool. Some distinctive pieces commonly associated with the Wincanton potteries – which, like Liverpool, were established during the 18th century – were decorated with motifs set in panels reserved against a background of speckled manganese (purple) colouring. The range of wares increased, but continued to include the large chargers, dishes and bowls familiar in the 17th century. These were now often decorated with a variety of rural scenes showing countryside activities (ploughing), historical events such as Lunardi's balloon ascent in 1784, and portraits of the monarchy, although the Hanoverian Georges were never as popular as their Stuart predecessors. The most widespread motifs continued to be drawn from Oriental porcelain. In particular flowers such as peonies and prunus blossom and trees including bamboo, willow and pine, feature along with naively painted Chinese figures and temples painted in the form of pagodas.

While bottles made of green glass replaced the earlier distinctive delftware bottles, there was a considerable increase in the range of table wares, tiles and small decorated hollow bricks. These last were intended either to hold flowers when filled with water, or quills when filled with sand. With the increasing availability of tea, coffee and chocolate came teapots – round and bullet-shaped; coffee pots – tall and cylindrical; cups and saucers, cream jugs and sugar bowls, despite the fact that these examples of low-fired earthenware were not very suitable for hot liquids. Punch was a popular contemporary drink and delftware punch bowls, monteiths and ladles were made, as well as tankards, puzzle jugs and attractively decorated wine bottle labels which hung round the bottle neck by slim chains.

Astbury, Whieldon and Wood

During the 18th century Staffordshire rose to become the industrialised pottery-making centre in England, producing many famous potters such as John Astbury, Thomas Whieldon, the Wood family and Josiah Wedgwood. The staple product of the potteries in the first half of the century was stoneware, although most potters also combined this with making traditional lead-glazed wares. Like delftware potters they gradually had to adapt their products in order to compete with the newly manufactured porcelain. Decoration continued in the form of stamped and applied relief motifs which later were made from small moulds. Popular motifs included rosettes, baskets of flowers, vine leaves, hunting and drinking scenes; these last were often picked out in bold relief on large mugs of the period. Another type of decoration, associated with the work of the potters Astbury and Whieldon during the second quarter of the century, made use of bold relief decoration but in contrasting white-coloured clays. This type of ornamentation, applied to the red brown clays of the stoneware body, was also used on contemporary lead-glazed eathenwares. Similar effects were achieved by making the handles and spouts on items such as

Cream ware basket dish decorated with pierced and fluted sides and a blue underglaze border pattern. Simple but attractive, such pieces can be acquired inexpensively. About 1775.

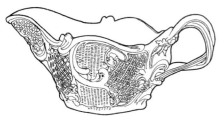

Salt-glazed stoneware sauceboat with moulded decoration. It echoes the typical mid 18th-century forms used in silver. Leeds, about 1770.

jugs, coffee and tea pots in a white-coloured clay which contrasted with the darker colour of the body.

Astbury and Whieldon are also associated with techniques introduced to make a whiter, more refined, eathenware. As early as the 1720's potted wares were being coated with a thin white slip over the new earthenware to simulate the fine white-bodied porcelain from the Orient. This method was later improved upon by adding ground flints to the white (Devonshire) clays, producing a material suitable for making both stonewares and lead-glazed pottery such as creamware. It was also an appropriate medium for newly-introduced moulding techniques. Their inception brought about a rapid increase

in production of all types of wares from the middle of the century.

The slip-casting method brought over from France in about 1745 was used to make 'hollow wares' such as jugs, mugs and pots. Not only were these pieces characterised by their very high quality and thin potting, but the shapes were no longer dictated by the limitations of the potter's wheel. Animals, houses and plants provided the inspiration for a wide range of items, such as teapots, in the shape of camels and houses. A number of these fanciful pieces are associated with Wood family of potters who produced them throughout the 18th century. Subjects varied from the well-known saltglaze Pew Groups, usually depicting two or three rather rustic-looking men and women leaning back against a settle, to single figures of birds, domestic animals and humans. Early examples in the 1740's were decorated with dabs of colour, but improvements in the use of metallic oxides led to the overall use of greens, yellows, browns, blues and greys. Other favourite products of the 1740's

and 50's were the agate wares made by kneading together different coloured clays to create a marbled effect. Later, tortoiseshell effects were also achieved by means of mottling the glaze.

The Hearty Goodfellow toby jug, possibly modelled by Aaron Wood, younger brother of Ralph Wood Snr, the proprietor of the well-known Staffordshire factory. c 1775.

Contributions of Wedgwood

The most important contributions to English earthenware in the second half of the 18th century were made by Josiah Wedgwood. One of a long line of potters, Wedgwood made Staffordshire synonymous with quality throughout the world. In 1759 he established the first in a group of famous factories, at the Ivy House, which he rented for £10 a year. This was followed by a pottery at the Bell Works (Brick House), which ran from 1764–69, and finally by his last and most famous factory at 'Etruria' (1769–1936). Wedgwood was noted for improving the quality of various glazes, particularly the greens and yellows which he used to great effect on the so-called cauliflower and pineapple wares made during the early years of the 1760's.

Another important contribution was Wedgwood's refinement of the common white ware, known as creamware pottery, which after 1760 began to oust other tablewares. Its clean colourless lines appealed to the neo-classical tastes developing in the 1760's and so keenly ware, most of the other five hundred potters in Staffordshire also made it too, the best of which is distinguished by its pale, milky hue and light weight.

Whilst the majority of ordinary domes-

Rare teapot made by Josiah Wedgwood and incised with his name on the base. Made of cream-coloured earthenware, decorated with applied motifs and Wedgwood's green glaze. c 1760.

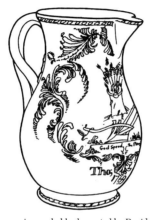

Cream ware jug probably decorated by David Rhodes, who worked for the Leeds factory. Leeds, dated and inscribed 'Thomas Store 1769'.

Small cream jug in blue jasper ware with white relief decoration. This example was made by the Turner factory, rivals to the nearby Wedgwood firm, in about 1790.

Teapot made at Wegwood's Burslem factory, showing characteristic mid-century form and decorated with lead-based green glaze. c 1763.

fostered by Wedgwood and his partner Thomas Bentley (d. 1780). Instead of the agitated animal and plant forms popular during the rococo phase, simpler patterns and shapes proliferated. Outlines and rims on pieces such as sauceboats, jugs and tureens were smoothed. Plates were decorated with a variety of classical scenes, either painted by hand or sent off to Liverpool for transfer printing. These scenes were usually encircled by restrained border patterns of fruit and flowers, or of abstract classical motifs. On many pieces these border patterns were used on their own, foreshadowing several designs still in use on creamware today. Following the success of Wedgwood's cream- tic items were made in creamware, Wedgwood developed several other materials for use in his luxury products. The most famous of these were the unglazed coloured jasper wares produced in crisp dark blue, soft pale blue, lilac, rose pink, green and black. These are still made today and are easily recognised by the application of small white jasper cameo moulds. These neo-classic cameos appear on the bodies of an enormous range of goods including tea services, vases, plaques and bowls. Other innovations developed by Wedgwood included the black basalt wares (stoneware) which could be cut and decorated on a lapidary (stonecutting) wheel, and buff-coloured 'caneware' (stoneware). All these are unglazed. Pieces made by Wedgwood at Etruria during the 18th century were always marked on the base of a piece with a variety of impressions, including 'Wedgwood & Bentley, Etruria', 'Wedgwood & Bentley' or, after 1790, 'Wedgwood and Sons'.

Josiah Wedgwood died in 1795, thus bringing to a close a period of outstanding artistic direction and business acumen. His influential career is ringingly summarised on his tombstone: 'He converted a rude and inconsiderable manufactory into an elegant Art and an important part of the National Commerce'.

Porcelain

Ever since oriental porcelain had been imported into Europe in the 16th century, this fine-bodied translucent ware had been highly prized. Many manufacturers sought to imitate it, but it was not until the early 18th century that the German factory at Meissen successfully developed a true, or hard paste, porcelain of the type produced in the Orient. Elsewhere, experiments led to the discovery of soft paste porcelain, and this became characteristic of the English factories which sprang up from about 1745 onwards.

Hard vs. soft paste porcelain

Hard paste porcelain consisted of china stone (petuntse) combined with china clay (kaolin). The two ingredients, which had been worked together, were covered with a chinastone-based glaze capable of total fusion with the body material. The paste was suitable for throwing, moulding and modelling, and when fired at a very high temperature produced a strong, largely translucent body. The makers of soft paste porcelain, particularly those in France and England, were under the misapprehension that true porcelain was a glass-based product, so instead of adding chinastone to their own attempts they mixed china clay with ground glass. The result was sometimes characterised by a rough gritty surface and is less brilliant than true porcelain, since it glazed only after a second (glost) firing with lead or tin oxides.

During the 18th century most of the porcelain made in England was soft paste. Exceptions were the hard paste porcelains made at Plymouth and Bristol, and later at Newhall, Staffs.

Dish in soft paste porcelain with scalloped edge, painted in enamel colours over the glaze. When flawed, a minor crack is probably preferable to rubbed enamel decoration. Chelsea, 1749–52.

Sauce-boat in soapstone porcelain, a type of soft paste body used at Bristol before the firm was amalgamated with Worcester in 1752. Painted in enamel colours and marked 'Bristoll'. c 1748–52.

Tureen in the form of a rabbit, naturalistically painted in enamel colours. Other creatures and vegetables used in this way include cauliflowers and hens.

Early factories

Many porcelain factories sprang up in London, Staffordshire and the West Country during the middle of the century, although by the close of the 18th century most of those still in production were confined to the Staffordshire (potteries) area. The first recorded piece of porcelain was made at Chelsea in 1745. Chelsea pieces are noted for their fine quality and sophis-tication, a factor reflected in the high prices which they usually obtain today. A large factory was established at Bow, in the east of London, in about 1746. Bow was noted for adding bone ash to its soft paste porcelain, a method which would later establish the foundation of the English bone china industry which flourished from the 19th century to the present day. Other factories were begun at Derby

Soft paste inkwell inscribed 'made at New Canton', a name of the Bow factory. Dated 1751.

Plate, *c* 1755, with moulded relief decoration of leaves with painted motifs in the centre. Typical of Longton Hall factory, whose wares often tend to be poor quality and gritty.

in 1751 (especially noted for its finely modelled figures), Worcester (at about the same time), Longton Hall (1749–60) and Lowestoft (1757–1795). This latter produced domestic wares intended for the locality, although some souvenir pieces carry delightful inscriptions such as 'a trifle from Lowestoft'.

At the end of the century factories were set up at Coalport, Spode and Minton

which, together with Wedgwood, firmly established Staffordshire as the pottery-making centre of England.

Decorative inspirations

The designs and shapes used in early porcelain production in England had no precedents. Manufacturers had to look, not only to the porcelain wares of the East and Meissen, but also to the shapes and motifs of mid-century silver. The closest that porcelain wares moved to silver designs were in some well-known pieces made by the Chelsea factory, modelled after silver salts in the form of crustacea.

Chinoiseries were the height of fashion, in keeping with the rococo tastes of the 1750's and 60's. In particular the *famille rose* patterns of China and the delightful asymmetrical Japanese Kakeimon designs, painted in a light palette, were imitated by painters decorating the pro-

ducts of factories such as Chelsea, Bow and Worcester. Cheaper wares were painted in blue under the glaze and often illustrated oriental themes. The fanciful chinoiseries of the French designers Pillement, and of the painter, Watteau, were popular in the 1760's, as were a whole range of exotic bird and plant forms. These chinoiseries are usually associated with pieces made after 1760, when the taste for strong, brilliant ground colours became prevalent. Rich claret, yellow, pea greens and turquoise had already been popularised by the Sèvres porcelain factory of France. A distinctive blue fishscale ground pattern appeared on Worcester porcelain after about 1765.

Although porcelain was used to make table wares and other domestic pieces like inkwells and candlesticks, it was also widely used in the making of ornamental figures. Early figure pieces were often

Mug with enamel overglaze decoration in the Japanese 'Kakeimon' style and mug in white-glazed porcelain decorated with applied prunus blossom. Bow, *c* 1750–1755.

Small cream jug in soft paste porcelain and painted in underglaze blue. The 'sparrow-beak' spout rising above the rim line is typical of Lowestoft wares. *c* 1765.

designed in the round and used as table decorations. But later these gave way to models intended for display on mantels, and in china cabinets. These were frontally modelled pieces whose elaborate scrolling rockwork bases were picked out in gold. The contents generally consisted of figures in the rather exaggerated poses popular in the 1770's. Other features of early figures included the use of a brilliant palette, and the fine modelling of intricately worked flowers and foliage (bocage) used on a number of models associated with the Chelsea, Derby and Bow factories. A wide range of subjects included those drawn from the Seasons, Aesops fables and the *comedia del'arte*, particularly the ubiquitous Harlequin figure. With the revival of neo-classical tastes in the last quarter of the century,

Worcester tea pot made in about 1765, with puce- and gilt-painted decoration. The finial is characteristic of Worcester pieces and is in the form of lop-sided opening flower.

pastoral themes came into prominence. Other stylistic developments of the 1780's and 90's included plainer bases and gilt scrolls, with shells and rockwork giving way to border patterns such as the Greek key pattern.

Improvements made in 1745 in moulding and casting techniques corresponded

Shallow dish moulded with rose leaves and buds, commonly known as Blind Earl pattern. Though most examples are painted overglaze in enamel colours, this piece shows underglaze blue decoration. Worcester, *c* 1765.

to the mid-century taste for natural forms. Several factories such as Longton Hall and Bow made tureens and sauceboats in a variety of animal, bird and vegetable shapes, although few equalled the quality and humour of those made at Chelsea. Shapes popular towards the end of the century reflected the simpler outlines associated with the neo-classical style, such as urns decorated with delicate swags of flowers. Plates and tablewares were also decorated in a restrained manner. Talented decorators including William Billingsley, William Quaker Peg and Zachariah Boreman, painted light-coloured floral festoons or classical landscapes and flowers within simple border patterns.

The production of porcelain in the 18th century was often hazardous, and the development of such fine products demanded great skill and patience and the finest pieces were expensive, highly prized and collected. Today this situation has not changed.

Ewer in the classical taste painted in enamel colours with gilt decoration. Made by the newly amalgamated Chelsea-Derby factory in about 1780–1785.

The New Hall factory was one of the few English firms to produce true hard paste porcelain, such as this jug. Manufacture of this distinctive medium lasted from about 1781 to 1810.

Eighteenth-Century Silver

During the 18th century silver plate was bought, not only by the rich and powerful big city corporations, courts, prominent nobles, wealthy figures or the church, but by an increasingly affluent and growing middle class. While much of the plate made for the former displays remarkable levels of craftsmanship and design, it is the less flamboyant and mainly domestic plate which holds such widespread appeal today.

The new silver standard

The first twenty years of the 18th century were dominated by the introduction of a new silver standard. Towards the close of the 17th century there was increasing concern for the rapidly dwindling supply of gold and silver coins. This reduction in the coinage was brought about by a ten-

dency among silversmiths to clip and melt down the coinage in order to supplement the short supplies of wrought plate then available and to meet the increasing demands of a rapidly expanding clientele. In order to counteract this state of affairs the Britannia Standard was introduced in 1697. This differentiated between the quantity of silver used in coinage and that used in wrought plate, by raising the standard of wrought silver from the old level of 925/1,000 to 958/1,000. (The balance consisted of various alloys which help strengthen and harden the silver which otherwise would be too soft to work satisfactorily and would also be easily damaged.)

Whilst the new standard did help to restore the coinage supply, it was never very popular among silversmiths and in

One of a pair of trencher salts in the typically undecorated style of the early Georgian period. Made by well-known salt maker, Edward Wood. London 1723.

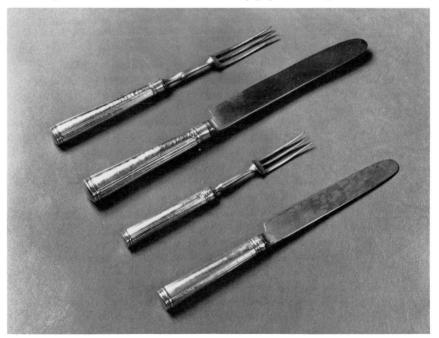

18th-century knives (cutlery), forks and spoons (flatware), can be acquired inexpensively one by one. These are from a large set for 12, and have silver handles and original steel blades. Sheffield 1797.

1719/20 the old Sterling Standard was restored. At the same time the Britannia Standard remained optional and is occasionally used even today. But the Sterling Standard had proved itself a more reliable and durable measurement for wrought plate.

The distinctive feature of the Britannia standard was the introduction of a new mark. The old marks of the Lion Passant and the Leopard's Head were replaced by the figure of Britannia and a Lion's Head Erased. They were accompanied, as before, by a date letter. But with the return of sterling in 1719, the Lion Passant was restored and in addition was accompanied by the assay office mark and a date letter. An optional fourth mark was the initials of the maker or makers, now that some firms were expanding and taking on partners.

Although London, since medieval times, had been the most important centre for gold and silversmiths, several towns in England acquired or regularised their own assay offices during the course of the 18th century. These included Exeter in 1701 (regularised: a three-towered castle replaced the X mark used since medieval times); Chester, 1701 regularised: City arms of a shield accompanied by date letters); Newcastle, 1702 (re-established: three castles in a shield); Birmingham, 1773 (established: upright anchor); and Sheffield, 1773 (established: crown).

The increasing demand for silver

The range of items made during the first quarter of the 18th century was limited when compared with the richness available by the end of the century, but much

Early 18th-century chocolate pot with the wooden handle placed at right angles to the spout. These pieces are increasingly rare and expensive. 1706.

George I tea caddy with two divisions by Joseph Farnell, London, 1717. Each division would contain a separate type of tea which, in the early 18th century, was very expensive.

of it was characterised by a simplicity of line typical of the Queen Anne style. Elegant proportions were enhanced by a lack of either applied or embossed ornament and engraved decoration was restricted to simple inscriptions, armorial bearings or the occasional border pattern.

Although dining rooms were not a distinctive feature of early 18th-century architecture, some items destined for the dining table began to make an appearance at this time. Cruet frames, casters and bottles for oil and vinegar, and sauce boats of the double-lipped type were all

early products of table service. Sauce boats were made either with separate stands or with feet, but these latter were not common before the 1730's. There was, however, a steady increase in items used in tea drinking, in line with the increasing availability of tea imported from the East. Newcastle became an important northern centre in the early 18th century for assaying a wide range of domestic

Bullet-shaped teapot of the early Georgian period, with an elegantly shaped handle fitted with a thumb grip, complemented by a straight, tapering spout.

The tall, tapering, straight sides of this coffee pot are typical of the first quarter of the century, as are the domed lid and finial.

articles such as two-handled cups, candlesticks, tankards, coffee and tea pots. Some early tea and coffee pots had handles set at right angles to the spout, but by 1720 these were usually set opposite the spout. Lids were generally domed but gradually became flatter, while round globular or bullet-shaped bodies were used for tea pots. Coffee and chocolate pots had tall, straight-sided bodies and were fitted with shallow, domed lids. Sometimes octagonal – and even hexagonal – forms were introduced by faceting the sides of the pot. The fashionable method of faceting was also used for many other wares, including candlesticks, tapersticks (small candlesticks used to melt sealing wax), castors, jugs and small table salt cellars which were now generally preferred to the large, old fashioned type.

The decade which followed the accession of George II in 1727 saw little change in the basic design of silver. But at about the same time that the Old Sterling Standard was revived, a gradual return to ornamentation was discernible on domestic plate. It had never really disappeared on costly ceremonial pieces. Much of this work was carried out by highly-skilled Huguenot craftsmen, many of whom had settled in England in the closing years of the 17th century. They made frequent use of engraved decoration, often in conjunction with flat chasing. Borders and panels were filled with intricate, delicate low-relief arabesque designs, set against diaper-patterned backgrounds. Although

An unusual silver octagonal-shaped salt for use more in the kitchen than on the table. William Darkeratt, London 1726.

Silver

Silver taperstick by James Gould of London, 1738. Tapersticks followed the same style as candlesticks but were used to melt sealing wax. They are sometimes found with standishs.

Undecorated pear-shaped cream jug similar to the coffee pot (right). This is an early example made by Ralph Maidman, 1732.

Coffee pot by William Shaw and William Priest in 1758 showing the characteristic 18th-century pear shape.

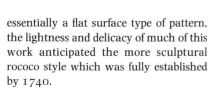

essentially a flat surface type of pattern, the lightness and delicacy of much of this work anticipated the more sculptural rococo style which was fully established by 1740.

The rococo expression in silver

Lightness and movement are characteristic elements of the style predominant between 1740–60. Known as rococo, it was certainly evident in the work of several leading silversmiths during the 1730's but it did not become wide-spread outside London until the middle years of the 18th century. Although the rococo style was very much an ornamental one, it also affected the form and outline of much wrought silver. The straight recti-linear outlines of the early 18th century gradually gave way to agitated, sometimes asymmetrical, curvilinear lines. Hollow wares such as jugs, castors, tankards and coffee pots became increasingly pear-shaped, and by the late 1750's a further bulge sometimes appeared at the

base, giving it a characteristic dropped-bottom appearance. Bombe shapes were fashionable as well, and were used on large and costly tureens as well as on much smaller caskets and even tea caddies. Not only were forms affected but rims and edges were often treated in an exaggerated way. Broken curves and scalloped edges were used in complex and imaginative ways. The helmet shape, introduced in the late 17th century, was now a particularly fashionable form for jugs and handles became an increasingly decorative feature in the middle of the 18th century. Not only were they made up of a number of broken curves, but on some elaborate and costly pieces they were finely modelled and cast in the form of figures, beasts and mythological animals and birds. Many items, particularly those designed for the table, were raised up on feet placed around the circumference. This was widespread, not only on small pieces such as table salts, increasingly elaborate cruet frames, baskets and cream jugs, but also on larger pieces such as tea

kettles, the newly introduced epergnes, tureens, trays and salvers.

The rococo was a complex style affecting all the decorative arts. But silver was a medium exceptionally well-suited to the highly fanciful range of rococo form and ornament. While flat chasing and engraving had given adequate definition to the linear arabesque decoration fashionable during the 1720's and 30's, during the mid-18th century silversmiths made use of more complex techniques. Embossing

One of a pair of sauce boats decorated with scalloped edges and a double-scrolled handle. Its lively treatment is characteristic of the mid-18th-century style. London 1774.

One of a pair of silver gilt candlesticks in the rococo style, vigorously decorated with repoussé decoration. Thomas Howell, 1771.

and applied cast decoration were called upon to achieve the rich, more sculptural, quality then popular. Motifs were drawn from a wide range of sources. Plant and flower forms were often used singly or in sprigs to decorate the bases and bodies of inkstands, candlesticks, tea and table wares. Crustacea and, in particular the shell motif, was another source of inspiration to many famous silversmiths such as Nicholas Sprimont (later involved in the Chelsea porcelain factory), George Wickes

Richly decorated silver tureen made by Frederick Kandler of London in 1761. Kandler's reputation as a fine silversmith would considerably enhance the value of this piece.

(founder of Garrards) and Paul de Lamarie. These three are arguably the finest craftsmen of the first half of the 18th century. As in contemporary porcelain manufacture, some items such as sugar bowls, sauceboats and jugs were cast in the form of sea shells and cabbage leaves. They are today rare and costly. One of the most distinctive sources of inspiration came from the exotic chinoiseries which had fascinated Europeans for over a century. The newly introduced and very costly epergne – an elaborate table decoration – and even tea caddies, appeared in the form of pagodas with rooftops equipped with tinkling bells.

One of a pair of George III gentleman's hairbrushes displaying the neo-classical decoration fashionable during the late 18th century. Made by Hester Bateman.

The development of Sheffield plate

By the last quarter of the 18th century, silver production had gradually developed from being a small family-based concern to production on a large scale. London, traditionally the heart of silver manufacturing, continued to be the most important centre, but by the second half of the century it was seriously challenged by the emergence of important metal-manufacturing towns such as Birmingham and Sheffield. Not only were signifi-

Sheffield-plate epergne with cut-glass bowls. This piece served as an elaborate table display. It would, however, realise less than a solid example. Late 18th century.

cant developments in production techniques made during the course of this period, but the competition offered by Sheffield plate did much to increase the production of silver items.

This relatively cheap method of plating silver, which effectively sandwiched a sheet of copper between two thin sheets of silver, had been invented as early as 1742 by a Sheffield cutler called Thomas Bolsover. However, it was not until the 1760's that it was taken up and used on a large scale by a number of firms. The most important to use this technique was that headed by Mathew Boulton (1728–1809) who, like Josiah Wedgwood in the field of pottery, was largely responsible for establishing the Midlands as the industrial metal-making centre of England by 1800. Together with widespread improvements made in machinery, such as the development of a machine in 1769 which enabled whole sections of silver plate to be stamped out and pierced with accuracy, the introduction of Sheffield plate helped to meet increasing public demand both at home and abroad for a wide range of small and relatively cheap goods like buttons, buckles and mounts as well as domestic plate.

Neo-classical designers

At about the same time that large-scale mass production techniques were implemented, the neo-classical taste became fashionable. Although it was the rich and influential aristocracy who tended to spearhead the newest fashions, the style was taken up quickly and was well established by the late 1760's. The simple, clear outline and uncluttered appearance was easily adapted for mass production and was fostered early on by both Boulton and Wedgwood. But such a style could not have succeeded without the concensus of architect-designers such as Robert Adam, who had done more than anyone else in England to introduce neoclassicism, and leading silversmiths of the day like Hester Bateman, Thomas Hemming and later, Paul Storr.

Forms such as urns and columns were drawn from antique artefacts, and these same motifs also appeared in the work of craftsmen in other fields. Echoes of antique design were also expressed in bead mouldings, reeding, bay leaf garlands, Greek key patterns, paterae, ram and lion heads, and various forms of foliage. Outlines were no longer agitated and irregular. Instead shapes were based on ovals and circles, or squares, with their variant polygonal outlines. Such shapes were well suited to small items like tea caddies, on which the only decoration was often the new bright-cut engraving technique. This produced deeper, more angled and curved, cuts than traditional engraved decoration had done. Bright-cut engrav-

Boat-shaped sugar basket decorated with a reeded rim and bright-cut engraving, which was very popular during the last quarter of the 18th century. 1793.

ing, which was very popular in the 1780's, imparted a livelier, jewel-like sparkle to the flat surface. Not only did wrought silver achieve a lightness and delicacy of design not seen before, but many pieces were actually lighter in weight. This trend was also visible in the cheaper wares made in both Sheffield plate and the newly-introduced Britannia metal.

Some of the more intricate examples took the form of baskets, used both for bread and cake. Often circular in shape but becoming increasingly elliptical in the

Silver table salt by a leading 18th-century maker, Robert Hennell. A blue glass liner is used for the salt, while the bowl is decorated with pierced motifs. 1774.

1780's and 90's, these swing-handled baskets were frequently constructed of delicately interlaced ornamental wires, or executed in solid silver with delicate pierced patterns. Similar patterns were used in the decoration of salt cellars and sugar baskets, both of which were generally fitted with blue glass liners. A characteristic found on silver made after 1784 is the sovereign's head, which signified that the tax at 6p for every ounce of silver had been paid in accordance with the act of 1784.

A very wide range of items was now made in silver. They included not only traditional table wares but also many smaller items and decorative mounts intended for objects such as walking sticks. There was a demand for large and elaborate dinner services, and a number of small table wares – beehive-shaped honeypots, fish slices, egg cruets and butter dishes – began to appear at the close of the 18th century.

Eighteenth-Century Glass

The invention of lead glass in the late 17th century established England as a leading centre of glass production during the next hundred years.

Whilst lead glass, or white glass as it was sometimes called, provided the impetus needed to bring about the development of a national English style, there was at the same time an increase in the production of the more traditional and cheaper green glass. This type of glass came from the so-called green glass houses which made a variety of objects including bottles and window glass. Due to the prohibition of the sale of bottled wine by tavern keepers in the early part of the 17th century, wine was sold by the barrel direct to the customer from the vintner. This state of affairs evolved because of abuse of the franchise by taverners, who were notorious for watering down wine as they bottled it. Instead it was now the customer who provided his own bottles direct to the vintner. Such bottles, which varied from a light green to a dark green almost blackish hue, usually carried the name or seal of the owner impressed on a small glass disc. The bottles were produced in very large quantities from the turn of the 18th century and approximately three million were made annually by some forty-two glasshouses. These bottles were similar in form to those made during the second half of the 17th century, and were characterised by their thick-walled, squat-shaped bodies fitted with tapering necks of various lengths. Some were provided with a 'kick' or depression underneath the base of the bottle which gave it added stability and also helped the cooling processes of the glass. Those made from about 1720 up to the end of the third quarter of the century were more cylindrical in shape, with a sloping shoulder to the neck. This form, similar to wine bottles widely used today, was capable of binning on its side, instead of neck down as had been done before. Many were produced from bottled moulds which came into use in the middle of the century. Seals and names (and occasionally dates) impressed on small round blobs placed in the centre of the body or just below the shoulder line were used up to the 1830's.

Developments in drinking glasses

Drinking glasses continued to form the largest category of glassware made throughout the century and many are still available today at a wide variety of prices. In the early 18th century forms were fairly limited and only a few are particularly associated with popular tipples of the period. One such example is the tall, elegant, narrow-bowled champagne flute of a type known since the 17th century, which is becoming increasingly fashionable now. This shape was in use up to about 1715, when a wide shallow-bowled glass became stylish. Other wines in the early 18th century were often drunk from plain, funnel- or bell-shaped bowls standing on thick massive stems, decorated with a variety of balusters and knops. Cordials and ales, both of which were strong alcoholic drinks, were imbibed in similarly-shaped glasses, whose correspondingly smaller bowls reflected the potency of their contents. The foot of all these glasses was commonly of a conical- or domed-shape, and the rim was often turned under (to a width of approximately 0.5 cm) for strength. The folded foot was less

Nailsea jug in green bottle glass with blobs of opaque coloured glass marvered into the body. Late 18th century.

Large lead glass goblet showing the heavy, almost massive, proportions of early 18th-century glass decoration.

common after about 1745 when the introduction of a tax made it uneconomic, although it reappeared later in the century and was also used in the 19th century. It was necessary to raise or dome the foot, as the rough surface of the pontil or puntee mark at the base of the stem (the point at which the glass was broken off from the iron rod) would have made the glass unstable. After about 1780 this rough surface was usually ground down, thus enabling the foot to become flatter. Other features associated with early 18th-century glass is a type of moulded stem in the shape of an inverted baluster with ribbed polygonal sides. This is commonly known as a Silesian stem, though it was actually of German origin, and was introduced to England following the accession of the Hanoverian monarch George I in 1715. It is a device found on wine glasses to about 1740 and on candlesticks and sweetmeat glasses to about 1760, after which it went out of fashion.

By the middle of the 18th century there was a growing demand for lighter, more delicate shapes and copious decoration better suited to the increasingly popular rococo style. Coincidentally, at about the same time as this style was becoming widespread, a tax was levied on the weight of glass. There had been a similar tax raised in 1695 by William III to obtain funds for the war against the French, but this had been rescinded within five years. The tax introduced in 1745–6 required payment by glass makers at the rate of 9 shillings and fourpence on every hundredweight of raw glass material. Despite vigorous protests it remained in force throughout the 18th century, with ensuing increases in the rates levied in 1777, 1781 and again in 1787.

Elements of the new form were first noticeable in the stem. Like the bowl, which gradually became thinner and smaller, stems became more slender and attenuated. Instead of the monumental

character of the earlier Queen Anne style and of the slightly less massive forms of the 1720's and 30's, the style of the mid-18th century concentrated on lighter forms and the use of decoration within the glass and on the surface. Air trapped within the body of the glass had been used in early baluster stems to form teardrops and occasionally to encapsulate coins. But now the glassmakers evolved a technique which enabled small bubbles of air to be pulled out so that they formed delicate cables inside the otherwise solid cylindrical body of the stem. These air cables could be twisted and, when combined with two or more air twists, formed decorative and intricate patterns. In the late 1740's twisted threads of opaque white glass (a category of glass exempt from taxation under the 1745 Excise Act) replaced air twists stems and remained popular up to the 1770's. On more elaborate pieces, different coloured enamels were added and were occasionally com-

Candlestick in clear colourless glass with a moulded, polygonal stem commonly known as a 'Silesian' stem. Also described as a shouldered stem. c 1720.

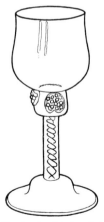

Wine glass with a bowl and foot made in cheap green glass and with a clear glass stem decorated with opaque spiral twist. Not an uncommon combination. c 1750.

Pair of wrythen ale glasses of the late 18th century. Ale was a stronger drink than it is today and was taken in smaller quantities. About 1790.

bined with the opaque white twists. Examples with colour twists in greens, red, blue, black, and less commonly yellow, are now increasingly rare finds and have become correspondingly costly. These patterns were employed mainly from 1755 to the late 1770's, when they declined following the increased levy of the 1777 Excise Act extended to cover all enamel glass.

Engraved examples

Both diamond point and wheel engraving had been known in England since the 17th century. In the early years of the 18th century these skills were still largely carried out by foreign craftsmen whose work was superior to our own. In particular Dutch and German craftsmen were noted for their skills and many German decorators came to England in about 1715 following the accession of George I. The family coat of arms was a widespread form of engraved decoration on glass during the 18th century. Other devices included the emblems of loyal Williamite and Hanoverian supporters, as well as those of the Jacobites. Symbols such as the rose, the oakleaf, the thistle of Scotland and a star, representing the light of the cause, were all part of the Jacobite liturgy to appear on glass. This particular group of glass made between 1745 – 65 has been well studied and collected for many years. It is doubtful that there are many finds still to be made, and numbers of forgeries have more recently swelled the market.

Other motifs characteristic of the first half of the century are the delicate arabesque border patterns which in mid-18th century examples merge into a freer pattern of leaves, fruit and flowers, in keeping with contemporary rococo styles. Also used are the occasional chinoiserie figures set amidst picturesque landscapes or the more common hops and barley motifs used on the bowls of mid-century ale glasses. Whilst English engravers had evolved their own style of decoration by about 1735, they were never really as skilled as their continental competitors. Much undecorated glass was exported abroad to Holland and Germany to be worked upon by Dutch and German engravers.

Enamelling and gilding

In addition to engraved decoration, enamelling became popular by the middle of the century and to begin with was used on opaque white glass in imitation of contemporary china. Some of this glass is attributed to the hand of Michael Edkins who painted pottery as well as glass, although other centres are now thought to have decorated similar wares. Enamelled opaque glass decorated with chinoiseries and flowers gave way to gilt decoration, particularly on the blue glass so fashionable in the second half of the century.

Gilding was a delicate technique and

Goblet in clear colourless glass decorated with stipple engraved scene of a man holding a 'Romer'. Stipple engraving was commonly carried out by Dutch engravers. Signed 'F Greenwood 1728'.

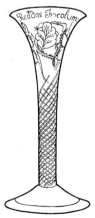

Jacobite wine glass engraved with loyal symbols and spiral twist stem. This example shows the Jacobite rose. About 1745.

Scent bottle in opaque white glass with enamelled decoration. About 1775.

when gold leaf precipitated in honey was used as the agent, did not last very long. A simple design of grapes and leaves with scrollwork borders became a favourite motif and was occasionally used to frame the delicate coloured enamel paintings of the Beilbys. But the Beilby family of Newcastle continued to use enamel colours, often in conjunction with gilding, on plain clear glass. Their work was especially sought-after during the 1760's and 70's.

In keeping with the neo-classical style

Decanter in the dark blue glass often associated with Bristol. Gilding was commonly used for decoration and a well-known gilder was Michael Edkins. *c* 1795.

which came in during the course of the 1770's, gilt borders often imitated classical patterns such as the Greek key.

The evolution of cut glass

The last method of decoration which developed during the course of the century was cutting. Like engraving it was a process designed to remove part of the surface of the glass. Iron or stone wheels of varying sizes and contours were used for this

technique. The process of cutting not only added new dimensions to the surface of the glass but also greatly increased the light refraction of the glass itself, and remains the method of decoration best suited to English lead glass.

Cutting, like engraving, was of German origin and was known to be used from early in the 18th century, although the earliest extant examples only go back to about 1725. At this time cuts were very simple and restricted mainly to the thick-

Scent bottle in blue glass with the facet-cut decoration popular during the second half of the 18th century. Each diamond-shaped facet is decorated with a gilt motif. *c* 1770.

er, more accessible sections of the glass. The brims and feet were incised with long shallow scallops and notches, whilst the thicker stems of wine glasses were occasionally covered with a shallow all-over diamond pattern. Glass cutting did not really develop as a craft, however, until about the second quarter of the 18th century when fashion catapulted it into prominence as the most widespread decorative medium. The range of patterns

increased between about 1745–70 to include diamonds, and scale and segmental cuts (also called lunate). These, together with the continuously popular fluted decoration, which carried on as a rather shallow form of cut decoration on its own, combined to produce a rich overall effect.

With the increased levy on glass by weight in 1777 there was a decline in cut glass made in England. But many English glasshouses re-established in Ireland soon after 1780, the year when free trade restrictions were lifted between the two countries. It was Ireland which continued the tradition of cut decoration of glass and huge quantities were imported to England. The patterns of this period were particularly deeply-cut and fluted, with relief patterns made up of small pointed diamond shapes. An example is the hobnail pattern. It was this type of crisp relief cutting which led to the all-over diaper patterns fashionable at the turn of the century.

Apart from wine glasses many objects were made in both lead glass and coloured glass during the 18th century. The decanter was in widespread use by the 1750's. Small glasses were made for syllabubs, jellies, custards and sweetmeats which often formed a special feature at the end of a meal called a 'banquet'. These small glasses were piled high in pyramidal formations to provide a magnificent centrepiece, a feast for the eyes and the appetite. Glass played an important part in the making of lighting equipment throughout the century. The refractive quality of the cut glass from the mid-century on was admirably suited to use in a wide variety of candlesticks and candelabra.

Eighteenth-Century Smaller Collectables

Treen

The word 'treen' is loosely applied to a very wide range of objects. Usually it applies to all small wooden objects, but is also frequently extended to include artefacts made in other materials such as ivory, horn and bone.

Treen objects have been made since medieval times although pieces surviving from before 1700 are increasingly rare. They constitute the cheap end of a very wide range of objects made in superior materials for a wealthier market. They include dairy and kitchen aids and those items associated with the eating table, but also extend to feminine artefacts and commemorative tokens.

The dairy was an essential part of the country community. It provided milk, cream, butter, cheese and whey. The implements used in the dairy represent a way of life which has since largely disappeared with the advent of mechanisation though, like other pieces of treen, they can capture in a flash the feel of a bygone age. Cream skimmers, bowls, butter pats, whey strainers and cheese scoops are still easily come by and are not prohibitively costly. Kitchen and eating implements are other types of popular collectables. Pestles and trenchers provide good, if simple, examples of cut and shaped woodwares, but more elaborate pieces may be found in the wide range of turned woodwares: table salts, spice boxes, funnels, goblets, even coffee or spice grinders and large punch bowls.

Woods used for treen objects vary considerably but those associated with food and drink tend to be woods which would not impare the flavour of the contents. Sycamore, sweet chestnut and certain fruitwoods – like pear wood – were ideal.

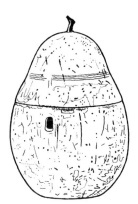

Tea caddy made in pearwood in the shape of a pear. Other fruit shapes include melons and apples. Third quarter of 18th century.

These woods did not warp with the constant change from dry to wet. Other woods included *lignum vitae* – particularly popular for punch bowls and goblets – boxwood and beech. Treen is frequently connected with special activities such as pipe-smoking or snuff-taking, and treen boxes provide interesting objects for collection. Feminine artefacts, particularly toilet articles – paste or rouge pots, combs, busk stays and glove stretchers – are all much sought after. Many of these pieces, such as busk stays (particularly fashionable between 1760–1800, when prevailing dress fashions favoured small waists and wide skirts) were decorated with chip-carved motifs in the form of flowers and hearts. They also conveyed love messages such as 'When this you see: Pray think of me' and sometimes the name and the date when such a piece was given to the loved one. Other erstwhile 'tokens of esteem' were the well-known Welsh love spoons, but these are now highly prized and good examples are expensive. Further small collectables include wool winders and some very decorative knitting sheaths.

Fans

Fans have been used since ancient times, but early references to them in England do not appear until about the 9th century. But it was not until the reign of Elizabeth I that they became regarded as an essential part of feminine attire, gradually developing a complex social language of their own.

The 18th century was the heyday for both makers and collectors of fans. Examples surviving from 1700 are rare. Fans were made in two forms: rigid fans, circular in shape, which could also be

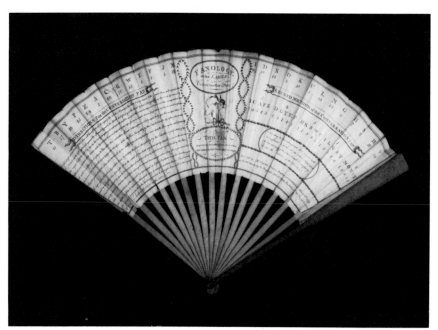

Paper fan printed with instructions for use as a 'conversation aid'. The instructions include a code of fan signals. Published 1797.

used as a face screen, and the folding fan. The latter was introduced to England during the Restoration (1660–85) and became the most typical type used during the 18th century. It was characterised by a number of sticks which could be opened to form a semi-circle, mounted between two outer sticks, or guards. The number of sticks used varied with different periods, but they helped to determine the overall size, or spread, of the fan. In the early 18th century a typical fan size was equal to one third of a circle and used between 12 and 18 sticks, whereas those made in the middle of the century with between 18 and 21 sticks had a spread of half a circle.

During the 18th century a fashionable fan was the so-called brisé fan, made up entirely of sticks in materials such as ivory, tortoiseshell, mother-of-pearl or horn, linked together with tightly-woven silk ribbons. These 'leafless' fans were made throughout the 18th century, although the decoration varied. Early examples were decorated with delicately cut and pierced designs resembling fine lacework, while later brisé fans, in which the sticks overlapped each other, were painted. By the end of the century bone was used to replace the more expensive ivory and mother-of-pearl. Other favoured materials included sandalwood (also noted for its light perfume, which wafted out as the fan waved) and cut steel, which was a fashionable material widely used for making buttons, buckles, châtelaines and the 'costume jewellery' of the last quarter of the 18th century.

The alternative folding fan popular during this period was made of sticks partially covered with a leaf, or mount. The materials which formed the leaf could be fine vellum, (also described by fan-makers as chicken skin), lace, silk or paper. It was usually of double thickness, covering both sides of the sticks, so that two decorative surfaces were provided. The subjects and themes of that decoration varied widely, but frequently reflected topical events of the day as well as popular fashions. Some mounts could be easily removed and replaced by others to meet the demands of particular occasions. Engraving, or hand-painting in mediums such as watercolours or gouache was the norm. Mythological or classical subjects – often used on mourning fans in the last quarter of the century – were also painted *en grisaille* (ie: black-and-white). Other forms of decoration included gilding, and the use of sequins in tiny sun and moon motifs in gold and silver. The pivot, or handle-end of the fan, was also subject to embellishment, and elaborate examples were set with precious and semi-precious stones.

Samplers

Samplers were small needlework panels worked by the young daughters of well-to-do and aristocratic families from the early 17th century onwards. Although their purpose varied they were intended primarily either as a reference sheet of patterns and stitches or as an exercise for young girls in order to improve their sewing skills. By the 18th century these sewing exercises were frequently combined with the basic educational skills of reading and writing. Letters of the alphabet as well as numbers were standard sampler fare. The youthful needlewomen

Sampler which displays both educational and devotional preoccupations. It also shows the passage of generations, since it appears to have been started in 1733 and reworked in 1784.

were proud of their work and many examples are signed and dated.

In the 18th century square panels of loosely-woven linen or canvas were often preferred to the long rectangular shapes popular in the second half of the previous century. Silk threads were used in a number of clear bright colours, but the themes covered a wide spectrum. At the beginning of the century they included stories taken from biblical texts. As in carving and silverwork, the Fall proved exceptionally attractive, with the naive figures of Adam, Eve and the Serpent clustered under a stiffly-shaped tree picked out in cross stitch. Other subjects were based on popular verse, prayers, and even contemporary hymns such as those of Charles Wesley. Later in the century purely pictorial motifs became the vogue. The can-

vas teemed with figures, animals, birds and houses, sometimes in imitation of contemporary embroidered needlework pictures. Pastoral themes were also fashionable, showing shepherds, shepherdesses and their sheep in front of a cottage set amidst rolling hills. The most common stitch was cross stitch, but others included satin, chain and lace. This last was also popular for trimming baby linen. Samplers invariably have a whimsical charm and can be endearing items to collect. In part this is probably due to the fact that they have been diligently worked by a little girl, usually well under the age of ten, and sentimental attachment over the years has assured their care and preservation, despite the fragility of textiles.

Battersea Enamels

English enamels were produced from the 1740's onward to appeal to a middle class

market who were unable – or unwilling – to pay the very high prices demanded for similar trifles made by gold and silver-smiths.

Decorated enamels are a form of opaque flint glass. This brittle top layer could be fused to a very thin sheet of metal – usually copper – at a prescribed temperature. Decoration was added by brushing on enamel colours, or by transfer print. Other ground metals used were gold, silver and pinchbeck.

For a short three year period, 1753–56, some of the finest examples of English enamels were produced at York House, Battersea. These so-called Battersea enamels were noted in the 18th century – and continue to be so – for the high quality of enamel and for the high artistic standards achieved in their decoration. The

Enamel necessaire with gilt mounts. Inside the necessaire are gilt blue-glass ink bottles and writing equipment and a small patch box (shown). c 1760.

factory turned out a wide range of mainly small-sized goods such as those which appear in the *Daily Advertiser* of 28th February, 1756, the year in which the factory stopped production. These included 'snuff boxes of all sizes and a great variety of Patterns, of square and oval pictures of the Royal Family, History and other pleasing subjects, very popular ornaments for cabinets for the curious, Bottle tickets with chains for all sorts of liquor ... watch cases, Toothpick-cases, Coat and Sleeve Buttons, Crosses and other Curiosities, mostly mounted in metal double gilt'.

The factory at York House was opened by Stephen Theodore Janssen, a younger son of a prominent and wealthy city merchant. Jansen himself was a notable patron of the arts and knew many of the finest artists, engravers and decorators of the time. It was largely due to such contacts that he was able to recruit the services of engravers like Robert Hancock, John Brooks and Simon-Francois Ravenet, the most famous name to work at Battersea. Brooks was also an important figure at Battersea as it was probably he who first mooted the commercial feasibility of using transfer prints, taken from copper engravings, to decorate enamel wares. The creamy white enamel backgrounds, which are a characteristic of all Battersea enamels, provided an excellent ground for decoration by this method. Both monochrome and coloured decoration was used. Colours used for monochrome transfer printing included a purplish black, mauve, a soft warm sepia tone and a rich crimson. Gold was also used – although with great restraint, when compared to later Staffordshire enamels. Landscapes, figures and floral designs were used to decorate the entire surface of these small, dainty trifles.

Japanned Metal Wares

Throughout the 18th century, the Welsh town of Pontypool (Mons) was famous for its production of high-quality japanned metal wares. Japanning, a technique which imitated Oriental lacquer work, had been fashionable in England since the Restoration in 1660, but initially was used on wood. Only later was it appreciated as a decorative possibility on metals such as iron, tin and copper. The lacquer was a type of varnish which could be coloured to produce an opaque ground with hues which changed with the dictates of fashion. In 1680 John Allgood discovered a heat-resistant varnish. This enabled each layer to be individually dried in an oven, then buffed and polished to produce a smooth lustrous surface for gilt motifs and, later painted colours. High quality items had as many as fifteen layers with as many stovings, and were correspondingly expensive. In 1760 an elaborate Pontypool tray was advertised for sale at fifteen guineas.

In the early 18th century demand for japanned metal wares was such that by 1730 Edward Allgood (1681–1763) had established a factory at Pontypool to supply japanned metal wares to the landed gentry and the aristocracy. In 1760 the factory was taken over by his eldest son Thomas, but two other children set up a rival factory seven miles away at Usk. These two operations continued to make the best japanned metal wares in the 18th century, although by the middle of the 19th century both had gone out of production (1820 and 1860 respectively). In the middle of the 18th century other competitors opened factories in Bilston, Birmingham and Wolverhampton, but despite their adoption of the word 'Pontipool' (complying with unwritten trade's description act of the time by using an 'i' instead of a 'y'), the work of these rival workshops remained inferior. But by the close of this period Birmingham was the largest centre in the country for japanned metal ware production, exporting both to America and to the Continent.

Pontypool wares made up to about 1760 were decorated with gilt chinoiserie scenes. Grounds ranged from crimson, black and chocolate to mottled ground made up from all three colours described as tortoiseshell by the makers. In the second half of the century, with the increased competition from centres in the Midlands, a greater variety of decoration and ground colours appeared. Painted floral clusters were popular, as well as seascapes and landscapes. By the close of the century the latter, together with hunting scenes, had become hugely successful and could cover entire flat surfaces of pieces like trays from rim to rim. The range of japanned wares was large and included tea equipment such as trays, waiters, caddies (or canisters), and both tea and coffee urns. Other items were cake baskets, cheese coasters (also called cheese cradles) snuff boxes, decorative urns, candlesticks, snuffers, dishes, bottle coasters, and knife boxes. Metal finials and iron animal masks for ring handles were also made. With the introduction of die-pressing techniques in the second half of the century (c 1770's) pierced decorative patterns, such as palings, were used on the rims of trays with an effect similar to that of contemporary Sheffield plate and silver forms.

Basket in dark-blue japanned tinware with gilt
decoration. The shape is similar to contemporary
silver forms. *c* 1760.

Eighteenth-Century Antiques
What To Look For

Viewing and Buying

Museums, special exhibitions, specialist dealers in London and the provinces, leading auction houses.

Furniture

Predominant woods: Walnut, Mahogany, Satinwood and Oak.
Can be broken down into at least 3 categories, each well represented by dealers and auction houses nationally.
i Fine furniture: commonly characterised by good timber with the addition of fine gilt decoration, exceptional marquetry, well-cast metal mounts, good carved decoration. Provenance often available.
ii Good furniture: is generally of good quality timber and sound craftsmanship. Represents largest category. Generally made by leading London and provincial makers.
iii Traditional and country furniture: commonly made of oak or other indigenous woods, often showing simple – even crude – carved decoration.

Points to Watch
Handle replacements: these may well detract from the aesthetic and financial value of a fine piece, but is less important on medium-range or country furniture. Detection can be made by the appearance of more than one set of handle fixings, clearly seen on the back of the drawer front.
Condition and extent of restoration (see 17th century).
Some 18th-century pieces decorated during late 19th century followed fashion for 'medievalising' everything. Generally this took the form of deep all-over carving in the Jacobean manner.

Pottery and Porcelain

i Fine porcelain typified by rare examples, early works from factories such as Chelsea, Bow and Derby; good polychrome decoration, decorative pieces including vases and figures.
ii Medium range pottery and porcelain includes blue-and-white underglaze decoration, mostly transfer printed (this is principally overglaze though blue was also used under).
iii Traditional wares – principally pottery – blends well with country furniture, characterised by deep, earthy colours.

Points to Watch
Small chips and hairline cracks. Same method of detection as used in porcelain or glass (see below).
Old restorations tend to discolour over period of years but modern methods using epoxy resin adhesives are much more difficult to detect, though can be seen under ultraviolet light. Other methods used include teeth rubbing and clarity of ringing tone. Those using their teeth detect a lifelessness to the touch, but not everyone finds this a satisfactory method.

Silver

Fine silver: made by well-known craftsmen. Mainly large decorative or commemorative pieces with high quality of decoration show fine embossed, engraved, repoussé work. Often gilt.
Good silver: pieces are mostly domestic and small wares showing less flamboyant decoration.

Points to Watch
Wear at base of joins, particularly around handles, spouts and stems. The removal of engraved crests or initials can seriously weaken the metal. Thin metal indicates considerable wear and is

a potential weak spot.

Pieces made up of more than one section generally display an assay mark on individual sections – ie a teapot is generally marked on base and cover. Beware those that have too few marks. Other pieces such as a tankard may show 3 marks on base, body and handle. The handle mark may well be different to the other marks indicating that it was made by a specialist small worker possibly making only handles.

Glass

Predominant glass: types of drinking glasses.

i Fine glass is characterised by rarity, fine colour and exceptional decoration – generally by a well-known decorator eg: Beilby or James Giles. Includes good examples of commemorative and decorative glass, including those commemorating Jacobite cause (beware of fakes and copies, however). Other unusual features include complex twist patterns, occasionally using colours such as black and yellow.

ii Medium range glass shows less elaborate decoration. Includes most decorated glass such as spiral twist, shallow-faceting and moulded patterns. Some coloured glass, such as coloured decanters – commonly in blue or green – with gilt name labels.

iii Country and traditional glass includes a wide variety of drinking glasses used by pubs and hostelries. Tend to be poor in colour, thick-walled and have impurities in the metal. Variable lead content can be judged by the length and tone of ringing sound when struck. The low cost of this glass makes it comparable to cost of modern good-quality lead crystal but in addition each glass is unique and individual.

Points to Watch

Hairline fractures: if not easily visible can be heard by the buzzing sound made when the glass is struck.

Chips: these are often ground down, but usually leave the rim slightly unbalanced and can be sharp to the touch.

Later decoration: usually etched but can be engraved.

Fusing or 'marrying' two separate pieces to create a good new piece. Especially common in drinking glasses (which are generally made in three parts). This latter point is a major alteration and should be avoided. Detection can be difficult as the glass fuses under certain temperatures, but can be ascertained in the unbalanced design or under an ultraviolet light.

PART THREE **The Nineteenth Century**

The Nineteenth Century
Historical and Social Background

Pen-and-ink drawing by George Cruikshank for *The Yule Log* by L. S. Chamerozow. Cruikshank was the doyen of mid-Victorian illustrators, providing light relief and satirical commentary for the books of Dickens, as well as for tracts on temperance, fairy tales, and in political and social cartoons. The Victorian preoccupation with hearth and family is well portrayed by the artist; the smell of roast goose, steamed pudding and mulled cider almost wafts off the page.

Dramatic changes followed in the wake of the Napoleonic wars at the turn of the 19th century. The campaign, begun in 1795, dragged on for a further twenty years before Wellington's brilliant victory at Waterloo in 1815 finally brought to heel the fabled Napoleon Bonaparte, Emperor of France since 1804. At home the war had started a tide of rising inflation. This, set against the quickening pace of the Industrial Revolution, was to introduce to established society a new and vociferous rich. Furthermore the population, despite the exigencies of poverty, disease and even war, increased at a steady rate throughout the period, so that the population of about 10 million people at the beginning of the century had all but quadrupled by the close. Such expansion, augmented by fresh markets overseas, brought about a continual demand for economic growth. The ensuing note of materialism, with its counterpoint of ever-constant search for change and novelty, are among the chief strains running through the 19th century.

The fruits of the Industrial Revolution

The success of Britain's industrial boom lay in the availability of resources, particularly coal. Hitherto this had been only tapped by laborious and dangerous methods. The use of Humphry Davy's new 'safety lamp' improved safety standards of mining in deep underground coal pits. For it was coal above all which enabled the great industrial centres – already established since the close of the 18th century–to accelerate production with the changeover from water power to steam. This in turn, radically affected all forms of industrialisation. It also initiated a new system of transport and communications in the form of the train, powered by the newly-invented steam traction engine. Initial success was achieved by George Stephenson, whose famous 'Rocket' set speed records of 30 miles per hour in 1829.

The opening of the first railway line from Stockton to Darlington four years earlier had already sealed the fate of the waterways and canals which, since the second half of the 18th century, formed the principal network for transport up and down the country. By the middle of the century, following two decades of frenetic and large-scale building programmes, some 5,000 miles of railway had been built, just in time for the real of prosperity in the third quarter of the 19th century.

The unfortunates of progress

But the 19th century, contrary to popular belief, was not always prosperous. The slump brought about by the end of the Napoleonic Wars and the corresponding inflation also meant unemployment, particularly among the

Mid 19th-century Staffordshire portrait figure of Napoleon – probably a reflective study of the exiled Emperor. Napoleon was a very popular subject. About 1850.

soldiers from the national armies recently demobbed. At the other extreme the flagrant extravagance and moral lassitude exhibited by the Prince Regent – appointed to that title in 1811, following the worsening insanity of his father George III – can have done little to assuage the ire of those around him as well as that of the common people. Stabbing taunts concerning the conduct of the Prince were readily accessible through the publication of pamphlets, broadsides and the political cartoons of James Gillray and Thomas Rowlandson. But while the Regent demanded that funds should be found to meet such projects as his Brighton extravaganza – built in the form of an Indian mogul's pavilion at a staggering cost – the less fortunate, especially in the depressed rural areas and in the hideously overcrowded slums of the new urban centres, were suffering from quickly-rising prices and ever-higher rents.

For those at the bottom of the social scale, life in the big cities was especially grim. According to a census taken for Liverpool in the middle of the century, life expectancy itself was short, with only about half the babies born expected to live. The survivors were fortunate indeed to live to forty. It was not only poverty that caused such hardship but also the fact that the few urban centres – particularly the new towns such as Liverpool, Birmingham, Salford and Leicester which expanded at a terrific rate during the 19th century – could cope with the consequential social problems. Malnutrition, slums, poor sanitation – due to open sewers which were still commonplace up to the middle of the century – and a frequently foetid water supply did little to forestall the onset of diseases such as cholera, tuberculosis, diphtheria, typhus and smallpox. Even the Houses of Parliament suffered during the summer of 1858 when they were unable to sit due to the 'Great Stink' caused by the overpowering smell of effluent rising from the River Thames. Desperate overcrowding ensured that infectious illness spread like wildfire through the warrens of the Glasgow Gorbals or the East End tenements of London. Whole families lived cramped together in tiny garret-like dwellings with often more than half a dozen people to a room. These were the very poorest, who lived well below the official poverty line, in conditions of extreme hardship and starvation. They were fortunate to possess a single bed and the very meanest utensils necessary for domestic existence.

But not all the working classes were so poor, so seemingly beyond redemption. For those who could lay claim to a skill, or indeed, who might run some small retail outlet such as an ironmongery, life at least was tolerable. There was also a host of new jobs available during the course of the century, brought about by the development of railways, the post office, the police and even the spate of department stores which grew up during the 1860's and 70's, such as Whiteleys, Harrods and the Army and Navy Stores, an early form of co-

Mid-Victorian centrepiece with a cut-glass bowl supported by three putti. The piece shows the indiscriminate use of earlier styles typical of much Victorian silver. Steven Smith 1869.

operative. A small but steady income meant a fire in the grate and food on the table. The paraphernalia of respectability came with the clutter of cheap china ornaments displayed on the mantelpiece and the framed prints hung on the wall.

The energetic bourgeoisie

Life for the established working classes was moderately comfortable by the standards of the very poor, but compared to middle-class life it only illustrated the growing gap between the social divisions in the Victorian period (1837–1901). Just as the successful working classes reached out towards the 'respectable' way of life entrenched in middle class morality, so too did the middle classes look towards gentility and upward mobility.

But middle class respectability was powerfully bolstered by a widespread reverence for piety and the church. More churches were built during the 19th century than at any other time since the Middle Ages. It could not accept with an easy conscience the frequent displays of dubious morality, licentiousness, and selfish eccentricity that was exhibited by many of the landed gentry.

The central ethos of the Victorian middle classes was work – an idea that was essentially anathema to the upper classes, living comfortably if not always luxuriously, off the fruits of their landed inheritance. To these privileged few any attachment to work – especially 'trade' – smelt ominously of money-grubbing. But the inventive middle classes transformed this necessity into a virtue, and they did not hesitate to uphold their mode of life as exemplary to the working classes and the aristocrat alike. At the root of their success was the development of private business. A thriving trade brought gain and plenty for the owners, while at the same time extending the benevolent arm of paternalism over the workforce – an idea regarded as wholly admirable during the Victorian period, some years prior to the Welfare State. While the great majority of the middle classes were content to live within the solidly suburban perimeters of the industrial and commercial centres, a few who became really wealthy were bent on breaching the privileged citadels of the upper-class way of life.

Life at the top

Despite all the power and influence that 'earned' money brought in its train – backed as it was by the resources of the Industrial Revolution in the form of mining, banking, shipping and manufacturing – the prestige, if not the power, of the landed gentry remained undiminished in the 19th century and if anything was actually increased. But new money could buy ancient privilege, either by marrying into it – linking fortune with 'family' – or by entering into the country

Historical Background

Painted tin carrier for two dozen eggs. Late 19th century.

house market and developing as quickly as possible those attributes deemed necessary for the life of a country squire.

Beyond the necessity of establishing a country seat, life for the upper classes was one of organised leisure. To a great extent even the education of the young continued to endorse the value of leisure. Education for the wealthy middle classes and the gentry became increasingly biased towards sport, rather than the intellectual and cultural pursuits which had so enlightened the 18th-century mind. For sports were accepted as gentlemanly pursuits during the 19th century, regarded as the foundation not only of a healthy body but also of a strong, upright character and a steady moral outlook. Of course sports had been among the pastimes of the gentry during the previous century, but often the element of gambling – particularly strong in horse racing and wrestling – had been the motivating force. The Victorians, as an adjunct to healthy body, found the idea of competition morally uplifting. Games such as cricket and rowing, both stressing the team spirit, were particular favourites for school and university gamesfields but at home in the country more traditional sports such as shooting and the chase were eagerly taken up. It was in the 19th century that the sports club in town and country developed and fostered such wide ranging activities as tennis, cricket and golf – though lawn tennis was equally fashionable within the capacious grounds of suburban villas and the country houses. Like croquet, tennis was deemed suitable for women, and later in the century the widely popular bicycle was also adopted by the feminine contingent. Games became part of the social life of the leisured classes, favoured both for enjoyment and for encouragement of group participation.

Social life among the upper classes was as organised and as formal as it had been in the previous century, only some of the forms had changed. 'Morning calls' were now made in the afternoon and were apt to be stiff and rather boring. Tea, which had during the previous century been growing in popularity, particularly among women, now became a recognised social gathering and by the end of the century afternoon tea had become a large and elaborate meal taken indoors or out between midday luncheon and evening dinner.

But it was dinner that provided the formal high point of the day, provided of course that it was not displaced by a ball or – in a large town like London – a visit to the opera. Formality in dress, punctiliousness and great capacity were the major demands made by this formidable meal which might encompass at least a dozen courses. Endless house parties, made viable by the growing arms of the railways, were organised around picnics, cricket matches, musical recitals, gargantuan meals and the occasional ball. Sporadic trips to an increasing number of spa towns and watering holes both here and on the Continent were undertaken to break the pattern and helped to revivify the body against the physical cost of the high life. At the same time, coastal resorts such as Brighton – first popularised by the Prince Regent early in the century – came into their own as the holiday resorts of rich and poor alike.

Mid 19th-century doll's kitchen showing the wide range of equipment necessary for even the modest home. The doll is a German import.

Nineteenth-Century interiors and furnishings

The social turmoil which racked France following the revolution in 1789 and the growing impact of the Industrial Revolution at home did much to disturb the confident fabric of English society at the turn of the 19th century. The well-ordered symmetry visible in classical architecture no longer reflected the solid virtues and balanced harmonious way of life which had characterised English society for much of the previous one hundred years. By the last decade the picturesque style in architecture, which stressed irregularity and 'a sort of loose, sketchy indistinction', was gradually emerging. It would soon explode into a full-blown romantic revolt. The steady abandonment of the classical rule brought a number of cultures into prominence as models for inspiration.

The eccentric Regency

The diversity of tastes that emerged from early in the century became, as the century wore on, increasingly more complex and bewildering. At the outset, the Prince of Wales – later to become Regent from 1811 to 1820 and King George IV from 1820 till his death in 1830 – indulged his personal fancies by building a most exotic oriental creation in the form of the Brighton Pavilion. But while the external appearances of the pavilion displayed the most flagrant abandonment of pre-established, accepted order, the interior and decorations still owed much to the formality of the previous century.

Part of the reason for the divergence in house-building and decorating can be ascribed to the fact that the 18th-century idea of a country house was gradually being displaced by the concept of a private domain belonging to the owners, a personal kingdom subject to their whims and tastes, rather than a monument to political interests. To put it another way, the country house of the 18th century, surrounded by its parkland and estates, became in the next century a private house set in the country. This even held true for Osborne House, built for the Queen and her consort, Albert, in 1848. It was conceived as the *home* of the royal family, rather than as a palace, despite its considerable size and a choice of style strongly reminiscent of a 16th-century Tuscan palazzo.

Wyatt and Pugin – Gothic masters

The preponderant architectural nuance for much of the 19th century was the 'Gothick' style. Already there had been an early re-introduction of the form in Horace Walpole's fantasy at Strawberry Hill, Twickenham (begun 1750), but its orderly composition betrays its 18th-century origin. Later examples broke increasingly with 18th-century classical planning, becoming more extravagant and eclectic. By the late Regency, these were conceived on a truly enormous scale. The eccentric and fabulously rich William Beckford's passion for the

Page 94: The Drawing Room, Cragside, Northumbria. Its massive alabaster inglenook fireplace dominates the far end. The inglenook was a distinctive feature much used by the architect Richard Norman Shaw and many versions are complete little rooms in themselves.

The Drawing Room is top-lit and augmented only by a bay window and a small peep-hole in the inglenook. The deployment of the furniture is characteristic of the High Victorian interior. The house was the first in England to install electric lighting.

Large dinner plate with blue-printed scene showing the signing of the Magna Carta. This comes from one of the historical series produced by Jones & Son. About 1825.

medieval style induced him to create Fonthill Abbey (built by Wyatt in the 1790's) along the combined lines of a medieval castle and cathedral. Its most striking feature was the enormous octagonal tower, the height of which seriously threatened to rival that of nearby Salisbury Cathedral. But while Fonthill was breathtaking in its vertiginous escalation (though the tower collapsed in 1825 due to non-existent foundations, some seventeen years after its completion), there was an increasing tendency to return to the 17th-century horizontal plan of building in a series of rambling and seemingly dislocated buildings. Ashridge Park, another house designed by James Wyatt, but this time for the Earl of Bridgewater in 1808, was an early 19th-century example of such horizontal planning. It was also a perfectly conceived asymmetric design and bore very little relation to 18th-century concepts of design.

James Wyatt was most noted for his classically-designed buildings, however, the greatest of which was probably Dodington Park, based on the somewhat severely-correct Grecian style. This was a treatment later adopted by the Prince Regent's favourite architect, John Nash, for his dramatic town planning schemes, among them the enormous Metropolitan Improvements undertaken in London between 1812 to 1828. This encompassed what is now Regents Park all the way to Buckingham Palace. The Grecian style was also used by the gifted Thomas Hope for the design of his country house, Deepdene, situated just outside Dorking in Surrey (now demolished). But in general, classicism, although it enjoyed its most archaeologically-correct interpretation during the Regency period, was really the final flowering of a style conceived in the previous century which played a diminishing role during the 19th century.

By the time Queen Victoria came to the throne in 1837, following the death of her uncle, William IV (younger brother of George IV, who had died in 1830), Gothic architecture was well and truly established. It was greatly popularised through the romantic fiction of such writers as Sir Walter Scott, whose novels are copiously sprinkled with Gothic and Elizabethan baronial mansions furnished with the ancient accoutrements of an earlier age. In reality their eager imitations came from dubious antique shops along the environs of London's Wardour Street. The style was even imbued with a sense of religious rightness under the guiding hand of the architect A. W. N. Pugin (1812–52), whose own deep religious leanings led him to adopt the Roman Catholic faith while still a young man. Because to him, as to many others, a 'Gothic building announced its purpose clearly and unambiguously', not only was it an expression of faith at a time when religion and faith were increasingly the bulwark of the middle and upper classes, it also provided an opportunity to build in an honest and craftsmanlike way in the manner of the medieval guilds.

Upstairs, downstairs

The irregular appearance and rambling exteriors of many 19th-century houses, both large and small, belied the careful organisation of their interiors. The greatest division to emerge in contemporary house planning was a purely social one, irrevocably dividing servants from the masters and served by the barrier of the green baize door. The irregularity was a sham to conceal the complex social structure hidden within the walls. In general the divisions were threefold, dividing servants, family and guests. In the larger establishments such distinctions became unremittingly clear when the distance to be crossed between dining room and kitchen was often the length of a football pitch.

The number of servants employed in a fashionable and wealthy house, particularly one in the country, varied considerably depending on the means of the owner. Between twenty and thirty were typical, although in a few of the really large houses at least fifty were employed. But the hierarchical structure of life in the 19th century was as clearly defined within the servants' quarters as it was on the other side of the green door. Furthermore the necessity of separating the men from the women on moral grounds added further complications to an already complex structure. In some cases it led to complete segregation – exacting separate quarters for each sex with access to bedrooms above the workrooms via separate staircases. The principal rooms in the servants' quarters were divided between housekeeper, butler and cook. The former two head staff were largely responsible for running the household and took control of the indoor female and male staff, respectively. The cook, either male or female, was in charge of the kitchens, sculleries, bake house and a variety of larders and pantries, as well as of the kitchen staff who worked under them. The 'upper servants' – which included nannies, governesses and tutors – lived an awkward life, caught as they were halfway through the green baize door.

The kitchen itself was an impressive room and its large size reflected not only the number of staff required to run it but also the scale of entertainment enjoyed on the other side of the house. The dominant feature – apart from the battery of cooking aids which were necessary to the 19th-century cook such as mixers, mincers, pots, pans, fish kettles, bain maries, baking trays, and moulds – were the large and spacious ovens with an elaborate range of spits for roasting. These required the constant attention of at least one kitchen maid. Even in a modest middle-class home employing at least two or three servants, the duties of the 'skivvy' were onerous and often unpleasant. One of the major changes to emerge towards the end of the century was the appearance of gas and later electric cookers, but these were regarded as new-fangled ideas and were slow to be adopted. Gas, for instance, had been introduced early in the 19th century, and

Country-made armchair in elm with a rush seat. These simple, robust pieces were widely used in cottages, pubs, and in the servants' quarters of large houses. Early 19th century.

mains supplies were being laid as early as the 1820's in some towns, but its use on a widespread domestic scale – and then mainly for lighting – did not occur until well into the middle of the century.

Once beyond the confines of the servant's quarters – which were cut off from the guarded domain of the rest of the house by a labyrinth of interminably long and gloomy corridors smelling of the linoleum – the rest of the house was generally comfortable and crammed with sentimental clutter, fashionable knick-knacks and overstuffed furniture. Clutter was a particular feature of the Victorian period, although it was to be found mainly in the main reception rooms, but the sense of disarray had been apparent from the beginning of the century. In her novel 'Persuasion' Jane Austen describes how in an old-fashioned parlour 'a proper air of confusion' was achieved by 'a grand piano-forte and a harp, flower stands and little tables placed in every direction'. There was a concerted march of furniture away from the walls toward the middle of the room. It was only a short step from the discreetly haphazard arrangements found in Jane Austen's novels to the overcrowded maze which characterised many interiors by the middle of the century.

The evolution of living space

Carrying on from the last quarter of the 18th century, the drawing and dining rooms continued to develop as the most important areas for the entertainment of visitors. The same lavish treatment was accorded them, only the neo-classic tastes of the previous century gave way to a whole gamut of new fashions. The neo-rococo taste was especially favoured for drawing rooms. Combining the formality of the heavy well-padded giltwood furniture with the rich crimson damask coverings used for walls and upholstery, the effect was sumptuous and stately. These rooms now tended to reflect the tastes of the lady of the house and increasingly became more and more the domain of women. It was in the drawing room that the 'morning' caller was received in formal state on her arrival in the afternoon.

On the other hand the dining room and the library became more and more masculine in appearance. Massive carved furniture – usually in mock Jacobean or Gothic styles – and large sprawling Turkey carpets on the floor married well with the smell of cigars and old books. Even so, the library which had played such an essential part in the education of the 18th-century century man of taste, became less important. This coincided with the growing stress on outside activities at the end of the century, and so the library was often displaced in importance by the smoking or the billiards room.

But it was really the revival of the great hall that characterised many later

Oak tantalus with three decanters, which could be locked when not in use. The decanters have spherical, facet-cut stoppers and are cut with alternate panels. About 1890.

Regency period work table decorated with parquetry (geometric) patterns of differently-coloured veneered woods. The silk bag underneath is attached to a moving slide and pulls out – but this is often missing. About 1810.

19th-century houses, though it had enjoyed a vogue some years prior to Victoria's succession to the throne in 1837. The great hall was especially reminiscent of the impressive baronial interiors so aptly described in the novels of Sir Walter Scott, and of the halls to be found in late medieval and Elizabethan houses. At the same time it recalled with nostalgic pride the great days and entertainments of a bygone era. By the middle of the century, however, the large open space of the hall – surrounded by leaded windows filled with fine examples of modern stained glass in the Gothic taste, and roofed by massive rafters – was filling up like the rest of the house with more comfortable pieces of furniture to augment the baronial armchairs and 'refectory' tables. By the close of the century the great hall not only provided an imposing entrance (shielded from the outside drafts by a small vestibule), but also a large and comfortably informal reception room for friends and family to gather in. Even in the smaller middle-class villas of the mid 19th century, the hall became a major addition, housing the large hall stands for raincoats and galloshes.

The biggest change in 19th-century interiors became apparent in the layout of the bedroom. The formal arrangement of this apartment, which had characterised many 18th-century interiors, was with few exceptions abandoned in the 19th-century. Bedrooms became increasingly private. Nor did they provide the sort of sitting room space, popular particularly among women, as they had done earlier on. Instead the bedrooms, positioned above the main reception rooms, were used in much the same way as they are today. The addition of dressing rooms for both husband and wife was fairly common, and with the benefits of modern plumbing by the middle of the century bathrooms became more widespread – though bathing in a hip bath in front of the fire was probably still more prevalent. Children became more visible – still preferably not heard – and were accorded their own nursery suite situated close to their parents but even closer to the nanny responsible for their care. Indeed there was a new attitude to children which further underlined the growing concern among Victorians for greater domesticity and the advancement of homely pleasures.

Nineteenth-Century Furniture

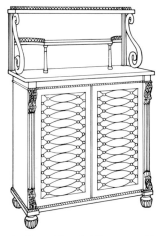

Rosewood cabinet with typical Regency motifs such as the brass trellis-work doors, usually backed with pleated silk panels, and a gilt metal gallery at the top. c 1815.

Mid 19th-century lacquer cabinet with chinoiserie decorations. About 1860.

The early 19th century was dominated by the Regency style, so-called after the then Prince Regent. But the style overlapped the strict limitations of the Regent's term of office, which lasted from 1811–20. It can be said to have begun in the closing years of the 18th century and to have lasted throughout his reign as George IV (1820–30).

The neo-classicism of the early 19th century proved to be a much more austere and archaeologically correct form of classicism than that espoused in the 18th century. Among those to anticipate the new style was Thomas Sheraton who published his Cabinet Dictionary in 1803, three years prior to his death. But none compared with the spirit of historical verisimilitude displayed in Thomas Hope's book entitled 'Household Furniture and Interior Decoration', 1807.

The Greek ideal

The elegant simplicity of Grecian forms was paramount in Regency furniture design. But ancient Roman and even Egyptian motifs and shapes made a first popular appearance in England. Gothic and Chinese styles, intermittently fashionable since the mid-17th century, enjoyed a revival, particularly under the patronage of the Prince Regent, both at his earlier residence, Carlton House (London), and at his later Brighton extravaganza, the Royal Pavilion. Real bamboo furniture imported from China was seen for the first time and quantities of imitation bamboo furniture were made, principally out of woods such as beech. The imitation furniture was then painted and grained to look like real bamboo, a technique also employed to imitate several other woods such as ebony and rosewood.

In the first decade of the century furniture was characterised by a simplicity of outline and a bold but sparing use of ornament. What ornamental features existed were more boldly carved and displayed than before and tended also to be larger in scale. Depending on the style favoured, such motifs might include Grecian philosopher's heads, lyre supports, lion masks – which generally had rings in their mouths when used as handles – lion-headed monopodia used for table and chair supports, stars, lotus leaves, Egyptian mummy heads and even crocodile heads and feet. These Egyptian devices were especially popular after Nelson's great victory at the Battle of the Nile in 1798.

Many of the smaller pieces of furniture introduced during the second half of the 18th century continued to be fashionable, but there were a few additions. Little work tables fitted with a silk bag which hung beneath a small frieze drawer became increasingly common and remained so well into the earlier years of the Victorian period. Small nests of tables, called quartetto tables were used, as were a number of other occasional tables. Pedestals became the most widespread means of supporting table tops. Elegant circular and rectangular pedestal tables were made in mediums such as rosewood, enlivened with ebony stringing or crossbanding. Dwarf bookcases and cabinets fitted with doors were intended for display in drawing rooms rather than in libraries, and were fitted with pleated silk panels behind gilt metal grilles.

The paternalistic style

But in general much furniture, particularly dining and library furniture, became more masculine and heavier in appearance. Large uncluttered areas of plain solid wood or veneer dominated. Strikingly marked and grained woods were in demand and richly-coloured dark woods like rosewood and mahogany were once again pre-eminent, replacing the paler golden colour of satinwood and harewood favoured during the last quarter of the 18th century. Gilt and even brass decoration often provided a strong contrast to these sombre tones. Simple plain ebony stringing was used between 1800 and 1810, but later inlaid decoration became more elaborate and, following the fashion popularised by the Prince Regent, brass inlay was used. To begin with it was used sparingly but gradually it became more elaborate. Complex patterns similar to *boulle* appeared; the latter was a form of decoration then fashionable on the Continent.

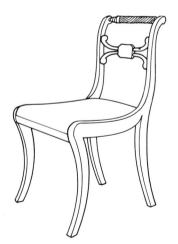

Trafalgar chair, so-called because details such as rope moulding (top rail) and anchor motifs recalled Nelson's famous sea battle. c 1805.

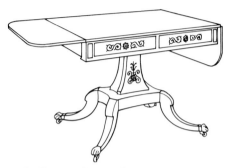

Sofa table, originally owned by Princess Charlotte, veneered with amboyna and kingwood with brass inlay decoration. Made for her wedding in 1816.

Several new styles of turning were introduced, including the scimitar or sabre leg used principally on chairs. This outcarved form was adopted from a famous Grecian prototype, the Klismos chair, which also provided the inspiration for another distinctive Regency chair design: the tablet- or yoke-shaped chair back. During the 18th century the emphasis of the back splat had been vertical; that is, there was a linear emphasis running from the seat rail to the top rail. The wide, curved, tablet-shaped back of the Klismos chair ran not vertically but horizontally, and many variants of this form were used on Regency chairs and on examples made well into the early Victorian period. Caning, principally in the form of caned panels, was also used. The increasing emphasis on comfort contributed to the popularity of the Regency sofa. Early 19th-century examples, whether in rosewood, mahogany, ebony or even giltwood, are widely sought after, though this type of sofa remained in use throughout the century and many later examples can still be found. During the Regency period these sofas were normally accompanied by sofa

tables – essentially a form of elongated Pembroke table – fitted with flaps at either end and supported on splayed legs or lyre-shaped supports.

Many mirrors, particularly pier-glasses, were designed to enhance the spatial dimensions of rooms, and this taste for mirrored expanses continued into the Victorian era. Gilt circular, convex-shaped mirrors, some surmounted by eagles, were introduced in about 1800. The most typical form of decoration was an inner frame of gilt balls. Such mirrors were generally small but could be anything up to 7 or 8 feet high. Cheval glasses

Circular, convex mirrors with giltwood frame were very popular from about 1800–1830. c 1800.

were also in vogue and continued to be made well after the Regency period, as were gilt overmantel mirrors. These latter examples were relatively commonplace during the Regency and William IV periods. Their restrained use of decoration, often in the form of a simple bead or rope moulding around a plain or tripartite mirror plate, make them an attractive addition to the modern interior.

By the end of the second decade it was increasingly apparent that the stylistic uniformity visible throughout the 18th century was fragmenting. The elegant lines became more stolid and bulbous as the taste for richer, more florid forms set in. Not only were the styles more elaborate, even coarser, but, by the end of the 1820's, there were several new, patently disparate, styles which were not only fashionable but fashionable all at once in the same room. This was accompanied by

Mahogany davenport, with its characteristic sloping top and drawers, which were complemented on the other side by dummy drawers. c 1820.

a steady growth in the population and a visible rise in the prosperity of the middle classes whose demand for novelty was insatiable. Similar versions were also produced in a horizontal design, often supported at either end by classical gilt columns.

From Greek to Gothic

By 1835 the main styles which many tend to associate with the early Victorian period (1837–51) had already emerged as Grecian, Louis Quatorze, Elizabethan and Gothic. The Grecian was the most popular, but it was really a continuation of the Regency style. If anything, the forms were heavier and carved applied ornamentation – such as the anthemion – bolder, but it was often less vigorously carved. Legs, particularly on chairs and sofas, when not of the sabre shape, were generally straight and reeded. Rather thick spiral reeding was also widely used in conjunction with

Mahogany chair showing the neo-classic ornament in the Grecian taste popular during the second quarter of the century. This robust example would be used in the dining room. 1834.

classical motifs to decorate the whole leg or a small section of it. Furniture in this style tended to be ponderous and masculine and was well-suited to the heavy dark woods, principally mahogany and rosewood which continued to be thought the most desirable though other timbers were

also employed. Of these walnut came back into prominence for the first time since the early 18th century, and was used in all the styles then fashionable. By the middle of the 19th century the Grecian mode was in decline.

Furniture in the Grecian taste was destined for use in such masculine domains as the library or dining room. It was to lighter, if incorrectly described, Louis Quatorze styles that designers turned for furnishing boudoirs and drawing rooms. This style was also variously described as Old French, Louis XIV and rococo, though in reality it more resembled the mid-18th-century rococo style rather than late 17th-century Louis XIV styles. The rococo influence remained until well into the 20th century and is still used for some bedroom furniture today. Like 18th-century rococo it has a 'characteristic roundness of members', a profusion of naturalistically carved decoration, frequent use of gilding and lightness of design. Other characteristics include an elegant use of cabriole legs, generally decorated with a bold cabochon motif on the knee and a well-scrolled foot. The rococo style declined in popularity during the middle of the century and during the 1850's the naturalistic style of carving became more popular and more sculptural. It also made good use of narrative or anecdotal subjects, but these pieces were very costly to make and comparatively small amounts were produced. One famous school, at Warwick, was renowned for a magnificent buffet (or sideboard) carved by William Cooke. Called the Kenilworth Buffet, it was exhibited at the Great Exhibition in 1851 and depicted scenes from Sir Walter Scott's novel of the same name.

The Victorian-Elizabethan idiom

Although there was some serious furniture scholarship during this period, there is also little doubt that a considerable amount of confusion and muddled thinking concerning historical styles was prevalent among both designers and makers in the 19th century. Nowhere is this better seen than in the style of furniture which purported to be based on that used by the Elizabethans. What the early Victorians believed to be Elizabethan was actually closer to the furniture made three quarters of a century after Elizabeth's death in 1603. Turning – especially spiral twist turning – was used to decorate

'Elizabethan' chair with spiral uprights. This differs from its 17th-century predecessor in its padded back panel and cabriole legs. *c* 1840.

arms, legs, back supports and decorative posts. Other motifs included cup and cover designs and strapwork decoration. To add to the confusion a good deal of furniture was made up from genuinely old fragments of 17th-century pieces.

Woods used in this way were invariably oak or walnut, since it was felt, and rightly so, that mahogany was inappropriate for the historical spirit of the style. But little did they realise that walnut was barely appropriate either, since in the late 16th and 17th century this wood was reserved only for the very finest pieces of furniture, although it became the most popular timber following the Restoration of Charles II in 1660.

Among the characteristic examples of 'Elizabethan' furniture are numerous chairs. Large quantities were made for use in libraries, halls and in dining rooms and were generally constructed with high, straight back panels in the manner of late 17th-century models. They were decorated with carved and pierced backs and twist turned legs and uprights. A distinctive 19th-century feature on this type of chair is the addition of a comfortably-upholstered back panel, in velvet or embroidered Berlin woolwork, which became fashionable in about 1845. Furniture in mock-Elizabethan style continued to be made through the remainder of the century and enjoyed a revival during the 1880's. As an alternative to upholstery, seat and back panels were also more appropriately caned.

The Gothic style – like the Grecian, rococo and Elizabethan styles fashionable during the 30's and 40's – was distinguished by a profuse accumulation of carved stylistic detail: pointed arches, cusps, columnar legs and crenellations. Oak and walnut were the most widely-used woods. Gothic taste reached its apogee during the 1860's and was adopted by several important designers and architects seeking to reform furniture design in the second half of the century.

New materials for new modes

Not only was there a diversity of styles in the 19th century, but the many developments in materials, techniques and machinery combined to make the choice even more complex. Among the most popular enthusiasms was the papier mâché pieces made by firms like Jennens and Bettridge of Birmingham. Although the use of papier mâché in furnishings was not new, the firm contributed significantly to its development by firstly patenting the use of mother-of-pearl inlay in 1825 and, later in 1847, a new method using coloured glass inlay which they described as 'gem inlaying'. In general papier mâché was used to make small items such

Prie-dieu chair made in papier mâché with padded back covered with Berlin-woolwork. Characteristic features are the low seat and padded top rail. *c* 1850.

as trays, tea caddies, boxes, letter racks and coasters, but limited amounts of furniture, reinforced with wood or metal carcases, were made. These consist chiefly of decorative chairs, stools, and small tables. Black was the most popular ground colour, but others included red, cream, green and, very rarely, blue and yellow. Metal furniture was also greatly developed during the 19th century and the Coalbrookdale Iron Company was the most prominent firm in this field, making cast iron furniture intended principally for use in gardens and hallways. Metals such as brass and cast iron were also common during the second half of the century in the making of bedsteads, particularly as it was believed to be more hygienic than wood. In the middle of the century strapmetal rocking chairs were made which resembled the graceful curving lines of bentwood furniture invented by the Austrian furniture-maker Thonet.

of the period. Since the early 19th century there had been a revival in the use of marble, particularly for plain and inlaid marble tops. This fashion continued into the reign of Queen Victoria, when elaborately inlaid marble tops were decorated with both floral mosaics and geometric devices.

The evolution of comfort

Thickly padded, comfortable upholstery is the outstanding feature of Victorian seat furniture. It became widespread following the invention of coil springs patented by Samuel Pratt in 1828. This type of seating, though remarkably comfortable, blurred the outline and imparted a round-

ed, low-seated chairs with flat, padded top rails, to be used either as chairs or in religious devotions. Easy chairs, library chairs and even club chairs were, in the mid-19th century, given padded arm rests and were frequently deep-buttoned. From about 1850 upholstery tended to be confined within the carved or moulded wooden framework of the seat and back. Good examples of this type of upholstery can be found in the companion 'spoonback' chairs. When fitted with arms these chairs are known as gentlemen's chairs; without they become ladies' chairs. They are now relatively expensive due to their long-standing popularity. Though generally associated with the middle years of

Bentwood rocking chair with cane seat and back. Developed by the Austrian firm of Thonet, these chairs were widely copied in the last quarter of the century.

Comfortable upholstered armchair showing neoclassic ornamentation typical of the William IV period. Variations were made throughout the century. Loudon's Encyclopaedia 1833.

Balloon-back chair popular from about 1830 to 1870. c 1850.

Marble – and cheaper variants such as slate – were used on pieces such as heavy half-round cabinets and sideboards. These were topped with equally large half-round mirrors, and both pieces were much used in dining and drawing rooms

ed, squashy and somewhat shapeless appearance. With the invention, several new types of upholstered seat furniture appeared, such as the 'Ottoman', the 'sociable sofa' and the 'tête-a-tête'. Prie dieus were well upholstered, high back-

the century, they were made and advertised well into the final quarter of the Victorian period despite the fact that they no longer were the *sine qua non* of fashion.

Another chair design popular during the Victorian period was the 'balloon' back. This design evolved from a late Regency type and was made throughout the rest of the century for use in bedrooms, drawing rooms and dining rooms. The introduction of the cabriole leg in the middle of the century was especially favoured for the lighter drawing room or bedroom chairs, although nowadays these delicate, sometimes spindly examples are expected to do robust service as dining chairs, a function for which they were never intended.

The heritage of the Great Exhibition

By the middle of the century there was growing concern over the wild eclecticism displayed in furniture design. The Great Exhibition of 1851 sought to encourage innovation, but instead it helped to highlight the low state to which furniture design had sunk. In the aftermath of the Exhibition a two-tiered system of furniture design and manufacture emerged. On the one hand the mass producers, growing in number all the time, sought to satisfy increased public demand for furniture by producing the styles which were known to be popular but which also tended to demonstrate the conservative tastes of the vast majority. On the other, idealistic level, were those reformatory designers and architects who sought to improve public taste and make what they adjudged to be good quality, honestly constructed, and well-designed furniture. The second half of the 19th century was a period in which the battle of the styles was fought. On one – the most productive – side, were the innumerable revival styles; on the other, the conscientiously and rather self-consciously designed pieces known as art furniture.

The range of mass-produced furniture provided a baffling array of styles. With the exception of the Grecian, all the other fashions produced before 1850 continued, even though many were no longer fashionable. Rococo furniture, opulently

This sideboard fitted with a large mirror is similar to designs published by William Smee & Sons in 1850. c 1885.

gilded or painted, was still very suitable for drawing rooms, and in the late 1850's the appearance of the neo-classically inspired Louis XVI-style re-inforced the domination of French tastes. Lighter-coloured woods were popular – in particular satinwood – but other favourites included walnut, ash and oak. Marquetry, inlay and painted decoration in the 18th-century manner was also used.

Other Continental influences were visible in the so-called Renaissance style which combined 16th-century French and Italian furniture designs. This style was sometimes barely distinguishable from 'Elizabethan' and 'Jacobean' imitations and was considered ideal as hall or dining-room furniture.

Late 19th-century innovations

The last quarter of the 19th century saw a resurgence of 18th-century English fashions by the mass-production furniture makers which realised a notable commercial success. The main styles were then described as Queen Anne, Chippendale (which was really a variation of the rococo), Adam, Hepplewhite and Sheraton, though few bore any real resemblance to the styles they purported to copy. Queen Anne dressing tables, chairs, bookcases and the highly desirable whatnot were thought to be achieved through the addition of curved broken pediments, dentil moulding, cabriole legs and scrolling end-gables. Chippendale 'copies' proved to be even more fanciful and exag-

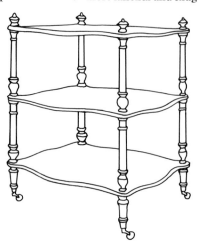

Whatnot veneered in walnut, with turned columns standing on casters. A useful addition to the drawing room. Mid 19th century.

gerated, but their basis in fact was somewhat more assured. These late 18th-century furniture revivals were among the best quality reproductions at this time.

Firms like Wright and Mansfield were making some very good copies of furniture in the 1870's and 80's and did much to popularise the Hepplewhite and Sheraton styles. There was a vogue for white-painted bedroom furniture in the so-

Satinwood armchair in the Hepplewhite style. This differs from earlier examples in its slighter proportions. Wright and Mansfield, London, c 1860.

called Adam style, and several chairs appeared with oval- and shield-back patterns.

In general late 19th-century furniture tended to be lighter and more spindly. Legs particularly became slimmer and were usually of the square tapering type. Overall dimensions were slighter than those found on genuine 18th-century pieces and the rounded curvilinear outlines of the early Victorian period gave way to rectangular linear forms. Although not strictly speaking antique – if the yardstick for such a description is taken to be 100 years – many good quality 19th-century reproduction pieces represent good value today. Not only

have they stood the test of time – although many have not – they can be acquired at very competitive prices when compared to similarly-styled reproduction furniture of today. A few 19th-century examples are such good copies of late 18th-century designs that they have on occasion been mistaken as such.

Following the Great Exhibition of 1851, a growing number of art magazines and journals appeared whose aim was to improve the level of public taste, then felt to be at a dangerously low ebb. This was thought to be particularly so with regard to furniture design. But as early as 1835, the architect designer, A. W. N. Pugin – who worked for much of his short life on the interior decoration of the new Houses of Parliament (burnt down 1834: rebuilt 1837–51) – had already expressed his dissatisfaction. Many of his ideas had a strong moralising content, and he proposed that furniture-making should return to the simple, honest methods of 'sound or rational construction' used by medieval craftsmen.

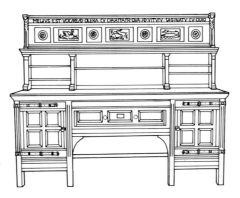

'Art Furniture' sideboard designed by Bruce Talbert admired for its 'construction honestly shown'. Made in oak with carved boxwood panels. Designed 1871.

The vehicle adopted for this return was, logically enough, the Gothic style. Pugin's ideas were later taken up by architects and designers in the 1850's, among them William Burges, Richard Norman Shaw and William Morris. Morris became the most vociferous and best-known champion of the reformist movement and many of his ideas were promoted through the firm he founded in 1861, later known as Morris and Co.

Morris was not himself a furniture designer. The man responsible for this field during the 1860's and 1870's was Philip Webb. The 1860's saw a return to a much simpler, more architectonic Gothic style based on 13th-century forms. This contrasted sharply to the fussy, over-decorated 15th-century Gothic popular before the 1850's. Moreover, the firm advocated two different types of furniture: that which Morris classified as 'necessary workaday furniture . . . simple to the last degree' and 'state furniture' by which he meant large, imposing pieces such as cabinets, bookcases and sideboards. These latter, like the pieces designed by William Burges in the 1850's, were illustrated with medieval narrative themes by leading painters of the day. They were very costly to make and fell far short of Morris' aim to make inexpensive quality items which could be afforded by the man in the street. Instead they contributed to the 'swinnish luxury of the rich'. Few of these extravagances were made, and they are now sought as much for their opulent beauty as for their relevance to furniture history.

Large quantities of the 'simple workaday furniture' were made from 1861 on, and many imitations made well into the 20th century. These pieces demonstrate the simple, open or 'revealed' type of construction advocated earlier on by Pugin. This shows clearly the maker's methods, such as peg jointing. Decoration was kept to a minimum and English woods such as oak, fruitwoods, elm, ash, beech and yew were typical. Traditional

A Sussex chair produced by the firm of William Morris & Co; an example of the firm's workaday furniture. They were produced in large numbers from 1865 onwards; this example is ebonised. *c* 1880.

cottage patterns were used, particularly in chair design, the best-known being Morris' rush-seated Sussex chair which enjoyed enormous popularity during the rest of the century. These chairs, which contrasted sharply with the formal rococo and French styles also then fashionable, were generally ebonised or stained green, and were part of the vernacular tradition

The 'smokers' bow' was a popular form of chair, widely used in kitchens, pubs and offices during the last quarter of the 19th century. They were usually made in local woods.

of turned chairs. Other classic cottage-style furniture, based on traditional designs, was associated with regions such as Lancashire, Windsor and Mendlesham (Suffolk) and were made throughout the 19th century, but the influence of Morris & Co helped popularise them further. Morris' firm also produced a bergère armchair and the Saville chair. The bergère – with caned or upholstered side and back panels – stood on square, tapering legs and remained popular up to the outbreak of the First World War. The Saville chair, made from about 1890 onwards, showed the typical square form of late 19th-century furniture.

The Japanese influence
The Gothic, or Early English style as it was also called, continued in vogue well into the 1880's. By the late 1860's a few commercial firms had turned their attention

Large, deeply-upholstered armchair on bulbous turned legs and casters, made throughout the second half of the 19th century. These can represent a saving on a comparable new example.

to it as a wider public became aware of this new 'art furniture'. The architect-designer Bruce Talbert worked for several prominent London firms, but it was Charles Lock Eastlake's enormously influential book on both sides of the Atlantic, 'Hints on Household Taste', first published in 1868, that popularised the art furniture of the late 19th century. Both retained the simple forms of 13th-century Gothic furniture used by Burges and Morris, but as well as Gothic decoration new forms of ornamentation appeared. Tongue and groove panelling was used on the backs of sideboards and washstands; enamelled and painted plaques showing sprigs of flowers and birds, some in the Japanese style popular during the 70's and 80's, were set into panels. Pierced fretwork decoration and rows of spindles provided decorative friezes, helped by the widespread use of fret-cutting machinery.

One of a set of four satinwood dining chairs in the style of the late 18th century. The painted decoration is a trifle over fussy and the proportions – particularly of the front legs – too delicate. Such examples are generally well made and were often produced by leading 19th-century furniture makers such as Graham & Jackson, Edwards and Roberts and Wright and Mansfield. *c* 1900.

The principal wood continued to be oak, but it was frequently left unstained and was treated only with hot oil. Pigeon holes and little shelves appeared and brackets were used instead of the 'un-meaning scrolls' associated with mass-produced furniture. Ebonised wood, often decorated with some gilding, became fashionable on cabinets and overmantels. By the end of the century the style had become debased, and was frequently merged with other early English styles such as Tudor, Elizabethan and Jacobean.

Ladder-back chair with rush seat, designed by Ernest Gimson in about 1888. Made in ash, he called it 'wonderful furniture of a commonplace kind'.

109

Popular versions of the Art Nouveau style were made in large numbers by firms more interested in commercial than in aesthetic considerations. This example made in about 1899.

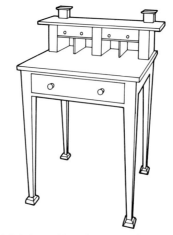

Oak desk designed by Arthur Macmurdo and made by the Century Guild in about 1886, showing simple rectilinear outline, square-cut tapering legs and flat mushroom cappings characteristic of much Arts and Crafts furniture.

The predictable result was a 'mass of elaborate gimcrack cabinets, whatnots, corner cupboards . . . with spindly supports, a profusion of pigeon holes divided off by little railings of turned balusters'.

The 1870's and 80's saw a re-emergence of interest in foreign influences, of which the Japanese was the most prominent. E. W. Godwin was the designer most associated with this style, but very few of his severely linear, ebonised structures were made. Quantities of bamboo furniture, none of which bore any resemblance to real Japanese furniture whatever claims its makers made, have survived to bear witness to the common preoccupation with the Orient. Bamboo furniture was produced mainly in London and the Industrial centres of the Midlands, from the 1860's up to about 1930. The raw materials were largely bamboo poles, woven grass panels or matting, and lacquer panels imported from Japan at very low cost. This range of furniture was enormous and encompassed whole suites of furniture intended for boudoirs and bedrooms. Because of its delicate nature little bamboo furniture today is in good condition, but quantities of small tables, hanging shelves, magazine racks and cabinets have survived. Interest in late 19th-century and early 20th-century bamboo furniture in recent years has led to some increase in its cost but it is still a bargain-hunter's delight.

The last quarter of the 19th century witnessed the development and growth of the Arts and Craft Movement, whose high ideals were based on the principles of the early reformist designers. As early as the 1880's some leading figures in the movement were using forms which already foreshadowed the Art Nouveau style of the 1890's and early 20th century.

Nineteenth-Century Pottery and Porcelain

White-glazed earthenware dish decorated with oxide of gold to produce a soft pink lustre. The grape motif was popular during the Regency period. *c* 1815.

Earthenware

By the close of the 18th century the Industrial Revolution was already evident in the Potteries. This had come about largely through the establishment of a factory-based system of production, such as at the Wedgwood factory, Etruria. Growing demand throughout the 19th century, from more people with more money, encouraged a steady increase from the manufacturers in both the range and the volume of their goods. This, coupled with a steady flow of technological improvements and the ever-constant need to lower costs, resulted in the manufacture of a bewildering wide variety of ceramics. The product displayed a high standard of technical virtuosity but often at the ultimate expense of taste.

By about 1800 the majority of porcelain and earthenware potters were based in Staffordshire. Though this area, known as the Potteries, dominated ceramic production in the 19th century – as it still does – a variety of mainly earthenware goods were also made elsewhere, as far away as Yorkshire, Sunderland, Derbyshire, Bristol and London. Furthermore, it was common practice among many pottery firms, by the beginning of the century, to produce a very wide range of goods in both the finer porcelain-based ceramics and in the coarser earthenwares. This naturally tended to bring about a merging of styles between the two mediums.

Lustreware and ironstone

Creamware, popular at the end of the 18th century, was replaced by the more refined Pearlware, which had the additional appeal of being tougher and less fragile than the earlier form. It had been developed by Wedgwood in about 1779 and was taken up by many factories during the 19th century. One of the most distinctive examples of earthenware made in Staffordshire, Sunderland, Bristol and Swansea, was lustreware. It was particularly popular during the first quarter of the century and was made into any number of small domestic and decorative wares including jugs, mugs, cups and saucers, vases, plaques and watchstands. Their distinctive feature is the delightful pearly shimmer of the metallic oxide or lustre, which comes in a myriad of colours from rich reddish-gold, to purple, gold and silver. Gold-base lustres range from coppery tints to the softer pink lustres associated with Sunderland potters. By the middle of the century cheaper copper oxides were used to produce similar lustres, but these tend to have a brassy tinge and, in general, the potting was coarser. Silver lustres were made from platinum oxide which, unlike real silver oxide, did not tarnish, though some early silver coloured lustres are rather grey in colour. While many lustre wares were decorated all over with a thin coating of metallic oxide, others were more restrained and the lustre controlled to cover only specific areas. These are known as 'resist lustres', and were introduced towards the close of the first decade. The lustre was restricted by using an inhibiting waxlike agent on those areas which were to be coated. While the agent resisted the lustre, it was also easily removed and could be later washed away. Apart from some lustre pieces made by large firms, such as Wedgwood, few samples are marked.

By 1804, Miles Mason, proprietor of a pottery at Lane Delph, Staffordshire, had developed a tough earthenware body suitable for withstanding everyday usage without damage, He called it ironstone. The patent was taken out in 1804 and extended in 1813 by his son, Charles James Mason. But when the patent expired in 1827 other competitors began to manufacture ironstone, despite the fact that the patented process had been deliberately obscured in order to prevent imitations. Ironstone, which resembles a fine stoneware, was made into every type of tableware service available, as well as some large decorative and architectural pieces, the best known of which were fireplaces. Quantities of Mason's ironstone china can be found today, including whole or parts of large dinner services, plates, meat dishes, variously sized and shaped jugs, bowls, basins and vases. Many of the pieces were in the octagonal shape popular during the first quarter of the century. Decoration took the form of vibrant colours, principally in bright orange-red and blue, with a frequent use of gilding. The strong simple shapes, combined with bold patterning and low cost, have made them sought after today. The vases are especially in demand for conversion into contemporary table lamps. Patterns are similar to the everlastingly-popular Japanese-inspired Imari patterns, repeating the same flowers – particularly peony and prunus blossom with appropriate foliage. Other motifs include Chinese dragons depicted in less common colours such as bright emerald green, yellow, black and gold.

The rise of transfer printing

Not only did a number of technical developments occur in material composition, but decoration in the 19th century

was also affected. The method of transfer printing had first been developed in 1753 at the York House of Theodore Janssen – otherwise known as the Battersea enamel factory. In the late 18th century Josiah Spode 1 had greatly improved transfer-printing techniques, but these improvements were not used on a wide-spread commercial scale until the early 19th century, when they were applied to both porcelain and earthenwares. The fine clear blues obtained from cobalt oxides were used for printing the blue and white wares now made chiefly in Staffordshire. Patterns varied enormously, but those inspired by oriental motifs predominated. The most famous design was the Willow Pattern, first used in the late 18th century, and it still remains popular today. Other options included romantic, pastoral and topographical scenes; hunting and

Transfer-printed tureen by Spode, made as part of a botanical dinner service. Each item is printed with a different plant, appropriately, in green. About 1830.

Large earthenware dish with underglaze-blue printed decoration, made by Copeland and Garrett, successors to the firm of Spode (1833–47). Spode was one of the earliest factories to introduce underglaze-blue transfer printing on earthenwares in the early 19th century. (L 18¾ in.)

zoological themes; Beauties of America, milkmaids, woodmen and floral designs.

By 1830 the development of multi-coloured printing on paper by George Baxter had led to the successful development of an economic underglaze method of printing on pottery. In 1848, Jesse Austin, the recently appointed head decorator of the firm F & R Pratt & Co, of Fenton, Staffordshire, was successfully using multi-coloured transfer printing techniques on the company's range of domestic and commercial earthenwares. The best-known earthenware pieces to be decorated in this way were pot lids. They were used on all sizes and types of containers, holding a wide range of products: hair preparations (bear grease), fish paste, potted shrimps, tooth paste, meat paste, rough and tobacco. Pratts were the largest single manufacturer of these lids. Up to this time they had been decorated chiefly

with monochrome colours – sepia red, blue and black. For a short time (1846–48) Austin experimented, using two colours on prints showing the well-known bear series. This theme remained very popular and inspired designs ranging from realistically portrayed bear hunts to sentimental bears' tea parties. As knowledge of Arctic regions grew, even polar bears joined the menagerie. By the middle of the century pot lids were slightly domed and were made in enormous numbers throughout the 1850's and 60's. Other firms produced these highly collected items including Ridgways of Hanley and, after 1859, their successors Brown, Westhead, Moore & Co.

Pottery and porcelain figures enjoyed an unprecedented vogue throughout the 19th century. The simple earthenware figures of the earlier part of the century are the work of a number of potteries, but

those of Enoch Wood and the slightly later samples of Obadiah Sherrat exhibit some of the fine qualities. Among innumerable subjects, portrait busts such as Wood's portrayal of the Reverend John Wesley are among the best portraits of the time. In the middle of the century the fashion for displaying modelled figures on an

Staffordshire flatback in the form of Dick Turpin on his horse. This group is typical of the numerous figures that were made as cheap imitations of finer porcelain examples. c 1830.

already well-cluttered mantel piece necessitated careful modelling on only one front. The back of the figures were left in a crude, often unglazed and unmodelled state. These statuettes are known as 'flatbacks' and provide an informative and entertaining reflection on the prominent and notorious figures in Victorian society. Animal subjects were also popular and among those most commonly used were wild animals such as deer, rabbits, lions and tigers, as well as domestic pets, dogs and cats. The firm of Sampson Smith, Staffordshire, produced large quantities of flatbacks and these are the most commonly encountered examples today.

Decorated earthenware pot lids were used for a variety of commercial jars and containers. This example bears a printed view of the Exhibition held in 1851 and was probably made by TJ & J Mayer in 1850. (D 5¼in).

Earthenware vase in the 'Etruscan' style, made by F & R Pratt with transfer-printed decoration. This proved a popular 'revival' during the 1840s and 50s. (H 4in).

'Gothic' and 'Renaissance' wares

During the 1820's the early bold, simple outlines of the Regency style gave way to more exaggerated forms and to an increase in applied ornament and painted decoration. Though pottery was less affected than the more fashionable and costly porcelain, the florid rococo style

Stoneware jug in the Gothic taste, depicting religious scenes in relief. These are set within an architectural framework of Gothic arches. Charles Meigh & Son, c 1850.

typical of the 1830's and 40's made itself felt. Historical revival styles were also evident and wares moulded in high and low relief reflected the various tastes for Gothic, Grecian and Moorish fashions. The firm of Charles Meigh and Son made a number of Gothic-styled stoneware jugs. These were decorated with moulded Gothic motifs revealing religious subjects framed within arched and pinnacled panels. Similar stoneware pieces were made by several other potteries from about 1835 and some tankards are fitted with hinged lids made of the newly-patented Britannia metal (1840). During

the 1840's the firm of Wedgwood revived their famous Grecian-styled 'Etruscan' range – popular also at the beginning of the century – though a number of other firms, such as F & R Pratt, echoed the style. The ceramic bodies varied considerably in quality; while the best were in the familiar black basalts, developed by Wedgwood in the late 18th century, cheaper examples were made in coarser earthenwares. Scale was another changing factor and many 19th-century examples are much larger than either the 18th-century, or indeed the original Pompeiian, models.

At the time of the Great Exhibition, 1851, Continental, and particularly French, influence was strong. The leading ceramic firm of Minton appointed the

Large earthenware ewer decorated in the manner of 'Henry Deux' ware, achieved by inlaying with differently-coloured sections of clay to form the pattern. Minton 1862 (H 15¾in).

Frenchman Leon Arnoux as their Art Director in 1848, the year in which French émigrés arrived in England following the turmoil caused by the collapse of the Third Republic. Arnoux, familiar

with current fashions in France, introduced several new ranges – including a revival of 16th-century Italian maiolica, although it more closely resembled the coloured glazes used by the 16th-century French potter Bernard Palissy (d. 1590). The first examples – a *tour de force* of ceramic artistry – were exhibited at the Great Exhibition, but several smaller Staffordshire firms continued to produce maiolica or, as it was popularly called, Majolica, for the rest of the century. Majolica remained not only common but quite acceptable to those who sought to improve what they considered to be the alarmingly low state of English taste, despite being mass-produced. C. L. Eastlake writing in his 'Hints on Household Taste in Furniture Etc.' in 1868 felt that the 'larger objects, such as vases, flower dishes and figure pieces in imitation of majolica are the most tasteful and effective in form and colour.' Another example of the popularity of earlier French earthenware styles of decoration can be seen in the imitations of Henri Doux earthenware, sometimes also known as Saint-Porchaire, a type of very thinly potted creamware decorated with incisions filled in contrasting coloured clays, black to reddish brown. Some of the best examples were made by Charles Toft, who worked for a number of leading ceramic firms including Minton's. Minton also imitated the terracotta figures and flower sculptures of the Italian 16th-century Della Robbia brothers. These are characterised by decoration in opaque and coloured glazes.

Though many potters marked their wares, either in full or with their initials, until 1842 there was no official form of registration. This resulted in widespread plagiarism and imitations of newly-developed materials and patterns. From 1842 manufacturers were able to register designs, which protected them from copyright infringements. The registration was accompanied by a lozenge or diamond-shaped mark with a loop at the top end, showing the letters Rd. (registered) in the middle. Each corner of the lozenge was bracketed and was marked with a letter or number from which it is possible to work out the exact class (metal (I), wood (II), glass (III), earthenware (IV)), day, month, year and parcel number of the piece. These marks were used from 1842 to 1883 in two cycles, which ran from 1842–67 and from 1868–83, as by 1868 it was necessary to start at the beginning of the alphabet again. From 1884–1909 the letters ran sequentially. In 1891 importation laws in the United States of America required that all ceramics be marked with 'England' and the mark 'Made in England', though this latter mark was not generally used on non-export wares until after about 1910.

The art potters

The overall proliferation of styles – especially the explosion of the many revivals which sprang up during the middle of the century – led to a gradual undercurrent of dissatisfaction among more discerning members of the Victorian public. One of the earliest to articulate these doubts was Henry Cole who set up 'Felix Summerly Art Manufacture' in 1847 believing that an 'alliance between fine art and manufacture would promote public taste.' Concern over the tasteless-ness and materialistic emphasis of so much Victorian industrial art brought about the Great Exhibition of 1851. Henry Cole again was a significant con-

tributor to its promotion and organisa-tion. Though many Victorians marvelled and applauded the exhibits, others were distressed by what they saw, since many pieces merely reinforced the criticisms which had brought the Exhibition about in the first place. Among those who al-most certainly visited the Great Crystal Palace show was the 17-year-old William Morris, who was to spend the rest of his life trying to promote principles of good taste, good design and honest craftsman-ship. Though his chief concern was furni-ture and interior design, not pottery, his innovative ideas influenced a youthful friend, William De Morgan, whom he met in 1863.

De Morgan (1839–1917) worked ini-tially as a decorator of furniture and only later became interested in pottery. But by 1870 he took up the craft, establishing a workshop in the house to which he, his mother and sister moved in 1872. His early work concentrated on decorating tile blanks, with characteristic motifs in the form of animals, especially rabbits, deer and exotic – even fantastic – creatures such as dragons and griffins. Birds and a variety of stylised floral motifs were also typical, many of them being recognisably based on carnations and the Tudor rose. It is in some of these floral motifs that Morris's influence is especially noticeable, reflecting some of his distinc-tive textile designs. De Morgan's early success brought more work, and in 1882 with an increased staff, he moved to his new Wimbledon workshop, Merton Abbey, where the range increased to in-clude tiles, vases and large dishes. The finely-decorated pottery wares were usually ornamental rather than utilitar-ian and demonstrate De Morgan's strong

interest in Moorish and Persian art. Many pieces were decorated with ruby and silver lustres, or were executed on bril-liant blue and turquoise grounds. In 1888 De Morgan moved to the Sands End Pottery, Fulham, where he was joined by the architect Halsy Ricardo. From 1898 to 1903 he carried on alone, but was forced to give up in 1907 due to ill health, though his assistants carried on the pot-tery for a further five years. De Morgan pottery shows a variety of name marks such as 'De Morgan', 'D.M.' or 'Wm De Morgan'.

Other firms making art pottery in the second half of the century included Doul-ton & Co, the Martin Brothers – best known for their outrageously grotesque

Modelled by Wallace Martin, one of the three Martin Brothers, this drinking vessel and cover is in the form of a grotesque bird and made in salt glazed stoneware. London, dated 1903.

animal and bird shapes – and a number of provincial art studio potteries. Among these was the Barnstaple pottery of C. H. Barnnam (est. 1879), who produced a range called 'Barum' ware. Pilkingtons, the glass manufacturers, established a pottery for decorative and tile wares in 1897; Harold Rathbone opened his 'Della Robbia' pottery in Birkenhead in 1894, and the Ruskin Pottery was set up in 1898 in Birmingham by E. R. Taylor.

Salt-glazed stoneware mug with 'scratch blue' or incised decoration. This was cut into the wares while in the unfired 'green state'. Doulton (London) 1874.

Doulton had been making salt-glazed stoneware since the pottery's beginning in 1815. In general they produced traditional buff-and-grey coloured stonewares for mugs, jugs and bottles to hold products such as ink, jam, vinegar, oil and shoe blacking. Many of the mugs intended for beer were decorated with applied relief moulding in the form of rustic and hunting scenes. Windmills were also a common motif. By 1820 John Doulton and his partner had become owners of the factory and from 1826–54 it was styled Doulton & Watts, after which it became Doulton & Co. From this time on, the firm increased its range to include art pottery and stoneware. Tankards, toby jugs, hunting jugs, loving cups, vases and claret jugs became

the general run while a number of old forms were re-introduced, including puzzle jugs and 16th-century Bellarmine shapes. Age-old methods of decoration were also exhumed, the best-known being the sgraffito technique, where the soft clay body was incised with patterns and the lines filled with colours such as brown, blue or black. Typical motifs included stylised floral patterns, which continued to be popular throughout the last quarter of the 19th century, and some freely-drawn animal and bird designs. The principle artisans were Hannah Barlow, whose pieces are generally initialled HB and with whom the animal and bird drawings are generally associated, and her brother Arthur. It was Arthur Barlow who introduced the form of decoration using tiny beads of clay to delineate the pattern, generally flowers. After 1882 Doulton and Co began producing bone china from their newly acquired Burslem factory (est. 1877), which reflected such trends as the Japanese style which was very influential during the 1870's and 1880's.

Porcelain

The Regency period, concurrent with the first quarter of the 19th century, saw the introduction and successful use of a new porcelain body in England: bone china. This was first used on a commercial scale by the Spode factory, founded in 1770 by Josiah Spode I. It was under his son, Josiah Spode II – who assumed control of the firm on his father's death – that the factory rose in prominence to become one of the leading producers of both earthenwares and fine bone china in the Regency period.

Bone china is a type of porcelain made

Cup and saucer in stone china, a type of cheap substitute for bone china consisting of hard white earthenware and china stone. Printed in underglaze blue and decorated with enamel colours. Spode (Staffs) c 1810.

up principally of china stone, china clay, and with the crucial addition of bone ash (Spode used calcined ox bones) in quantities of up to 40%. It remains today much as it was in Spode's day. It is characterised by a fine white paste which when thinly potted has a clear translucent body. When compared to other hard paste porcelains in use on the Continent, English bone china is stronger and is less brittle. Two other important contributions made in the early 19th century were stone china and felspar porcelain.

Regency fashions

The neo-classical style of the late 18th century remained fashionable throughout the Regency period but forms became more varied and decoration more elaborate and ornate. Rich gilding was widely used for both ornamental and useful wares, particularly those destined for the dining table and for the increasingly popular tea and coffee services. Designs were generally framed within gilt-patterned or plain borders made up of broad bands. Alternatively a design might encircle the body of the base. On plates, broad border patterns generally covered the entire rim or a thick band followed a thin gilt line. On hollow wares such as jugs, mugs, cups, vases and even ice pails, bands encircled both top rim and base. Floral and fruit designs were among the most common, though colour ranges and harmonies

Porcelain jug showing the little upright spur characteristic of many wares made by the firm of Mason. Decorated with a broad horizontal band of gilt fret. *c* 1800 (H 3½in).

were less garish and more restrained than the flower designs of the early Victorian period. The light delicate sprays and sprigs of flowers so favoured during the late 18th century, however, tended to give way to full blown bouquets and sprays; an especial favourite was the blooming rose. Other motifs included pastoral scenes – showing rustic folk among romantic landscapes – and natural flora and fauna – such as sea shells and interesting topographic views – framed within delicate white beads or 'pearl' borders. The topographic views encompassed many well-known English sites, as well as a number of American land- and townscapes. The two doyens of English porcelain, Worcester and Derby, pro-

duced some good examples of several of these designs, though Worcester continued to produce steatitic, or soapstone, porcelain until about 1820 when it began to concentrate on bone china.

Oriental fashions, based on Japanese Imari and Kakiemon designs, appeared on

Two-handled vase supported on a square pedestal foot, elaborately gilded and painted. The high quality of the vase is reflected in the value. Barr, Flight and Barr (Worcester) about 1810.

both porcelain and eathenware pieces, exhibiting the now familiar gold, blue and red. Patterns frequently covered entire pieces or were employed against richly coloured grounds.

Meticulously hand-painted decoration was the chief method of ornamenting porcelain. The high degree of artistic accomplishment required escalated the high costs involved in the production of bone

From 1783–1840 Robert Chamberlain, a former employee of the Worcester porcelain factory, operated a rival firm. This vase, marked 'Chamberlain's Worcester', was painted, in enamel colours and gilt, probably by John Barker. *c* 1815.

Thomas Baxter's London decorating studio was one of several independent firms which painted blank white china. This example is a fine Coalport plate painted by Thomas Baxter jnr, noted for his shell-and-feather motif. Dated 1809.

china. In general, transfer printing was used only for decorating the enormous quantities of mass-produced earthenwares, but the introduction of stipple-engraved bat printing in about 1820 allowed some cost-saving to manufacturers, from Spode to the smaller, unknown Staffordshire potteries. Stipple engraving superseded line-engraved transfer printing and was considerably finer than the earlier method. The stippled dots on the

Cup and saucer showing the characteristic ring handle produced by Minton during the early years of production. Bone china painted in enamel colours. *c* 1820.

engraving plate were filled with printing oil and the design transferred onto a thin sheet of gelatine, called a bat. A third process transferred the image from the bat onto the piece being decorated. The oiled image left on the ware was then carefully coloured with a fine dusting pigment

capable of being fired at a relatively high temperature. Firms using this method of printing included Spode, Minton, Swansea and Worcester.

Coalport and Parian wares

The rebirth of rococo in about 1820 found its expression in porcelain as in everything else. The first of many firms who were quick to develop this revival style was the Coalport factory of John Rose. Coalport had been established since 1795 at Coalbrookdale, Shropshire, but it was not until about 1820, when the factory began producing fine-bodied and glazed porcelains, that they achieved real prominence. It was at this time that John Rose

Part of a service made for Queen Victoria in about 1837 by Coalport, this jug is typical of the ornate floral decoration popular during the second quarter of the 19th century. Coalport were also noted for their elaborately encrusted wares.

acquired the stocks and moulds from the bankrupted Swansea factory which almost certainly contributed to the Coalport improvements. Rose's wares at this time were decorated with encrusted flowers and used characteristically flowing, curvilinear rococo forms. From the early years of Queen Victoria's reign, which began in 1837, the factory was principally occupied with reviving the full ground colours and lavish gilding associated with French mid 18th-century Sèvres styles. Colours included various shades of blue, turquoise and green. The name of Mme du Barry, mistress of Louix XV, was incorrectly adopted for Coalbrook's imitation of the famous rich pink used by Sèvres in the 18th century, but which was then christened Rose Pompadour, after Mme du Barry's predecessor. Coalport continued to produce high quality porcelain decorated in imitation of 18th-century rococo styles throughout the century. Though they did extend their production to Parian wares, they never made stoneware or earthenware. Other competitors making porcelain in the rococo style included the short-lived Rockingham works owned by the Brameld family from 1826 till its closure in 1842. Like several other porcelain firms, Rockingham produced small pastille burners in the form of cottages, houses, churches and castles. They also made similar models in earthenware. These small burners were fitted with a hole in the back panel through which the pastilles were inserted. A miniature chimney enabled the sweet, perfumed smoke to scent the air.

Parian ware, a type of unglazed porcelain, is yet another example of the 19th-century passion for imitating earlier styles, forms and materials. It was a type of biscuit porcelain which closely imitated those made in the 18th century by Sèvres and a little later by Derby. Its smooth, creamy-white body colour and waxy finish also made it similar to the fine white marbles used by sculptors. For a time it was known both as 'statuary porcelain'

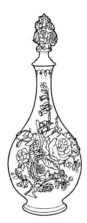

The Rockingham works at Swinton had been the site of a pottery since 1745, but the production of fine bone china did not begin until about 1820. This scent bottle, painted in enamel colours is marked with a griffin in puce enamel. c 1830–42.

Porcelain tureen, cover and stand made at the Rockingham factory at Swinton, decorated with painted and gilt floral motifs. c 1830.

and 'Carrara porcelain' after the famous Italian white marble of the region. Even the highly influential *Art Union Journal* of 1847 regarded it as scarcely inferior to marble as a material for art.

The popularity of Parian reflected not only a revived interest in figure modelling, much of it made inexpensively and thus suitable for even the modest home, but also the growing influence of mid-19th-century sculptors on the widening range of 19th-century artefacts. Its development in England is generally attributed to Copeland and Garrett, successors to Josiah Spode in 1845, though others, including Minton, made similar claims at the time and had Parian in production by 1848. Neo-classical themes were timely and characters such as Venus, Bacchus & Ariadne, and 'The Narcissus' appear. Portraits of people, particularly of the Royal family, were also popular, though they had to compete with literary favourites like William Shakespeare and Sir

Walter Scott. Other subjects, many of which reflect the Victorian love of the exotic and the sentimental, include 'Indian Fruit Girl and Water Bearer', 'Dancing Girl Reposing', 'Cleopatra', and 'Love Restraining Wrath'. Intricate and elaborate flower pieces were also made in the rococo style, some of them to be used as jewellery in the form of floral brooches.

Later in the century, modelled Parian figures were applied to larger pieces as high relief, though these rather elaborate pieces were costly to produce. Parian was made by many factories throughout the second half of the century but examples are difficult to distinguish between since only a few were marked. As production and competition increased forms became debased and quality varied considerably. Colours were introduced only towards the end of the century.

During 1869 the newly established factory of Beleek, in Co. Fermanagh, Ireland, began to produce good quality

Clytie was a popular subject for Parian ware busts. In Greek mythology she was the daughter of a Babylonian king who was tragically forsaken in love by the sun god Apollo. Copeland. 1855 (H 14in).

Pilgrim bottle showing the influence of Japanese 'Satsuma ware' from 1870 onwards. Made by the Worcester Royal Porcelain Company in about 1872 it shows scenes modelled in low relief, painted in enamel colours against an ivory-tinted background.

Vase resembling a pilgrim bottle in shape and decorated with pâte sur pâte, a type of low relief decoration built up in white slip, usually against a dark green-blue background. Minton c 1875 (H 10¼in).

Wares made at the Belleek factory in Northern Ireland are popular, but smaller pieces are still available at low cost. This elaborate sweetmeat dish in the form of a shell has the characteristic Parian body and irredescent glaze. c 1868.

Parian ware made distinctive by the addition of a creamy iridescent glaze. Many original patterns are still produced today and typical motifs include shells, rocks, coral, merfolk and flowers. Both glazed and unglazed types of Parian provide a relatively fertile area for the would-be collector.

Pâte-sur-pâte

One further addition to porcelain manufacture in the last thirty years of the century was the introduction, in 1870, of a complex and very expensive technique, *pâte sur pâte*. As its name suggests, it is of French origin and is quite literally paste on paste. It was, unlike Parian ware, a painstaking process involving the gradual building up of decorated areas with layer upon layer of slip; each layer being individually painted and fired. The product was a unique piece. The style – first developed in France – imitated earlier Chinese examples, and floral and leaf patterns were characteristic. As well as floral designs many examples reflect the sweet figure designs of contemporary book illustration. In appearance *pâte sur pâte* is not dissimilar to the expensive cameo technique used in fine glass production by leading firms such as Thomas Webb. In England the technique is particularly associated with Mark Louis Solon who worked from 1870 to the end of the century for Minton.

Nineteenth-Century Silver

The Warwick vase, one of a pair made as part of a service for Baron Berwick. This example was modelled closely on the original marble vase now at Warwick Castle. It is a fine example of a fashion which persisted untl the 1830s. The silver body is fitted with a liner which makes it suitable for use as a wine or a fruit cooler. Paul Storr, 1814.

Unlike his earlier Georgian predecessors, the man who was consecutively Prince of Wales (1762–1810), Prince Regent, (1811–20) and George IV (1820–30), was a keen and discerning connoisseur of the arts and played a leading role in the development of the tastes and fashions of the first thirty years of the 19th century. To historians a century later, the period reflects his influence, and they have repaid his lavish patronage by adopting his title of Regent to describe this thirty-year span. Nowhere was the scale of his patronage more evident than in the field of the silversmith.

Among the most influential craftsmen of the Regency period was Paul Storr and his occasional employer, the large firm of Rundell, Bridge and Rundell, goldsmiths to the Crown. Both gold- and silversmiths of this outstanding calibre were largely responsible for producing many of the finest pieces of the time. It was a period when keen interest and considerable expenditure was lavished on magnificent services of plate. The most notable was the superb service made principally by Rundell, Bridge and Rundell for the then Prince of Wales in 1805–6. The service comprised of several hundred pieces and was intended for State occasions, as nothing suitable had been made since the latter part of the 17th century.

The presentation piece

The Napoleonic campaigns or memorable races and hunts provided substantial excuses for commissioning magnificent presentation pieces. These generally took the form of large wrought cups or elaborately chased salvers. Classical urn shapes were popular but appear heavier and stiffer than the earlier neo-classical forms used by Adam. They were profusely decorated with classical motifs such as acanthus or vine-leaf patterns combined with martial and even nationalistic emblems in the form of Britannia. A good example of this type of formal, superbly-wrought silver plate is the Trafalgar Cup designed by the sculptor John Flaxman and made for presentation to the Admirals and sailors of that battle, by the Lloyds Patriotic Fund in 1805. Formal, ostentatious centre pieces and large dinner services persisted as the dominant trendsetter in silver during the whole of the 19th century. But due to their high cost they were generally subject to individual commissions.

Candelabra, epergnes and centre pieces were particularly spectacular in the Regency period, a time when lavish dinners and banquets were a popular form of entertainment. The fashion for highly sculptured forms is best seen in these large, often monumental, works. Classical figures such as muses support aloft finely-wrought bowls intended for festoons of fruit. Other subjects included bacchanalian revels and even military battles.

Since the late 18th century there had been a growing demand for more, but less expensive, silver. This, combined with technical developments available in machine production – first used on a large scale by Mathew Boulton at his Birmingham factory at the end of the 18th century – enabled a growing number of people to buy relatively cheap silver plate. Unlike the ostentatious and lavishly-decorated pieces ordered from some of the leading goldsmiths of the day, the use of machinery necessitated simple shapes and minimal decoration. A thinner gauge of metal was often used in order to lower the cost of production. By 1800 silver, which had formerly been the prerogative of the rich and aristocratic, was regarded as less exclusive. In order to cater for a rapidly-growing mass market, manufacturers – particularly around industrial centres such as Birmingham – increased their catalogues of useful, domestic and decorative wares. These continue today to find an enthusiastic and appreciative market.

Neo-classicism in silver

In general the neo-classical taste which had predominated throughout the end of the 18th century continued into the Regency period. The diversity of the Regent's own personal taste, admirably exemplified by his exotic pavilion at Brighton, ensured however, that it was not the only style of the early 19th century. Chinese, Gothic, Egyptian and even a revived rococo – visible earlier in silver than in any other material – are all styles which must be taken into account. Despite the occasional admixture of all these distinctive styles within a single piece, a characteristic feature of Regency silver is the extent to which form and ornament are subject to the restraints of symmetry and balance.

Regency tea pot supported on small bracket-shaped feet, resembling the rooftop of a pagoda. It boasts a mother-of-pearl finial and an insulated silver handle. 1809.

Unusually-shaped tea caddy with two divisions for different types of tea – commonly green and black. Made by Rebecca Emes and Edward Barnard. 1809.

The classical style of the Regency period was quite different in appearance to the neo-classicism advocated by Robert Adam. By 1800 Adam's style was attacked for its insipid prettiness and its light, linear form and decoration. The reaction brought with it a taste for heavier, sometimes massive pieces. Urn shapes were still popular but instead of the tall, graceful vertical elevations of the late 18th-century shape, Regency forms were low-bodied, even squat, with an accent very often on the oval- or circular-shaped horizontal plan. Ornamentation was revived and tended towards bold, sculptured forms in high relief. Broad bands of repeat patterns, such as vine leaves or anthemions, encircled square-shaped bases or circular bowls. Finely modelled and cast ornaments were applied and even gilding – the epitome of formal ostentation – was revived. Bacchanalian themes continued to grace wine coolers and wine labels. Bottle coasters were made of broad bands

One of the more elaborate variations on the fiddle pattern these fiddle thread-and-shell teaspoons were made by Benjamin Davis in 1828. Sets of flatware can be collected by selecting a pattern and gradually building up the numbers.

of finely chased leaves, though plain turned coasters with turned wooden bases were also common. Some fanciful imitation gun carriages in both silver and ebonised wood carried the military theme to its illogical conclusion.

Many new patterns were based on antique archaeological sources. Illustrations such as those by Charles Heathcote Tatham, who published his influential 'Designs for Ornamental Plate' in 1806, were always one of the most successful

methods of disseminating and popularising a new style. Though very little antique Graeco-Roman plate had even been discovered in the 19th century, other finds were inspirational – particularly the quantities of marble artefacts and statuary. Urns of various shapes and sizes were already familiar but the low-bodied, tall-necked amphora vases and the elegant design of Grecian – or as they were then believed to be, Etruscan – *oenochae* jugs were adapted for useful domestic wares such as tea and coffee services.

Teapots and tableware

In general these utilitarian wares followed the general form of the Regency style but were less elaborately ornamented. Tea and coffee sets were made in abundance to cater for the growing market. This was to some extent aided by the declining price of these hitherto expensive commodities, as colonial expansion overseas ensured a steady supply of tea or coffee to the home market. Sets were now made according to a single unifying de-

sign and the basic group of teapot, milk jug and sugar bowl could be augmented with additional water and coffee pots. The typical wide, low-bodied oval teapot shape was adapted for both cream jugs and sugar bowls. Spouts on jugs and teapots alike were commonly of a broad, flat D-shape, tapering towards the lip. Finials were more distinctive in the Regency period; like handles they were generally made of ebony or ivory, and were commonly turned. At their plainest these sets rely on their distinctive Regency form. The minimum of decoration might be as discreet as a simple gadrooned or reeded pattern around the rim or gallery of the shoulder or the base. Hollow wares during the first half of the 19th century were often raised off the table top on small feet, which, during the Regency period, were usually terminated in a lion paw or claw-and-ball. The elegant shell design came

A good tea pot of classic Regency shape. Guest and Craddock 1811.

Pair of candlesticks made by Thomas Bradbury in 1835. Decoration is restrained, confined to a simple gadroon pattern used on the base, column and sconce nozzle.

into its own during the rococo 1820's. Tea caddies and spoons were natural accompaniments to the tea ceremony. During the 19th century materials such as papier mâché and japanned metal were added to the more pedestrian wood, and the caddy spoon was produced in a variety of amusing and curious shapes: vine leaves, shell scoops and novelty shapes such as jockey caps.

Several new forms of tableware were introduced in the early 19th century. Toasted cheese dishes and toast racks are among the items collected today. The much copied and highly elaborate King's pattern appeared on flatware, as did the more restrained Queen's pattern. While leading fashionable firms such as Rundell, Bridge and Rundell dominated the top end of the market, factory-made plate and more desirable Sheffield plate enabled many more to buy silver for everyday use.

Since its invention by Thomas Bolsover in 1742 and its development by the shrewd Mathew Boulton, Sheffield plate had played an increasingly commercial role in the metalware market. From its foundation to the middle of the 19th century, it remained the most serious competitor to real silver. But in the 1840's, following the introduction of electro-

Decanter label or bottle ticket in the form of an S – probably for Sherry. Made by Rawlings and Sumner, 1845, not long before the compulsory use of printed bottle tickets made these labels obsolete.

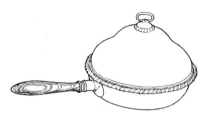

Silver-plated vegetable dish and cover. The wooden handle enables the dish to be carried easily to the table, but can then be removed. c 1860.

plating, the demand for Sheffield plate declined.

The rise of rococo

The purely symmetrical forms of Regency neo-classical designs showed signs of decline during the reign of George IV (1820–30). They were superseded by a revived rococo style which had already been used by Paul Storr as early as 1819. Despite the tendency at the time to refer to the style as Old French or Louis XIV, it was loosely-based on mid-18th century rococo designs and was to remain generally available, if not always at the height of fashion, well into the closing quarter of the century. Cast decoration continued, but the 1830's also saw a revival of embossed silver techniques which made use of machine-embossing rather than the old method carried out by hand. This fourth decade of the 19th century combined the rococo style with highly naturalistic floral decoration. Fruit forms – such as the melon shape – combined with fluted and panelled sides, were also prevalent. This style bore some similarity to the naturalistic style of carved decoration already noted on early Victorian furniture designs. Other styles popular from the reign

Pear-shaped ewer in characteristic Victorian neo-rococo taste. Edinburgh 1846.

of William IV (1830–37) through the opening of the Great Exhibition in 1851, included the Elizabethan and the Gothic. The latter was thought particularly suitable for ecclesiastical plate. There was also at this time a revival of the neo-classical style based on Grecian and Etruscan shapes similar to those found on the revived Etruscan pottery made by Wedgwood and Pratt's of Fenton, Staffs. The firm of James Dixon & Sons of Sheffield exhibited examples of this restrained Grecian style at the Great Exhibition in 1851. Dixons also produced Sheffield plate, but began to manufacture electroplated silver from 1848, when they obtained a licence to do so from Elkington.

The 19th century saw a move away from the 18th-century traditions of craftsmanship based on small family concerns. Instead the orientation was towards large factory and retailing outlets. This pattern was already established by the beginning of the century with the success of firms such as Rundell, Bridge and

An elaborate toilet mirror that was once part of a service. It is in revived rococo style which enjoyed intermittent popularity throughout the 19th century. 1870.

Rundell and it still remains today the standard format. Another change which became apparent as the 19th century wore on was the increasing competition which London manufacturers felt from from the burgeoning silver- and metal-making centres of Birmingham and Shef-field, particularly in the field of cheap mass production. The silversmithing partnership of Rundell, Bridge and Rundell, already in decline at the time of George IV's death in 1830, survived him by only nine years. But the style and size of this large and impressive early 19th-century firm was continued by their long-standing rivals R & S Garrard, who succeeded them as Royal Goldsmiths in 1830. Another influential firm was Paul Storr's successors, Hunt and Roskell. Garrards, Hunt and Roskell, and firms like them continued to produce both the large and impressive presentation pieces, fashionable since the early years of the century, as well as more ordinary useful domestic wares.

The emergence of electroplate

The successful development of electro-plating by the Birmingham-based firm of Elkington and Company in 1820, and their subsequent use of it on a large commercial scale radically altered the silver-manufacturing industry and enabled a flood of much cheaper and quickly-made silver to be made. It also spelled the end of Sheffield plate and the lesser-used Britannia metals, at least as items of worth in their own right.

One of a pair of entrée dishes in the mid 18th-century rococo taste. This example is in electro-plate and is therefore considerably cheaper than a silver example. Late 19th century.

Electroplating is a method whereby a thin coating of gold or silver is electrically deposited on a base metal. These under-metals varied but were usually of copper or copper alloy, nickel or silver. Britannia metal made a return as a base material after 1845. Marks such as EPBM or EPNS refer to the identity of the base metal. Unlike Sheffield-plated wares, electroplating enabled pieces to be fully finished prior to plating. Casting was the most common technique and models were based on pieces of sculptural or historic interest. The main drawback with this type of plating was the loss of precision and of the crispness of the initial casting, following the addition of a thin coat of silver.

Aftermath of the Great Exhibition

In the aftermath of the 1851 Great Exhibition, the lavish examples of embossed rococo and naturalist styles of decoration fell into decline, although examples in both these styles, which were commonly blended together in a single piece, continued to be produced for the rest of the 19th century. The Grecian *oenochoe* jug form – with its tall elegantly-shaped ovoid body, narrow neck and typical trefoil lip – remained prominent. This design was much-used for claret jugs and for coffee pots. A distinctive Victorian characteristic was the tendency to elongate these pieces by emphasising the length of the neck and the lower body. Early examples show a use of embossed decoration which slowly evolved into flat engraving and chased designs, with small moulded beads sometimes used to emphasise foot rims and lips.

But the new style which appeared to

This elaborate silver centrepiece possesses a mid 18th-century stand and basket in the rococo style, upheld by the three classical Graces. 1860.

cause the greatest interest during this very active decade between the Exhibition of 1851 and its follow-up in 1862, was that of the Renaissance. The cinquecento sculptor and goldsmith Benvenuto Cellini would seem to have been the inspiration for this type of work although few of his pieces appear to have been known at the time. Tall-stemmed, wide-rimmed and shallow-bowled tazza shapes – also much used in contemporary glass design – were typical of the lighter pieces made in this resurrected fashion.

The evident restraint in the decoration of domestic siver during the 1850's persisted well into the next decades. But though the elegantly-curved Grecian and Renaissance shapes continued to be popular there was a tendency for these forms to become increasingly more angular and to lose the graceful, curvilinear sweep characteristic of the *oenochoe* form. Tops and bases became flatter, and handles more angular. Engraved decoration was more fashionable than embossed, but instead of the familiar renaissance motifs a

Silver pear-shaped caster of early Georgian form, with engraved decoration to the body and narrow-beaded motif to the foot rim. London 1868.

tendency to revive the neo-classical designs of late 18th-century silver decoration prevailed. This 'Adam' style remained popular from 1870 through to the First World War.

Electroplate which, according to C. L. Eastlake was 'now so common in households' (1868), had enabled many more people to afford substitute pieces of silver at much cheaper prices. It followed the more expensive fashion of solid examples and a number of large manufacturing 'works' such as Elkingtons produced enormous quantities of both real and substitute silver. As with solid silver pieces the gauge of the sheet metal used was a practical guide to quality: the thicker the metal the better the quality, is a fairly safe rule of thumb, applying both to real and substitute silver wares. A characteristic of electroplated silver wares made in imitation of the neo-classical bright-cut engraved designs of the late 18th century is that the plating process reduced the crisp, jewel-like sharpness of this technique and renders it soft and flat in appearance.

Simplicity and the East

The preference for flat-engraved decoration, in place of the embossed rococo and naturalist styles familiar from about 1830–60, was due in part to the work of

Jug with engraved decoration showing exotic plant motifs of a form reminiscent of Middle-Eastern designs. By E & J Barnard 1875.

the architect designer, Owen Jones. Jones, in his book 'The Grammar of Ornament' published in 1856 was one of the earliest to advocate a return to linear patterns. 'Beauty of form' he wrote 'is produced by lines growing out one from the other in gradual undulations . . . In surface decoration all lines should flow out of a parent stem'. Furthermore he felt, as Cole had

done almost a decade earlier, that the shape of an object was more important than the decoration of the shape: 'Construction should be decorated. Decoration should never be purposely constructed' – a consideration that was fundamentally unsympathetic to the process of embossing. In particular he felt that 'flowers or other natural objects should not be used as ornament but conventional representation founded upon them . . .'. His ideas in turn were echoed a decade later by Charles L. Eastlake, and though his work was widely eclectic in style, it was always selective. His use of ornament was considered and intended merely to enhance the basic form.

The Japanese fashion, at its peak during the 1870's and 80's, had been stimulated initially by the 1862 Exhibition. It was well adapted to formal engraved patterns, particularly as it was the motifs of Japanese art which were assimilated, rather than the forms. The style, like many others during the 19th century, did not really go out of production until well

Selection of late 19th-century engraved silver and silver-gilt scent bottles, displaying the widespread influence of Japanese decorative art at this time.

into the 20th century, longer after it had passed from fashionable consciousness. Among the patterns were those based on stylised bamboo devices sometimes combined with storklike birds. But quite often the familiar chinoiserie designs of pagodas, Chinese figures and the 'dripping icicles' were embossed rather than engraved.

The move toward Arts and Crafts

The Japanese style not only influenced the designs for silver used by the large mass production silver companies, but also had some impact on the ideas of reformist designers such as Dr Christopher Dresser, whose work during the 1880's and 90's was considered to be far in advance of his own time. His severely functional, undecorated forms owed something to real Japanese metal work, which he may well have seen during his visit to that country in 1876–7. But Dresser, like a growing number of mid- and late 19th-century Victorians, had long questioned the quality and taste of ordinary mid-Victorian silver design. Unlike Morris however, Dresser did not despise machinery nor did he reject the benefits to be had from mass production. To the contrary, he designed for a number of leading manufacturers such as Hukin and Heath (he was art director from 1880), Elkingtons, and James Dixon & Co. These creations, carried out in silver and, more typically, in electro-plate – a reflection of his concern for an economic use of material – embodied his own maxim that 'siver objects . . . should perfectly serve the end for which they have been formed'. Ornament is almost entirely excluded, except perhaps for the exaggerated line of an

Late 19th-century dressing table set of hairbrush, clothes brush, and hand mirror. Such pieces can be picked up individually or in sets. 1891.

ing, but Ashbee encouraged his silversmiths to leave it untouched. The range of objects was limited to simple items such as bowls, cups, boxes, vases, plain teapots and tea kettles, table lamps, and stands for vases, jugs and a variety of dishes. By the 1890's much of the group's work – which, after all, had had its beginnings in the Arts and Crafts Movement – began to affect the sinuous curves and floral designs of the Art Nouveau style. By 1900 it had conquered silver design in England, America and Europe.

ebony teapot handle, the square outline of a bachelor tea set or the turned ebony finial on the lid of a soup tureen. Functional rivets were also accentuated, drawing attention to both their constructional and ornamental purpose, an idea similar to the revealed construction used in late 19th-century furniture. Dresser's distinctive work, which looked forward to the unconstrained designs of this century, is rightly considered to play an important part in the development of silver design. But his stark, uncompromising forms, though certainly collector's items, have a limited appeal. Another designer sympathetic towards mass production was William Benson (1854–1924). This was despite the fact that he knew William Morris and had been a founder member of the Art Worker's Guild, later taken over by the Arts and Crafts Exhibition in 1889.

It was not until the last quarter of the century that reformists such as C. R. Ashbee, inspired by the ideals of William Morris, began to have any real effect on the field of silver. Charles Ashbee shared Morris' distrust and dislike of machinery and mass production and advocated the return to early medieval principles of craftsmanship. To promolgate his ideas, Ashbee established the Guild of Handicrafts in 1888. His guild advocated simple shapes, which like Dresser's designs contrasted sharply to the over-decorated examples of the majority of mass produced wares. Many of the pieces were hammered out by hand. The hammered surface would ordinarily be removed with polish-

Small silver pair of grape scissors in their original silk- and velvet-lined case. Similar accessories were added to canteens during the 19th century, many more decorative than useful. London 1892.

Nineteenth-Century Glass

Glass manufacture burgeoned during the 19th century. It was made possible, not only by an ever increasing market both at home and abroad, but also by the introduction of new techniques and the widespread modernisation of factories. At the same time there was a growing diversity in styles and glass materials, as manufacturers sought to keep pace with the growing catholicism of public taste.

The era of cut glass

During the first quarter of the century, a period described in England as the Regency, the fashion for bold heavy, deeply-cut glass prevailed. Cut glass had been popular since the second half of the previous century, but none of the earlier 18th-century cut glass could compare with the weighty opulence so typical of the Regency and of the Empire style, its Continental counterpart. Despite the high tax on glass, the early 19th-century examples were characterised by thick-walled bodies profusely mitre-cut in diamond and hobnail patterns. Such prickly surfaces were given to a very wide range of glasswares, from those associated with drink and the table – including cut trifle dishes, celery glasses, butter tubs and cruets – to personal items in the form of toilet bottles, eye glasses and fancy ornaments.

The pre-eminence of cut glass was fully established by the end of the Regency period (c 1820) and despite noticeable intermittent fluctuations in public taste, which brought about the periodic demise of cut glass, it never entirely went out of fashion. It remains today the predominant method of decoration. Other patterns produced on the cutting wheel during this period included chequered, crosscut and straw-

Barrel-shaped decanter displaying deep mitre-cut decoration, neck rings and mushroom-shaped stopper characteristic of the Regency style. c 1820.

berry variations, all based on a diamond cut, while pillared flutes, reeding and prismatic decoration were also very fashionable. Often these deep relief patterns were arranged in horizontal bands encircling candelabra stems, jugs and squat barrel-shaped decanters. These decanters, many fitted with mushroom-shaped stoppers, were also generally fitted with neck rings, varying from one to five or six, and sometimes combined with horizontal step cutting. This horizontal emphasis was not only found in glass at this time but was also seen on contemporary seat furniture.

By the 1830's this gave way to a more vertical, cylindrical shape. The prickly surface patterns became smoother, but none the less massive, using broad facets and thick pillared flutes. Moulded glass – both blown and the newly-introduced press moulding – followed most of the same patterns and motifs fashionable on more expensive cut glass items. But moulded glass – unless further refined by a cutter – remains soft in appearance and slightly rounded at the angles, whereas cut glass is distinguished by its crisp, sharp edges and outlines. Arched pillar cutting became a favourite technique during the thirties and forties.

From the time of the Great Exhibition in 1851 to the end of the 1870's, cut glass decoration was unfashionable. It never entirely went out of production, however. Many, like the reformist John Ruskin, disliked this form of decoration. This reaction was exacerbated by the flood of cheap pressed glass which imitated the more expensive product. But cut glass did re-emerge during the last two decades of the century, when, due to technical improvements, cutters produced high quality work of a dexterity and precision not seen before. Furthermore, cutters were able to apply their skills to shapes which had previously been beyond their ability and their equipment. This particularly applied to the spherical and semi-spherical shapes found on bowls, baskets and dishes made at the close of the century.

Nailsea glass

Despite the continued pre-eminence of cut glass, regarded then and now as the 'old legitimate trade', the 19th century was a period in which experimentation and the demand for novelty led to the introduction and popularity of many new forms

Nailsea type frigger in the form of a clear, colourless glass pipe decorated with opaque white stripes, *c* 1860. Similar wares were made throughout the century. (L 1ft 3in).

and types of glass. In particular coloured glass came to the fore, catering for both rich and poor markets. Ironically the popular taste for coloured glass was generated in the early 1800's by those whose incomes had hitherto prevented them buying the more expensive flint and cut glass. A type of glass, generically describ-

ed as 'Nailsea', was made in the numerous bottle and window glass houses up and down the country. In addition to Nailsea (nr Bristol), it was produced in Wrockwardine (Salop), Stourbridge (Staffs), Newcastle-on-Tyne and Alloa (Scotland).

The base glass of Nailsea was the green type used principally in the making of bottles. It resulted in a cheap product, because the material was less costly and because such bottle glass was subject to about one fifth of the tax levied on flint or lead glass. The standard of bottle glass generally varied widely due to the impurities in the batch, and could range from light clear green to a dark green-brown, which was so dark as to be almost black in appearance. When used in Nailsea it was decorated with haphazardly splashed-on blobs or delicately combed and looped trails of opaque white glass marvered into the body. Nailsea wares were often both decorative and utilitarian, comprising round-bodied jugs and mugs. But not all Nailsea type glass was so functional. It had been a long-standing practice amongst glass makers to use up the remains of the day's batch – and, at the same time, demonstrate their own particular skills – by making a number of amusing, fanciful glass pieces known as toys or friggers. Some had a use but most were decorative objects intended to hang by the fireside or in a lover's kitchen. Good examples became a further source of income, as fairings for sale at local fairs. Today these fripperies are increasingly sought after by markets much more exclusive than those for which they were intended.

Popular collectables include walking sticks, rolling-pins, bells, tobacco pipes with long solid glass stems, and large

glass balls of between 8–18cms in diameter. These balls were known as witches' balls and were believed to have prophylactic qualities. Their plain or decorated surfaces in colours of blue, green or ruby red, were hung in entrance doorway in order to ward off the evil eye. To increase their colourful brilliance they were sometimes silvered. Walking sticks and rolling-pins incorporate ingeniously spiralled and combed threads of green, white, blue and red in a clear or pale-green glass body. It is more difficult to date these pieces or to attribute them to any particular glasshouse or area since they were made throughout the 19th century and well into the present.

Powdered glass decorated goblet *c* 1810, imitating engraved or etched decoration but resembling neither. The technique was developed by potter/ glass maker John Davenport in 1806.

Coloured and opaque glassware

The production of coloured glass received a tremendous impetus in 1845, when, one hundred years after its imposition, all duty on glass was lifted. The abolition paved the way for greater experimentation in design and manufacture, since glass producers previously had been reluctant to diversify and experiment because they were bound to pay duty on everything made, regardless of whether it was sold or not. Already on the Continent, several glasshouses – notably in Bohemia and France – were struggling to break away from the domination of cut glass which English taste had imposed since the first quarter of the century. A strongly-coloured marble glass called Lithyalin glass appeared in Bohemia during the 1830's, while at the same time in France a slightly translucent white and coloured opaline glass was made. It was not long before English glasshouses followed suit. At the Great Exhibition in 1851, examples of clear and opaque coloured glass were dominant in the display cases. But the range of glass available was enormous, catering for every taste and pocket, thus making it virtually impossible to label each and every nuance or fluctuation in style.

Together with widespread interest in English historical styles (Jacobean, Renaissance and neo-Gothic), there was also a revived interest in early Venetian glass and in the classical styles fashionable in other arts during the middle of the century. Some glass made for the Exhibition was decorated with scenes and motifs in imitation of Greek, Etruscan and even Egyptian pottery. In particular white-bodied glass in translucent opalines or opaque white glass was used for this type of decoration, painted or printed with enamel colours. Border patterns of neo-classical ivy leaves, key patterns and anthemions were used on necks of vases and ewers, and for framing decorative panels depicting classical scenes and figures. A number of well-known firms, mainly operating in the Midlands, carried out this type of high quality work in opaque white glass.

WHB & J Richardson was one such firm, and was also well-known for opaque white glass in other styles. Examples include vases which were painted with encircling floral motifs set within horizontal bands or which rose vertically from the base in brightly coloured posies. Pictorial motifs were also popular and much of the factory's work was enhanced with gilding or a type of frosted surface which gave an attractive matt background to such themes.

Layered vase with blue and opaque white glass over a clear colourless base, revealed through cut panels and decorated with gilt. WHB & J Richardson made this popular type of Victorian glass in about 1848.

Layering, casing and engraving

At the Great Exhibition of 1851 glass was advertised in a very wide range of colours, including opal (white), amber, turquoise, blue, canary (yellow), pink, light and dark ruby reds (light red is sometimes also known as cranberry red), brown, and various shades of green, purple and black. Experiments were conducted not only into textures, such as the frosted finish used by Richardson, but also into layering glass, one colour on another. Overlay – or cased – glass had been available on the Continent since the 18th century but was not made in England until after 1845. Many decorative wares such as vases and ewers were made up of several equally-thick layers of glass, depending on the complexities of decoration. On elaborate pieces several layers might be used, although two to three was more common. Further decoration was usually added. The best results were achieved by cutting through one layer to reveal the coloured or plain glass underneath. In the 1850's and 60's the decoration took the form of arched windows in the neo-Gothic style then enjoying widespread popularity, but floral designs, oval cuts and geometrically-cut panels were also common. Additional etching and/or engraving was sometimes contained within the geometric frames.

A slightly cheaper way of producing a similar effect was through the technique known as flashing. This involved dipping the glass vessel into molten glass in order to coat the base layer with a thin film of coloured – or opaque white – glass. This method was widely used for cheaper imitations of high quality overlay and cameo glass from about 1845–80. Because the outer film of glass was thinner than on a properly cased layer, the cutting was necessarily flatter and shallower. Engraved decoration was another popular form of decoration in use from the 1840's onward. It was particularly suited to depicting the tight and intricate floral and

Three drinking glasses from a set of six sherry, wine and liqueur glasses. Each has a broad band of diamond-point engraved decoration.

Straight-sided jug with slightly tapering sides, decorated with wheel-engraved fern patterns, a popular motif in the late 1800's when the hothouse and conservatory were fashionable. c 1880.

pictorial themes so beloved of the Victorians. It was also an attractive medium for the thin-walled, delicate shapes, reminiscent of Venetian glassware, which became fashionable in the middle of the century. During this period arabesques inspired by classical Renaissance artists jostled with Greek motifs, and the smooth oviform shapes of Greek pottery dominated cabinets and mantelpieces.

During the late 1860's and 70's floral and bird designs came into prominence as a response to both the Arts and Crafts Movement and the stylised flower designs of popular imported Japanese ware. Many of these motifs looked forward to the Art Noveau style. Plants associated with the hothouse environment of Victorian conservatories bloomed on glass. The fern became a special favourite, featuring as a

single leaf design on a humble pub glass and on elaborate flower vases. In the 1880's a new style of decoration called rock crystal cutting was introduced for use on high quality glass. Examples exist from firms such as Stevens and Williams, and Thomas Webb and Sons. Much of this work sought to imitate the deep sculptural cutting on real rock crystal, and was carried out by highly skilled immigrant engravers, among them Frederick Kny. It represents the highest point of 19th-century glass.

Etched and cameo glass

Echoes of the motifs employed by engravers in decorating the surface of coloured, clear and overlaid glass appeared in the newer technique of etching. This method was in use in the early 18th cen-

Shallow-bowled champagne glass, showing the influence of earlier Venetian styles of decoration in the double-looped stem decorated with twisted coloured threads. George Bacchus & Sons, c 1850.

tury, but despite attempts to commercialise it during the 1830's it was not until the 1870's that it became widely accepted. The surface of the glass was masked

Cameo glass vase titled 'Raising an Altar to Bacchus' executed by a leading glass carver, Alphonse Lechevrel, who worked for Hodgetts, Richardson & Co at Stourbridge. c 1878.

with an acid-resistant medium prior to scratching or cutting a design to reveal the glass underneath. When immersed in a solution of hydrochloric acid, the unprotected glass surface corroded, leaving the coated glass untouched. The depth of corrosion depended on the length of time that the solution remained in contact with the glass. A satin matt finish was achieved by fairly brief immersion. Etching was occasionally used in conjunction with engraving, but by the last quarter of the century it was generally employed alone. The advantage of etching was that it could be employed on a mechanical basis, using templates, and did not have to rely on the artistic skills required for engraving. It was thus a much cheaper medium for decoration. It is also charac-

terised by a freer line, quite different to the stiffness visible in engraved glass.

Cameo glass came into prominence during the last quarter of the century. This type of decoration greatly accelerated following the endeavours of John Northwood (1836–1902) in imitating the famous Roman Portland Vase in 1873. Cameo glass was produced through a type of casing process. An outer layer of opaque glass, generally white, was superimposed on another colour, rather like the earlier overlay glass. But then the background to the design was ground or cut away, leaving the white cameo to stand out in relief against a coloured (or occasionally clear) background. This type of glass inspired by the Oriental imports of the 1870's and 80's, became more intricate as more layers were introduced. The technique was both demanding and costly, involving, like Apsley Pellatt's exclusive *crystallo ceramie* pieces of fifty years earlier, a high degree of expertise. Firms such as Thomas Webb and Sons and WHB & J Richardson specialised in

Cup with small white paste profile face encrusted in clear glass by Apsley Pellatt. Sometimes these works are called sulphides. c 1820.

cameo glass during the last quarter of the century. But despite the introduction of the cheaper etching techniques at the end of the century demand declined quickly. Like Pellatt's 'glass jewels' (which were a type of encrusted cameo set within clear flint glass), cameo glass is today costly and increasingly difficult to find.

Cut glass decanter with deep rounded body and long neck decorated with 'printies' or small, shallow oval or circular facets. It was popular from the mid-19th century on. Apsley Pellatt, c 1851.

Apsely Pellatt is a well-known in the annals of the 19th-century glass industry. He was responsible for reviving or inventing several new techniques. In the middle of the century he reintroduced a type of ice-glass, known to earlier Venetian glass makers, and so-called because the rough surface and the fractured appearance of the glass were similar to shattered ice. Although Pellatt christened his improvement – which he displayed at the Great Exhibition in 1851 – Anglo-Venetian glass, the term was also used by other firms, including Richardsons and George Bacchus & Sons. But to confuse the col-

Clear colourless flower stand with ruby trailing, made by glass-threading process patented by Hodgett's Richardson & Co in 1878. These pieces were popular from about 1870. *c* 1878.

Vase elaborately overlaid with applied floral motifs, made by Stevens and Williams who described this sort of ware as 'art glass'. *c* 1895.

lector, they used it to describe glass which was decorated in an entirely different way. Their version was embellished with twisted multicoloured and white threads like latter day Venetian latticino glass. But this latter style did not really flourish until the 1860's, when other characteristics of Renaissance glass – such as the naturalistic curls and twists, and wavy bowl shapes decorated with wings and ears – were added. This type of applied decoration became increasingly exaggerated and by the last quarter of the century much of the elaborate 'fancy' glass was covered in trailing frills, blobs, and leaf and flower motifs.

The great American companies

Although links with the Continent became more distant in the second half of the century, those with America tended to improve. As a result a number of developments in glass manufacture were affected. In the highly distinctive Mary Gregory pieces, particularly the vases with frilled neck rims, the decoration was typically of whimsical childlike figures painted in white enamels onto plain-coloured green or red glass. At first glance these glasses are not very different from cameo glass but later imitations became cruder and the white enamel took on flesh-coloured tints. This type of glass was erroneously thought to have been first made at the Boston and Sandwich Glass Company, USA, during the 1850's. In fact it was widely made in Europe and America and is now very collectable. Another American glass house was responsible for introducing a type of art glass known as Burma, or Burmese, glassware. This variety is distinguished by subtle gradations of

Glass shade in Queen's Burmese 'art glass' made by Thomas Webb & Sons. This example, with its colours moving from yellow to pale pink, is overpainted with floral motifs. Late 19th century.

colour in the glass itself, shading from a pale cream yellow to a fairly strong pinky-red tone. It was patented by the Mount Washington Glass Company 1885. Similar glass was made by Thomas Webb & Sons who made a type of cased glass called Queen's Burmese ware. Among the innumerable items made in coloured glass

Vase in green glass with scene in white enamel colours. Described as 'Mary Gregory' glass, it is often attributed to the Boston & Sandwich Glass Company, USA, but much was also made in Bohemia.

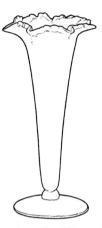

Vase in Burmese glass with a dull matt finish characteristic of much English Burmese glass. This was another type of 'art glass', which shaded from yellow to pink. Late 19th century.

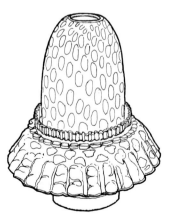

Pearl satinglass 'fairy lamp', striped in blue, rose, yellow and apricot and decorated with symmetrically arranged rows of trapped air bubbles. Late 19th century.

towards the end of the century were little fairy lights which were displayed in decorative formations on tables or used as night lights. These small domed candle shades were intended to fit over a special type of candle manufactured by the chandler Samuel Clarke during the late 1880's and 90's. They were fitted with a vent at the top and the glass shade was made in every conceivable colour, pattern and type of glass. One finish which is particularly sought after is that known as satin glass, its smooth matt surface achieved by dipping the glass into an acid solution. The lamps were made under licence in several other countries and the more exotic versions were moulded in the shapes of cottages and even elephants. They were very cheap and plentiful in the 19th century and can still be found today in large numbers, although they command considerably more than the 1p rate charged in 1880 for the simplest examples.

Pressed glass variations

Most examples of fairy lights were manufactured by the relatively new pressed glass method. Moulded glass goes back at least two thousand years and relies on each piece being made individually. Pressed glass techniques, on the other hand, introduced a mechanical process which finally led to full automation. Items were made by placing a blob of molten metal inside a pre-formed mould. A metal plunger, shaped in such a way as to form the inside of the object, was forced into the mould. Pressed glass differs from mould-blown glass in that the interior does not conform to the contours of the outside as it does on blown glass. Although press moulding was used for making the square bases used on large drinking glasses at the

Pressed sugar bowl made as an electioneering piece for Gladstone. Other pieces commemorated topical events, such as the Queen's Jubilee in 1887. Henry Greener, Sunderland 1869.

end of the 18th century, its potential was not recognised until the late 1820's when it became widespread in America. Within a few years it had travelled to Britain, but early examples were largely confined to imitating the styles of cut glass then popular. The technique opened up the glass market to a whole range of people who had hitherto been excluded from buying cut glass on the grounds of cost.

With the introduction of new techniques and the popularity of coloured glass in the second half of the century, pressed glass manufacturers turned their attention to utilizing coloured glass. During the third quarter of the century there was an attempt to imitate the textures and surface patterns available to etched and engraved decoration. In particular, the lacy patterns found on much glass manufactured in the 1870's and 80's was popular and is today relatively easy to find. The most characteristic motif was

Pressed glass sugar bowl with moulded floral motifs, showing the widespread influence of Japanese art during last quarter of the 19th century. Sowerby's Ellison Glassworks. *c* 1881.

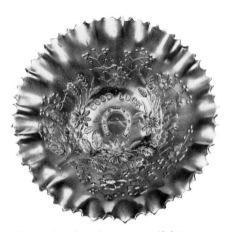

Carnival glass plate. These press-moulded pieces were highly coloured, exhibiting an orange-gold irridescence. They were mass-produced for fairs and carnivals from 1880 onwards. *c* 1800.

Opaque marbled glass dish better known as 'slag glass' or 'end of the day' glass. A number of firms such as Sowerby's, George Davidson and Greener & Co made similar pieces. *c* 1880.

the raised pattern of half round dots, which not only formed border patterns but was also used to make up the portrait profiles of notable figures such as Gladstone and Queen Victoria, together with the date and sometimes the event commemorated – for example, the jubilee celebrations of 1887. Commemorative pieces are always interesting, not only for their historical associations, but because they were intended to be eye-catching and decorative rather than purely functional. There is enormous scope in the commemorative field and anyone with a keen historical interest could well develop a particular theme taking in all the applied arts.

Another type of pressed glass which has recently attracted a considerable amount of attention is the opaque marbled glass known as slag glass. Traditionally this type of glass was said to be made at the 'end of the day' (another name for it), indicating that the glass was a trifle pro-

duced by the maker for his own amusement. However the high level of manufacture during the last quarter of the century would seem to contradict this. The marbling of the glass was due to the admixture of iron slag which was available in and around the smelting areas of Newcastle. In particular, Sowerby's Ellison Glass works – identified by its Peacock mark – and George Davidson & Co (both of Gateshead), together with Henry Greener and Co (Sunderland), are noted for making this type of glass. Much of it bears a registry mark. The colours used in the making of slag glass were generally confined to purplish black, blues and turquoise, orange browns and a near-black. Pressed glass in plain opaque colours was also made, ranging from a white to creamy ivory colour and a strong turquoise blue. Dating pressed glass is hazardous, as some styles are still in production today and others have recently been revived. A good example of this are the

elegantly-shaped grape dishes formed by a pair of outstretched hands. This design was first patented in Britain by the Edinburgh firm of John Ford in 1885. Other early examples tended to be fairly small and generally show signs of age and wear. They included straight-sided bowls raised up on small feet, candlesticks formed as classical columns, saltcellars modelled on late 18th-century pieces, milk jugs and sugar bowls (often part of a set), and baskets decorated in imitation of woven basketwork. A slight raised ridge is apparent on pressed glass, indicating the line where the mould was broken open once the glass had been shaped.

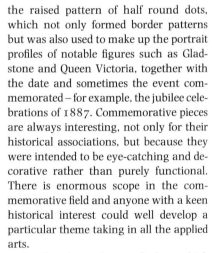

Nineteenth-Century Smaller Collectables

Kitchen Antiques

The kitchen has always been a focal point in the home. And in the 19th century, the staggering range of implements available to the cook multiplied dramatically. Even for the small kitchen, that doyen of 19th – century culinary art Mrs Beeton recommended at least 125 items as essential for producing anything from the simplest to the most sumptuous meals characteristic of the period.

Implements necessary for the production of dairy products are numbered among the items which once played a vital role in the 19th century but which have, by and large, passed out of daily use. Wooden butter pats, decorated with floral motifs or the more common ribbing are easily available today. Sadly, the small drum-shaped butter churns, which because of their size were for use in the kitchen rather than the dairy, are much harder to find and consequently more expensive.

The fireside or the kitchen range was the real centre of the kitchen in the 19th century. Brass or steel trivets stationed beside the kitchen range were, like the oddly shaped 'cat' or plate warmer, designed to keep food and plates warm. Another much more unusual aid in the 19th century was the iron hastener. This metal implement was generally shaped like a cupboard complete with door, but without a back. They were used for roasting large sides of meat, which were hung from a spit in the ceiling of the hastener. The backless side was placed in front of the fire and the meat would cook quickly and evenly; occasional checks on progress were possible by opening the small door on the front. These pieces are very rare and were generally associated with large household kitchens, such as the example at Ham House, and constitute a real find if discovered. Saucepans in brass, copper and iron were used in the preparation of preserves and jams. Though few suit the small size of the modern cooker, they are in demand as decorative jardinieres or as ornamental features in their own right. Similar use is also made of the larger iron cauldrons which were generally suspended above the fire. Other

Three kitchen collectibles: a tin two-piece jelly mould, a glass butter churn and a ceramic mould, all made at the turn of the century. *c* 1900.

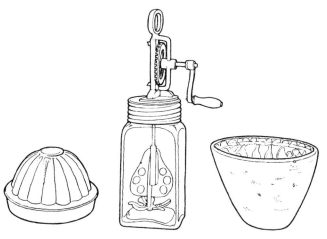

collectables include kettles, griddles, toasting forks and weighing scales – though beware the many modern copies which have been flooding the market.

Formal displays of food on a well-laid Victorian table demanded the preliminary use of moulds in a variety of materials and exotic shapes. They were used for everything including terrines, jellies and ice creams. The most common material was earthenware, but copper moulds have long been collected and are now relatively expensive. Moulds also come in materials such as silver, but Britannia metal was more typical in the 19th century. Pewter was not used as its lead content made it dangerous.

The kitchen was used for preparing food but in some cases it was also the room in which people ate their meals – either the owner in the case of a small cottage or servants in a larger establishment. Interesting items to watch out for might include coffee grinders, salts – and much other small kitchen treen – and, with the influence of the Arts and Crafts Movement towards the last decade of the century, the attractively decorated bread boards with flowers and wheatears round the border. These were made well into the 20th century but are now no longer produced commercially.

Smoking accessories

A steady accumulation of 'smokers' accessories' have grown up since the introduction of tobacco into Europe in the middle of the 16th century. Today they provide a wonderfully varied and fertile field for the potential collector.

Tobacco can be taken either as a finely-ground powder – which after mixing with herbs and spices is called snuff – or it can

be smoked. Early tobacco users smoked the tobacco leaves in pipes but by the late 18th century cigars and cigarettes were familiar.

An essential prerequisite for the smoker was a tobacco box. Early 17th-century examples were generally made of wood or lead and the drum-shaped box fitted with a tight lid. By the middle of the 19th century these boxes became more varied; brass and lead boxes in circular drum shapes, octagonal and oblong (coffin) shapes, were made throughout the century. Cigar boxes, or humidors, were also made in large quantities, and by the close of the century packets were the normal way to sell cigarettes. Other materials commandeered for smoker's paraphernalia included pottery, leather, wood (see treen, Mauchline ware and Tunbridge ware), japanned metals, papier mâché and the more expensive gold and silver. During the last quarter of the century Japanese influence was evident in the influx of lacquer cases and boxes and in the use of cloisonné enamelling decorated with oriental themes. Pipes were commonly made of fine white clay but meerschaum – a type of silicate which usually turned amber when in contact with heat and tobacco smoke – was also popular and many examples were carved in the form of grotesque human and animal masks. Wood and papier mâché pipe trays and stands were also made.

As well as a box in which to keep the tobacco, an instrument for lighting was essential. Thin strips of wood, called spills, were kept in jars and boxes amidst all the clutter of the mantelpiece, until matches made an appearance in 1826. Though even the first examples were called friction lights, matches tipped with phos-

phorous were not made until the 1830's, when the vesta match – which could be struck on the bottom of a rough surface – was invented. Vesta boxes came in all shapes and sizes, made principally of metals which varied from gun metal to gold and silver. Pocket boxes were generally small and oblong in shape, having a roughened edge on one side on which to strike the match. Many were fitted with a small ring which could be attached to the wearers' garments. Table models were also made of wood – especially *lignum vitae* – porcelain, pottery, cast iron and brass.

Tunbridge ware

Since the 1680's the small town of Tunbridge Wells in Kent had been famous for its health-giving chalybeate waters and as a fashionable holiday resort. Throughout the 18th century several notable visitors recorded that small, locally-made, wooden trifles were to be found for sale in the various retail emporiums found along the Pantiles, one of Tunbridge Wells' most

A Tunbridge ware writing slope with the back open to reveal the space for ink and pens. The floral panel and mosaic border patterns are typical of this work. *c* 1860.

select thoroughfares. Distinguished by their marquetry decoration, they subsequently became known as Tunbridge ware.

By the 1790's geometric patterns became à la mode for Tunbridge artisans. These took the form of veneered cubes in many differently coloured and grained woods, and a penant – or triangular – device often called the 'Vandyke' pattern. Both cube and vandyke marquetry were very popular during the last decade of the 18th century and remained in use throughout the 19th century. But whereas these patterns were used in the 18th century as principle motifs, in latter years they were invariably used in conjunction with mosaic patterns.

By the close of the 1830's the new mosaic technique had come into general use. It enabled manufacturers to produce Tunbridge wares more quickly and economically than had been possible during the Georgian period. The new method differed from the earlier veneered version by first gluing and pressing together a number of thin strips of differently coloured woods (spills) longitudinally to form a block. By cleverly arranging the various colours, a pattern was formed which ran through the block and was clearly visible at either end. These blocks, approximately 18″ in length, were cut into thin slices providing a number of perfectly repetitious 'end grain' mosaic-patterned sheets. They were then applied to the surface of the pine carcasses for decoration. After about 1845 these end-grain mosaics had a coarse appearance similar to the type of bold floral-patterned Berlin wool embroidery popular at about the same time. Despite the dominance of this coarser type of work, however, finer end-grain mosaic

was also used, the two running concurrently throughout the rest of the 19th century. With the introduction and widespread use of the new end-grain mosaics amongst Tunbrige ware manufacturers, the possibilities for introducing patterns were enormous. By the Great Exhibition of 1851 naturalistically portrayed birds, animals, plants, flowers and even insects such as butterflies were incorporated. The latter motif seems to have been a speciality of James and George Burrows of Gibraltar Cottage, who claimed to have invented the technique. These designs were used on a wide variety of objects as central vignettes. They also formed the basis of border patterns, although most borders were mainly geometric or floral. Views and buildings – particularly castles, ruined monasteries and abbeys – provided another source of inspiration in a century when romantic popular novels recalled an earlier age of medieval chivalry. Wood used for the background varied from pale golden-coloured bird's eye maple and sycamore to the rich, darker colours of holly, walnut and rosewood. End-grain mosaic and veneered cube patterns were deployed on an enormous variety of objects, the majority of them quite small, although some furniture – such as table tops and chair backs – was also decorated in this way. In the main it was used for boxes intended to hold letters, jewellery, tea, matches, cigars, perfume, and sewing and writing equipment. But really nothing with a flat surface was safe, and bookrests, clothes brushes, tea poys, pen-and-ink stands and trays fell to the Tunbridge craze. Even thermometer stands in the shape of Cleopatra's Needle – reflecting the interest caused by that curious obelisk

when it was set up on the Embankment in 1878 – took pride of place on Victorian desks.

Another method of using the blocks of coloured spills was to turn and shape them on a lathe into a whole range of small items: shaped pin cushions, watch-stands, thermometer holders, candlesticks, vases, tobacco barrels, and even spinning tops. These little fancies are also known as stickware.

Dolls

As well as providing companionship and forming part of the nursery furniture, dolls have played a number of roles. In early antiquity these small effigies of the

A Victorian doll's bed and French doll made by Jumeau, exhibiting her characteristic large almond shaped eyes. Late 19th century.

human form were often used as religious symbols and were significant participants in fertility, birth and regeneration rituals. In early medieval morality plays they did service as marionettes. Since the Renaissance, small pegged wooden dolls have been used as artist's models or 'lay figures' and several centuries's versions are still available. In the 17th and 18th century, dolls were used as tiny mannequins to model newly introduced fashions and for a time it was quite simply fashionable to own a pair of dolls.

By the 19th century the number of dolls and the variety of materials used in their manufacture had increased enormously. The simplest examples, which with the passage of time have usually suffered most, are the rag and cloth dolls. More robust materials such as leather were also used but these too have proved fragile. The peg doll, with simple joined limbs, was made throughout the century. Early 19th-century examples differ from later models by being given the appearance of a grown-up, rather than the baby faces which became fashionable in the middle of the century. The same trend also applied to china-headed dolls which were made in considerable numbers from about 1840, though a few Continental porcelain manufacturers made earlier examples. China examples differed from bisque dolls in that they are glazed and their delicate complexions varied from peaches-and-cream to a paler tone due to the whiter clay used in later examples. China hands and feet were often given to these dolls and were stitched onto their stuffed cloth bodies. It is not uncommon to find the extremities have been replaced, often with modern reproductions, since they are particularly prone to damage.

Bisque or unglazed dolls are probably the finest quality produced and the French firms of Jumeau and Bru are particularly noted for their models. These firms also made a number of automata dolls but fine examples are highly collected and expensive. Unlike china dolls, wax dolls were commonly modelled in composition and after painting were dipped into wax. The cracking of the wax surface, which is a common characteristic of this type of doll, is caused by the differing rates of expansion between the two materials. A famous wax doll maker was Madame Augusta Montenari of London who used real hair inserted individually with the help of a hot needle.

Paperweights

Paperweights, those small, spherical brilliantly-coloured glass objects that measure about 2 to 3 inches across the base, were first developed early in the 19th century with the introduction of crystallo ceramie by Barthelemy Desprez. But those encrusted cameos, a technique patented in England in 1819 by Apsley Pellatt, were difficult and expensive to make. It was not until the appearance of examples at the Austrian Industrial Fair held in Vienna in 1845, which used long-established Venetian glassmaking techniques like latticino and millefiori decoration, that their aesthetic and commercial potential was recognised.

Traditionally, heavy bronze ornaments were deployed to hold down stray pieces of paper but by 1850 three leading French glasshouses, St Louis, Baccarat and Clichy were making and retailing these attractively coloured, highly decorative, stationery objects for only a few francs each. Today, early examples from these factories command thousands of pounds at auction, especially those marked with their date of manufacture. By 1848 paperweights were made in England by firms such as George Bacchus & Sons, Birmingham, and were closely followed by a number of American glasshouses:

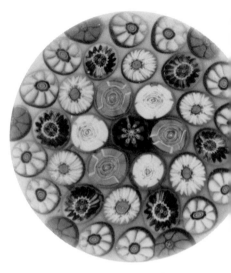

Above top: This millefiori weight, composed of 'Clichy Roses' and other 'flowers' is a much-loved and highly collected pattern. c 1845–60.

Above bottom: Sulphide portrait of Queen Victoria set in a bright red ground. The portrait is outlined within the 'printy' or faceted top. This example is rare. Clichy 1845–60.

the New England Glass Co (c 1852) and the Boston and Sandwich Glass Co.

The excellent artistic quality and skills displayed in paperweights caused these trifles to be collected for their intrinsic appeal not long after they were first introduced and by the close of the 19th century there were enormous quantities in circulation. Since the 1960's the growing interest in paperweights has caused some firms like Baccarat and St Louis to revive production and limited numbered series are now produced. Scottish firms, such as Perthshire Paperweights (Crieff) and Paul Ysart (Wick), have also started to produce examples, though some of the finest made today are made by the American botanist and glassmaker Paul Stankard of New Jersey.

Apart from the cameo encrustation of Aspley Pellatt, paperweights are decorated principally with floral, plant, millefiori and latticino patterns. 19th-century examples showing floral motifs tend to be much more stylised than contemporary paperweights, which often display superbly executed plant forms in a naturalistic way. Animal, insects and birds were also used but were less common. A more complex method involves the addition of another layer of opaque coloured glass on top of the dome of clear glass in which the decoration was embedded. Windows were cut or ground out of this overlay glass revealing the interior decoration.

Mauchline ware and Scottish tartan ware

In the early 1820's William and Andrew Smith of Mauchline began producing small boxes, principally for use as snuff boxes and razor strops. This Ayrshire-based industry quickly grew and by 1830

the brothers were manufacturing a wide range of small decorative items made of light, golden-coloured woods such as sycamore and birch.

Early examples from 1830 to 1840 were generally painted onto the wood. But a quicker method, introduced in about 1840, was to glue oval or circular pieces of paper, already painted, directly onto the item and seal it with a coat of varnish. Transfer-painting directly onto the wood was also introduced during the 1840's and Mauchline wares with this type of decoration became very fashionable as popular souvenirs among the resorts. Their success was due to the depiction of local interest or beauty spots, such as 'Black Gang Chine, Isle of Wight' or 'The Pier, Lowestoft'. Views of seaside resorts and spa towns all over Britain were used, as well as those on the Continent and in America. Souvenirs of the Continent showed resorts visited by British holiday-makers.

Another method of decoration to cover these small items, using Scottish tartans, was particularly well received. Its heyday was during the 1850's when Queen Victoria bought Balmoral Castle, her Scottish holiday home. The fashion was especially taken up by the monarchy-loving French and the production of these so-called Tartan wares continued through the end of the century until the firm stopped trading in 1904.

In the second half of the century other techniques were used to decorate these souvenirs. Photographs of resorts and well-known public figures were used in much the same way as the earlier paper cutouts. During the 1870's and 80's the fern motif made an appearance. Towards the end of the century increased produc-

tion provided a very wide and varied range of items both useful and frivolous. Aids for the letter writer (stamp boxes, letter racks and letter openers), for the seamstress (thimble boxes, needle and cotton cases), and for the smoker (cigar and cigarette boxes) all joined the list of 'necessities' which completed the well-furnished Victorian household.

Nursery toys and parlour games

The Industrial Revolution brought about mass production which, in turn enabled a much wider range of games and toys to be made. By the advent of the 19th century far more children and adults had the chance to 'play' in their leisure hours.

Every taste was catered for. The cupboards of a well-stocked 19th-century nursery were full of toys for boys and girls of every age. Little girls – including Queen Victoria – had dolls and doll's houses.

A selection of children's card games available from about 1875 to 1914.

Each room in the latter was thoroughly equipped and furnished, while the dolls themselves were often dressed in clothes made by the ingenious hands of their owners. Many of the dolls' houses give a glimpse of the duties involved in running a full-sized Victorian household, while well-fitted dolls' shops – set out as butchers, ironmongers or groceries – ensured the virtues of domestic economy from an early age. Indeed many toys made during the earlier years of Queen Victoria's reign emphasised an aspect of educational or moral training. For boys, toy forts filled with tiny soldiers were thought the perfect present in an age when the life of a soldier was considered a manly occupation for the second sons of the upper classes. Early tin soldiers – mainly imported from leading Bavarian toy makers – were of a characteristic flat type, but the

The Bunny ABC Picture Block made by the New York firm of Selchow & Righter in about 1895.

invention of hollow-cast lead soldiers by William Britain gave these little two-inch mimics of the British army a much more lifelike appearance. Toy theatricals were also popular, with miniature proscenium stages manufactured together with plain

or coloured printed cut-out figures and provided with scripts adapted from such well-known stories as Oliver Twist and Treasure Island.

Out of the nursery and into the parlour, games were just as prodigious for both child and adult. Quiet indoor games included simple picture blocks, each wooden cube decorated with a glued-on lithographic picture. Later jigsaw puzzles were made possible by the widespread use of new fret-cutting jigs. Family card and board games were endless in variety, with a typically Victorian emphasis on instruction in order to improve the mind or the morality of the participants. Board games came complete with every conceivable obstacle and encouraged a knowledge of history, religion, geography and the classics. On a more energetic note, indoor parlour games that imitated robust outdoor exercises could be found in such games as table croquet and carpet bowls, while hobby horses and hoops allowed the youngsters to let off steam.

Today, despite their tattered state, most of these Victorian toys are eagerly sought after as unselfconscious records of an era's social and moral preoccupations.

Beadwork

Beads of glass strung on thread or stitched onto canvas have been known since antiquity. But it was not until the middle of the 19th century that this decorative affectation reached its zenith as a popular English art form.

Since the Regency period there had been a noticeable increase in the variety of decorative jewellery worn by fashionable society women. Though valuable jewels such as rubies, sapphires and diamonds were still required for formal court

Stool with beaded upholstered seat and wooden legs carved and turned to resemble bamboo. Slightly damaged examples of this furniture can be very inexpensive but interesting. Late 19th century.

dress, cheaper semi-precious stones and even glass beads were introduced for less formal occasions and made up into fragile strings of necklaces, earrings, bracelets and brooches. It was not long before designs showing delicate sprigs of flowers or birds on branches superseded open-work necklaces. Instead these pastoral motifs were carefully stitched onto velvet bands to be worn round neck or wrist. Beadwork continued to make its impression on a growing number of trifles, so that by the early Victorian period any number of tokens were decorated with tiny polychrome glass beads. Beads often covered the entire surface of an object, giving it the appearance of heavily-worked petit point.

The craft was practised both as a cottage industry by lower-class women and by ladies as a skill developed during long hours of leisure. Perhaps for this reason many of the articles decorated with beadwork are of a feminine nature. Decorative designs on collars, cuffs, capes, belts and purses abound, as do beadwork fantasies embroidered on homely aids and household items. The range of beadworked objects destined for the sewing box was considerable – needle and thimble cases, pincushions, bodkin and scissor cases – useful protection against the sharp points of the two instruments. Other objects decorated with these tiny coloured baubles included tea cosies, and watch cases for protecting the delicate watch movements made during the Victorian and Edwardian eras. These accessories, like the decorated fire-screens, chair and sofa cushions, bell ropes (pulls), were made after about 1850. The earliest examples show a preference for lighter colours – pinks, pale blue and turquoise. Motifs are similar to those used in Berlin woolwork embroidery: flowers through hearts, hands joined, plant and leaf designs, and geometric patterns. After about 1860 colours became stronger and darker – rich wine reds, dark green, amber and black. The latter was much used following the death of Prince Albert in 1861 to augment dress decoration, shawls, parasols, and upholstery on chairs, sofas and foot-stools.

Ladies' work boxes/occupations

There were many things to occupy a woman from a moderately prosperous background in the 19th century. In the long years before the invention of television it was regarded as a virtue that every spare minute of the day should be usefully filled. The capacious needlework box became an essential possession for any household. Quite apart from the general requirements of repairing articles of clothing, household linens and upholstery, these boxes were a treasure trove of

Lady's work box with penwork decoration in black on a pale golden sycamore wood background. It displays the classical designs popular in the late 18th and early 19th centuries.

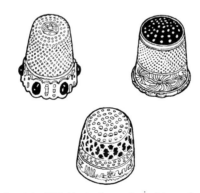

A variety of thimbles in silver and porcelain, made as much for the collector of these delicate objects as for use. 1740–1900.

skills. A glimpse at any book such as the 'Guide to Work Tables; issued by the Young Ladies Journal during the second half of the century, illustrates the very wide range of accomplishments to be acquired – including numerous types of embroidery, varieties of knitting, macramé, Berlin wool-work, fancy netting,

lace-making and tatting.

While many are familiar with the earlier disciplines, tatting and lace-making are now not so familiar. Both were regarded as suitable drawing room occupations, though lace-making, in particular, was also a thriving cottage industry. Tatting involved the use of a lozenge-shaped shuttle which, as the guidebook points out, were available in 'ivory, pearl, bone, vulcanite or tortoiseshell'. Using a fine cotton or silk thread wound round the shuttle, a series of knots created a delicate openwork pattern not dissimilar to fine crochet work or lace. Shuttles were sometimes decorated with incised floral or geometric motifs as was the lacemaker's bobbin.

Bobbins were more commonly made of wood, however – particularly fruitwoods such as may, oak, blackthorn or walnut – as well as bone. Decoration varied, though turned work was the most common. Inlay in a variety of differently coloured woods and even metals–such as pewter and brass – resulted in colourfully

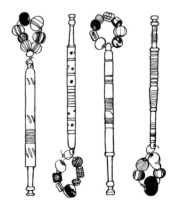

A variety of 19th-century lacemaker's bobbins. They are usually made in bone or wood. The colourful glass beads were used to weight the ends and were called 'spangles'.

patterned bobbins, while others were bound round with pewter or brass wire. Inscriptions of names and of love messages were also typical, since many examples were decorated by a lover and given as a love token, carrying such messages as 'may I have those in my arms that I love in my heart' or 'marry me my own truelove'. At the end of a bobbin hung a 'spangle' or circle of beads which helped weigh down the bobbin, though not all bobbins were finished this way. The glass beads were slightly roughened to allow for a good grip on the lace and favourite colours for the glass were clear and red of various shades. Sometimes a love-token in the form of a button or inscribed disk was attached to the spangle.

Needlework boxes were made in a variety of shapes and materials. Large, elaborate examples were incorporated into tables fitted with sewing bags. Smaller versions, veneered with a whole range of woods or mother-of-pearl, were made throughout the 19th century, while still others, imported from the Orient, were decorated with black lacquer and gold patterns. Inside, the profusion of trays and compartments, holding a complete set of accessories, indicated the range of its owner's abilities. Accessories were typically of wood or bone though more expensive ivory was also occasionally used. Scissors, needles, thimbles with and without individual cases (often dexterously stitched by the lady of the house herself or made by her daughters), thread-waxers, shuttles, pincushions, pin boxes, crochet hooks, reel holders and bobbins are but a few representatives of the wealth of collectables to be found in a lady's work box.

Photography

Over a century-and-a-half ago the medium of photography got off to a shaky and almost totally ignored beginning. The discovery of photography is credited to Nicéphore Niepce (1765–1833), whose picture of an indistinct primitive courtyard is the earliest photograph known to exist. It was taken in 1826, but it was

Photogravure plate by P. H. Emerson showing the Reed Harvest. Subjects such as this were used by Emerson for his book 'Life and Landscape on the Norfolk Broads'. 1886.

some years before any further success was made in the field. For the brief time until his death, Niepce worked with another famous figure, L. J. M. Daguerre, who had himself experimented with the *camera obscura* in trying to fix an image that would remain durable. After long years of experiment and some five years after Niepce's death, Daguerre successfully developed the process thereafter known as 'Daguerrotype', whereby an image appeared as a 'direct positive' on sensitized silver plate.

In England, however, a wealthy gentleman, Henry Fox Talbot, was also interesting himself in the possibilities of photography. The technique which Talbot developed by 1834 was later (1841)

christened by him Calotype, though it is also sometimes referred to as Talbotype. The method, which he described in his book 'The Pencil of Nature' (1844), enabled 'natural images to imprint themselves durably and remain fixed upon the paper' by producing a negative image on paper sensitised with silver salts. The most significant difference between the method devised by Talbot and that used by Daguerre was that the introduction of a negative image enabled numbers of positive prints to be made from the original, whereas the Daguerrotype, being a positive image in the first place, was unrepeatable and therefore unique.

By the middle of the century photography was becoming very popular. Already by 1841 the patent speculator Richard Beard had established the first commercial studio in England, though he used the Daguerrotype method invented in France. Famous figures, including the Queen, allowed their portraits to be taken. For the first time 'celebrities' were accorded a degree of recognition which is nowadays readily taken for granted. But hundreds of ordinary families had their portraits taken in the contrived stillness of the studio and many families today cherish records of such gatherings, in which grim-faced victims held their breath just long enough for the camera lens to 'delineate themselves without the aid of the artist's pencil'. But while photographs of families, views and landscapes played a most important part in the development of the art, photographic expeditions to the Middle East and beyond created instant and widespread interest in the styles and cultures of those areas. Social conditions were photographed and important social records published. An example was Jacob A. Riis' book entitled 'How the Other Half Lives', exposing conditions among the slums of New York in the 1880's. Early war photography was also developed during the 19th century, showing life on the battle front, from the American Civil War to the Crimea.

Many of the photographic milestones surviving from the third quarter of the century used the wet plate process developed by Frederick Scott Archer, which improved the clarity and precision of the print. By 1873 this was superseded by the dry plate process which enabled readymade plates, prepared by a gelatin emulsion, to be bought and stored for long periods before use. The introduction of the Kodak box camera in 1888 brought photography within the reach of the general public and the snapshot era began.

Among the best-known 19th-century photographers are Julia Margaret Cameron (began 1863), Lewis Carroll (began 1856), Oscar Rejlander (1813–75), Peter Henry Emerson (1856–1936), and the American Frederick Holland Day (1864–1933).

Jewellery

The rapid expansion of the middle classes, combined with a general move in the trade towards mass production techniques, resulted in an increasingly varied range of jewellery in the 19th century.

From early in the century the quickening shifts in fashion saw a corresponding change of jewellery styles. Precious stones, which during the 18th century had tended to be the preserve of the aristocracy, were augmented by a host of less costly semi-precious stones such as turquoise, topaz, amethyst, peridots,

aquamarines and agates. Gold and silver mounts became heavier and were sometimes accorded a granular surface. Furthermore, since the widespread improvements in glass-making in the 18th century, quantities of paste jewellery were made in emulation of the much more expensive diamond and precious stone jewellery which continued to command high prices.

The back of a small pendent containing plaited hair, possibly that of the Duke of Clarence, later William IV. This type of sentimental jewellery was popular throughout the 19th century.

Though much jewellery could be acquired in single pieces, the vogue for matching suites was revived early in the century. These *parures* generally contained a necklace, bracelet, earrings and brooch. A full complement might also include a tiara which, for much of the century, was regarded as an indispensable item of court dress. Styles reflected the more general fashions, and while Grecian neo-classic pieces remained popular during much of the first half of the century, Renaissance and Gothic influences became visible during the middle years. One item particularly popular during the first half of the century was the *ferronière* – a type of pendant which hung over the forehead suspended from a chain

encircling the head. It was particularly suited to the austerely romantic style of Grecian dress popular during the Regency period. The Grecian style, typified by a square neckline with a low-cut *décolletage*, a high bodice and hair swept off the face, was also found in the enormous selection of jewellery based on antique cameos. Though only a few genuine antique examples survived, brought back by early

Three examples of cut-steel jewellery fashionable from the late 18th century on. Included here are a bar brooch with ducks, buckles, and a butterfly brooch. Such items are still inexpensive.

travellers to Greece and the Middle East, a variety of cheaper substitutes were available. They utilized materials such as coral and lava, and the ceramic intaglios produced by Wedgwood – linked together with fine chains or later set in heavier mounts – were thought especially desirable.

During the third quarter of the century, the use of mourning jewellery reached a peak. The death of the Prince Consort in 1861 was the immediate catalyst but

Regency period earrings and pendant. Long drop earrings of hollow gold were very fashionable, embellished with flowers, filigree work or small stones. c 1830.

such *memento moris* had formed an essential part of an increasingly elaborate ritual since the early 1800's. Jet – a form of fossilised driftwood – became a major source of industry for the Yorkshire village of Whitby, where it was found in large quantities along the coastline. It was the most widely used material for mourning jewellery. Common themes used as designs for brooches, pendants, bracelets and necklaces show hands clutching flowers, simple bouquets or wreaths of flowers (particularly the rose), bibles and crucifixes. Other materials used in mourning jewellery included bog oak and black enamel set in gold or silver mounts. Some mourning jewellery also incorporated hair, a very personal form of memorium. Hair jewellery had been known since the previous century and continued to be popular throughout the 19th century. The majority of hair jewellery displays plaited or loosely curled locks trapped behind glass in lockets, rings or bracelets. More elaborate examples were woven from hair to make bracelets and watch cords.

Towards the close of the century the widespread manufacture of silver jewellery made it possible for even the working classes to afford simple love tokens, particularly brooches. In the main they show the recipient's name – Lucy, Annie, Ada, Baby, Mother, Nellie, Abigail and Desire – surrounded by forget-me-nots. Others convey friendship, affection and intimacy through love knots, hearts, flowers and clasped hands. Much of the jewellery fashionable during the later 19th century continued to find a market during the Edwardian period, but following the First World War the 'costume jewellery' we know today began to emerge.

Nineteenth-Century Antiques
What To Look For

Viewing and Buying

Museums and exhibitions. An increasing number of specialist dealers, specialist and most provincial auction houses, junk shops, street markets, jumble sales, rubbish tips and skips.

Furniture

Predominant woods: mahogany, oak and walnut.

Great scope for acquiring undervalued pieces of good quality furniture. But much 19th century – particularly late Victorian – furniture is badly made. Check quality of carcase – generally pine – for worm and damage. Restoration, recaning, or upholstery mean extra expense on top of the price, so take these details into account.

If it is a large piece and will not fit into the back of the car take into account the added cost of transport; this can turn a bargain into a headache.

Points to Watch

Conversions: occur in both the previous centuries, but are especially common in the 19th century. Obvious examples are late 19th-century washstands and pedestal dressing tables (less mirror), which convert readily into writing desks.

Marriages between two different pieces of furniture are also made and are particularly evident in bureau bookcases. Less frequent attempts include breakfront bookcases. One example seen recently was actually a converted Victorian wardrobe using only the base cupboard section complete with shoe rack made up with new glazed bookshelves above.

Pottery and Porcelain

Wide variety of types available, many still undervalued. These include good examples of fine porcelain wares made by principal factories.

Points to Watch

Numerous fakes, especially earthen-wares. Reproductions appear as values of particular types rise. Examples include altered marks by erasing original mark and substituting one which is better known. But several factories – eg Coalport and Minton – during the third quarter of the century copied Sèvres type and well-known English late 18th and early 19th-century types.

Other examples include lustreware copies but these tend to be crudely made with blotchy splashing, dull, dark lustre surrounds and highly finished backs. In contrast, the backs of originals tend to be crudely finished.

Silver

Many hundreds of mainly small items to be found for under £100 despite the increase in silver prices over the last few years. Good examples made in 18th-century styles are only a fraction of the cost of the originals and are usually well made.

Points to Watch

Several items have been subjected to widespread conversions. These include hatpins. Many have valuable and beautifully worked heads which have been cut off and turned into rings or other items. Unfortunately these conversions do not always meet the high standards visible in the original work.

Glass

Many good examples of 19th-century glass are currently undervalued. But much of it is difficult to date, although many well-known firms marked their glass. eg: Thomas Webb.

Nailsea type glass made over very long periods 1790–1925.

Points to Watch

Replaced decanter stoppers: this will affect the value of a fine example but not radically an ordinary example. Check that the stopper fits properly – you may loose the contents as well as the stopper itself!

Hairline cracks which might be difficult to see but which render the glass useless. Ringing tone should be as clear as a bell.

Reproductions: eg of Queen's Burmese ware. 19th-century examples made by Thomas Webb from 1868 were always signed but many 'unsigned' copies have been made in the 20th century.

PART FOUR **The Twentieth Century**

The Twentieth Century
Historical and Social Background

The twilight years of the Victorian era and the flowering of *fin de siècle* fashions had laid the foundations of change in British society heralded by the brief heady years before the outbreak of War in 1914. Already, in the 1890's, there was a growing desire to throw off the cloying sense of caution and stuffiness which seemed to characterise so much of the old Queen's reign. Her subjects wished to enjoy the self-confidence – and indulge the growing complacency – of a nation whose imperial ambitions, at least, had reached their summit.

A new century's euphoria

In the world of art and design the traditionalists' ideas of taste had early been challenged by the 'art for arts sake' message of the Aesthetic Movement. Meanwhile supporters of the Arts and Crafts Movement, firmly rooted in mid 19th-century concepts of John Ruskin and William Morris, preached a continued faith in the *social* significance of art. For many the new bible was 'The Studio' magazine. First begun in 1893, by the turn of the century it was enthusiastically promoting the Art Nouveau style so popular on the Continent. But despite its patronage Art Nouveau continued to be largely ignored by leading English artists. Like the First Impressionist Exhibition in 1905, its tenets were regarded as too extreme for conservative artistic taste.

Not only was the Edwardian era an exciting period for the world of art and design, it was also an age of considerable technological and industrial advance. The impact of the train earlier in the 19th century had done much to speed up travel, making it possible for many more to move quickly and efficiently from town to country and back again all in the space of a day. The displacement of steam and gas by electricity was another great step. But the motor car was the 20th century's most radical contribution. Its advent produced a way of transporting people not only more quickly, but also to those places which formerly had not been reached by the long arm of the railway. Before the First World War 1914–1918, however, the car remained the luxury of the rich whose main pre-occupation was to take family and friends for a 'drive' and was used principally for pleasure rather than for work. Only later in the century did its emphasis change. With a token speed limit of only 20 mph and a network of indifferent, albeit empty, roads, these early cars could do little else than putter along at a 'touring' pace.

Though some of the rich upper classes had been affected by the slump in land prices – particularly from the fall-off in rents received by the end of the 19th century – many continued to live in the manner to which they had become accustomed during Victoria's reign. The harsh reality of life at the other end of the scale continued to be much the same too. The vast majority of the workforce

Enamelled street signs were commonplace on street corners and above shop windows at the turn of the century, often lending a touch of colour to the otherwise drab, dirty inner city and suburbs. Examples were displayed on the risers of steps, particularly on public transport. This example advertised Rowntree Pastilles, a type of sweet still made today. *c* 1900.

remained concentrated in the towns and major industrial centres in London and the North. By the end of the 19th century a small but steady influx of immigrant workers mainly from Germany and the Jewish communities of Eastern Europe boosted their numbers.

Disease was slowly brought under control but one common complaint, particularly among the children of London East End, was rickets. Overcrowding in the poorer boroughs of the capital was appalling, but the impression given from contemporary accounts and drawings shows at best a lively sense of community spirit, humour and support which made such a life bearable. The more prosperous and respectable suburban areas which mushroomed during the late 19th century and the early years of the present one, showed a standard uniformity that makes these endless streets of identical housing and large mansion blocks of flats seem dull and lifeless. But whereas the slums have largely been cleared away, these neighbourhoods remain in large quantities.

'Country Life'

The standard suburban house design, which enabled people from the struggling lower middle classes to afford more space for less money, retained the front and back parlour, with a kitchen, scullery and coal shed beyond. Where this design differed internally from the 18th-century model was by a downgrade in scale, and the frequent addition of bay windows which broke the uniformity, at least in the front rooms of the house. Upstairs the main bedroom, straddling both front parlour and entrance hall, represented the largest room in the house, and the remaining bedrooms, usually two or three, were for the children and servants. Internal plumbing was hardly known and a tap in the scullery and an outside lavatory provided the most modern sanitary arrangements.

At the other end of the social scale, revolving not so much around the rather old-fashioned members of the gentry, as around the smart set and court circles, was an exhausting round of afternoon teas, house parties, evening soirées, gala occasions and balls. Many of the newer members of high society reflected the 'faster', cosmopolitan outlook of Edwardian society. Quite apart from the old family names were those of a sprinkling of financiers, bankers and business men, some recently elevated to the peerage. New money from new fortunes was needed more than ever to bolster the flagging fortunes of older families. A few of the eligible young men of old blood, bright enough to realise that land was not the only source of wealth, even joined the boards of established and acceptable business ventures, while others condescended to marry the daughters of wealthy businessmen drawn from among the *nouveaux riches* at home and from America. But in the midst of prosperity was an empty, vacuous sort of life. Unlike earlier generations, their busy idleness produced little of the brilliant patronage of former centuries. This was despite the inevitable excitement caused by the appearance of a fashionable painter or a budding young writer at some select gathering. But in retrospect, the 'glittering' Edwardian era is largely an illusion of the literary celebrants of an age who, according to J. B. Priestly, a boy at the time, 'look back not only at their own youth but also at a scene all the more radiant because it is the other side of the huge black pit of war'.

Society after World War I

The war brought many changes in its wake. Not least was a wave of 'new rich', followed by a swell of the socially conscious in their wake. Ironically, this tragic period, which had seen the flower of its youth die in the trenches in the name of patriotism, had acted as a catalyst for the sufragettes. Under the inspired leadership of Mrs Pankhurst, the bitter battle to give women the right to vote was brought to a head, though the right was not granted until 1928. Sudden emancipation necessitated during the war had seen women working on the trams, in industry and on the land, where formerly such jobs had been the preserve of men. The shortages of war had also introduced shorter dresses. For the first time ankles and calves were exposed. By the 1920's dresses were even shorter and the 'flapper' evoked the new excitement and zest for living which characterised both the 20's and 30's – at least for those who could afford it. Cigarettes – formerly the preserve of the rich and principally of the all-male smoking rooms in large town and country houses – were increasingly available and much cheaper. Even women took to smoking, with the cigarette poised carefully on the end of an elegant holder.

Improved communication was symbolized by the wireless set and the real impact of advertising began to make its mark. Distances were covered faster and faster by aeroplane, though on the ground more people were availing themselves of the motor car. The car was still a fair expense, however, and it was the bus, which by the 1920's was superseding the earlier tram, that was becoming the most widespread means of transport. Buses were even found in country districts, which trams and trolley buses had never managed to conquer.

In the world of entertainment the music hall gave way to film, and the coming of sound in 1928 sealed the end of the silent movies and brought in the 'talkies'. Music boogied to the sound of jazz. At home people with less money and smaller space resorted to the cocktail party in place of the more lavish pre-war entertainments, and the 'living room' became a room 'where people live – and work – not a withdrawing room for best clothes and conversation'.

A Royal Doulton figure of 'Miss 1927', which captures the glamorous woman of the post war period.

Twentieth-Century Interiors and Furnishings

The tendency for people to live in smaller and smaller houses, and the emergence of the flat, were two of the most striking features of life at the beginning of the 20th century. Many of these houses sprang up around the leafy suburbs of towns and cities while others, built at the terminus of some railway line, caused by their gradual proliferation, new communities and towns to grow up around them. The majority of these new properties were designed more for the comfortably well-off middle classes, whose occupations – mainly within the professions – enabled them to have a house surrounded by trees, but without the attendant responsibilities of landed estates encumbent on the more traditional country-house owner. The large sprawling mansions which had featured so strongly among the wealthy Victorians continued to be built during the Edwardian era, though never on quite the same excessive scale. The economic restrictions brought about by the land slump at the end of the 19th century and the Great War of 1914–18 ensured that such lavish domestic architecture and way of life was soon to be a thing of the past.

The advent of the small house

An early example of a characteristic small house of the twentieth century, had already been designed and built by 1860. In 1859 Philip Webb, the architect, designed a small house for his friend William Morris, on the occasion of his marriage to Jane Borden. For its time it was conspicuously compact, when compared to the expansive townhouses and ostentatious mansions of mid 19th-century industrialists. Not only was it small, it was also decidedly unpretentious for its time and even the servants' quarters did not share the degree of exclusion typical of other contemporary house designs. Though both these features were to be seen in many buildings by the end of the century, the 'Red House', as it was called, was nevertheless firmly rooted in its own time. It was, as Morris himself said, 'very medieval in spirit', with its Gothic-looking high pitched roof, eccentric shape and irregularly-placed windows.

By the turn of the century similarly modest country houses were being built on the fringes of rapidly-developing commuter belts–particularly those around London and the south east of England. They were being designed and built by architects both in the traditional 17th-century and 18th-century-based style of Edwin Lutyens or in the more progressive styles of men like C. F. Voysey. Details included solid buttress-like supports, clean unfussy triangular gables, deeply-projecting eaves, steeply-pitched roofs, and massive chimney supports (often combined with the buttresses). Plain, regularly spaced windows, often in long horizontal strips, were characteristic of Voysey's work as well as of many other architects during the first quarter of the century.

Pre-War interiors

Entrance fronts rather than being imposing were often rustic, picturesque and rather homely. They served to remind their owners of the traditional values of peace and tranquility which were, and still are, so highly valued in country life. A popular device was to give the front door a corner position, under a long and deeply sloping roof. According to the 'Studio Year Book of 1907' this gave it 'a pleasant old-fashioned effect'.

Similar regard for comfort and homeliness was to be found in the hall, which continued the late-19th century concept – albeit on a smaller scale – of forming an additional, but deliberately informal living room. The hall of course was also where the staircase was situated. It was a challenge to the architect to prevent the staircase from obtruding directly into the middle of the hall space. Newel posts were given dramatic floor-to-ceiling treatment or as 'The Studio' suggested in 1907 'a picturesque appearance may be obtained by a screen running to right and left in line with the bottom step'. Cosy corners were created by the use of window recesses filled with window seats and comfortably stuffed cushions, and by inglenooks. The latter device had been popular since the middle of the previous century, following the building of 'Cragside', the enormous house perched on a hillside in Northumberland designed by the architect Richard N. Shaw for armaments baron Sir William Armstrong.

Leading out of the hall were the principal rooms of entertainment which, depending considerably on the means and social standing of its owner, might include morning rooms (still sometimes referred to as front parlours), and for more informal calls, a drawing room, and a smoking room. As in the previous century these latter rooms served also as an informal sitting room for the gentlemen of the house. Informality was also echoed in the alternative use of the words 'sitting room' which were less formal than 'drawing room'.

In decoration historicism was blended with the modern look. Rustic traditionalism was achieved through the use of 'exposed' beams, the aforementioned inglenook and leaded lights in the windows. Polished floors covered with sprawling Turkey carpets and panelled walls continued to demonstrate love for the natural qualities of wood, even if it did give the interior a darkened feel. Conversely light, airy white interiors were also a fashion well before Syrie Maugham designed her all-white drawing room in 1927. Ceilings were plain or decorated with plaster reliefs reminiscent of Elizabethan and Jacobean interiors. Ornaments and knick-knacks were crammed onto shelves and mantelpieces which became the colourful focus of the room. An added eye-catcher were the coloured tiles to be found around fireplaces, as well as in entrance porches.

Furnishing varied widely according to taste. Some achieved historicism by

Page 154: The Large Hall, Rodmarton, Gloucestershire. This vast country house, which embodies many of the old traditions of country architecture, was designed by Ernest Barnsley in 1909. The house was still not finished at the time of Barnsley's death in 1926, and is in many ways unique. It was made up entirely of local materials by artisans using traditional methods of handcraftsmanship. The simple white-washed interiors, reflecting starkly against exposed beams and panelled walls, provided a homely setting for the furniture. Most of the latter was designed by the Gimson and Barnsley Brothers for the house.

The Hall was frequently used as an informal sitting room, which easily converted into a music room or theatre. A Punch and Judy puppet theatre and the piano illustrates the many uses to which these rooms were subjected in the late 19th and the 20th centuries. (Courtesy of Country Life)

blending late 18th-century furniture with earlier 17th-century and even 16th-century-styled pieces. Others indulged in the 'total look' afforded by the new styles of such firms as Liberty's. Many of these designs incorporated quantities of built-in units, including cupboards, bookshelves, panelling, and inglenook fireplaces, complete with seating. Examples of this type of total design were also found in the work of architects like Charles Rennie Macintosh.

Economy of line and space

After the war economy of space and of labour was increasingly at a premium. Labour-saving devices, such as hoovers, washing machines, polishers and a host of other domestic equipment took over from the armies of servants which had been readily available even in the first few years of the century. The impact of this social upheaval was to have immediate effects on interiors. Kitchens, which had formerly been the preserve of 'cook', banished to the end of some dim and distant passageway, now, literally, came to the fore as a more prominent room, staffed as often as not by the owners themselves. Gone was the homely kitchen with its ranges, dressers full of crockery, and 'sand-scrubbed kitchen table'. In its place was one that reflected the streamlined 'functional' look of the 1920's and '30s, so much so that it led 'The Studio Yearbook of 1938' to comment that 'the cook and kitchenmaid appear to have fled and left the machinery to get on with it'.

Bathrooms also received more attention and by the 1930's these rooms were becoming streamlined. Instead of heavy ungainly baths with brass taps, the emphasis was on marbled or tiled walls and floors in light bright colours, and matching bathroom suites with chrome fittings. Though the result was an impression of hospital-like cleanliness in both bathrooms and kitchens, and to a lesser extent even bedrooms, this concern for designing a 'machine for living' did not extend to the reception-rooms. These were now principally reduced to two, in the form of a dining room and a living room. The dining room continued to reflect the formality of a way of life familiar only a relatively short time before, but the living room had moved on to provide a milieu which was thoroughly modern.

The post-war years, 1920–1930, brought baser metals and electroplate to the attention of reputable designers and silver manufacturers. Tea and coffee sets appeared in chrome, pewter and often more exotic mediums. These, unsigned pieces of a tea/coffee set in silverplate, show the exaggerated angles of Art Deco.

Oak chair with a pierced motif in the back and a leather seat, designed by M. H. Baillie-Scott in about 1895.

Mahogany bureau bookcase in the Edwardian style, showing characteristic neo-classical inlaid decoration on the slant top. The cost of such pieces is rising rapidly. *c* 1910.

Reproduction of a chair designed by C. R. Macintosh for the Argyle Street Tearooms, Glasgow. Original examples of his work are few and prices exorbitant, reflecting his importance as an individual designer, as well as the influence he exerted on Art Nouveau trends in Europe.

Twentieth-Century Furniture

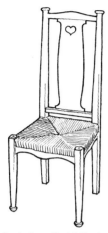

Chair made by Ambrose Heal & Son in the English Arts and Crafts style, showing a rush seat, cut-out heart motif and straight tapering uprights with mushroom cappings.

At the beginning of the century the enormous output by manufacturing firms of all sizes, two-thirds of which were based in London, concentrated on the ever-popular revivals of earlier centuries, while a handful of dedicated fringe designers and craftsmen, working in the tradition of the Arts and Crafts guilds, maintained the ideas and principles of reformists such as William Morris and John Ruskin in the previous century.

The rise of the retail showrooms

Retailing and manufacturing concerns such as Waring & Gillow (which prior to 1903 was styled Gillow & Co), Maple and James Shoolbred & Co were typical of the large emporiums which had developed during the last quarter of the Victorian period (Victoria d. 1901) and which reached their peak in a period of national self confidence, and prosperity, 1900–14. Most firms relied on the distribution of lavishly illustrated catalogues, to inform potential customers of the staggering variety of furniture in all the revival styles to be found in their West End showrooms. It had been customary among several firms since the 1880's to display particular furniture styles in 'specimen rooms'. James Shoolbred, who had their showrooms in Tottenham Court Road, referred in their catalogue of about 1910 to 'the growing love of the antique and genuine ancient pieces of furniture. . . . As far as style and taste are concerned' the catalogue continues, 'within a few minutes of entering the Specimen Rooms you are face to face with all that is graceful and beautiful in the decorative epochs known as those of Louis XIV and Louis XV in France, and of Queen Anne and the first

two Georges in England. From the masterpieces of Adam, Chippendale, Sheraton and the English Renaissance generally, one passes to the practical solidity of early Victorian times, now once again attaining a certain vogue'.

Particularly popular in the revival were the Sheraton and Queen Anne styles – the first more typically found in mahogany, the latter in walnut. Neither represent accurate renderings of their 18th-century prototypes but both distilled essential features and added any other form that appealed, so that it was not unusual to find an incongruous mixture of styles and periods on a single piece. The Sheraton style was used principally for drawing room or bedroom furniture. Seat furniture shared the characteristic square outline of the 18th-century designer's work, but splats were generally thinner. Chair and table legs often were made too thin by designers who believed this to be synonymous with elegance; it was also however an attempt to cut down the high costs of timber at the turn of the century. Satinwood banding and thin boxwood stringing on mahogany furniture were typical of the late Victorian and Edwardian Sheraton style. Shell motifs or the Prince of Wales' feathers, reserved within oval panels, were invariably used to decorate table tops of delicate occasional tables or the slope top of a bureau based on traditional 18th-century lines.

The more elaborate pieces, now generally described as in the Edwardian style, were closely based on Sheraton forms but details from Adam, Hepplewhite and even Chippendale were sometimes added. They were of good quality, made in expensive timbers such as mahogany, rosewood and satinwood, and were distinguished by the

A typical example of commercial English Art Nouveau, displaying such characteristics as a curvilinear back superimposed on an otherwise Edwardian settee. The inlaid decoration is in 'late 18th-century style'. *c* 1900.

addition of delicate, even fussy, inlaid patterns principally in bone and boxwood. Classical motifs included urns, links of wheat ears (husks), and flowers similar to the harebell. The latter were typically used on the tops of legs. Very expensive satinwood pieces decorated in a grand Edwardian manner are often decorated with painted designs and panels in the 18th-century style. Similar pieces, painted or enamelled in white, were favoured for bedroom suites.

A formal settee dimly reminiscent of Louis XVI, showing the turn-of-the-century fondness for inlaid details. About 1900.

Elegance was essential to the Edwardian interior, often at the expense of Victorian concepts of comfort, but the large deeply-padded and well sprung chesterfield type of settee was also very popular during the early years of the 20th century and remains so today. Characteristic examples show upholstery with and without deep buttoning, and arms and a back rest of a uniform height. Legs are typically of the dumpy turned form resting on castors fashionable during the Victorian period and the early 20th century. Several models have the helpful addition of a drop arm which can be let down by either pushing a button or pulling a lever which

turns the settee into a type of day bed suitable for reclining on at full length, a function that had earllier been served by the chaise longue.

Washstands and wardrobes

A number of new furniture forms developed towards the close of the 19th century and were used well into the early years of the next. It was usual for revival-style furniture to be made in suites. Cost for different rooms varied enormously but a dining room, drawing room or a bedroom in 1910 might be equipped for as little as £35 or as much as several hundred pounds. Bedroom furniture, even in a very modest house or flat, included a wardrobe, chest of drawers, the newly fashionable wood bedstead and a washstand fitted with a marble top and tile splashback; by the turn of the century it was characteristic to see an additional towel rail fitted to the sides of these otherwise Victorian forms. By the turn of the

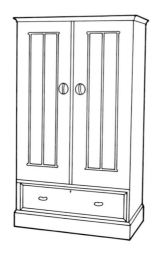

Simple, uncluttered wardrobe designed by Ambrose Heal in unstained oak. c 1905.

century, the dressing chest was fitted with a mirror and occasional small drawers. A combination of the dressing chest and the washstand was a useful if rather mundane development of this piece. The wardrobe, a large rectangular piece of furniture, incorporated drawers, cupboards and door which was generally fitted with a looking glass.

The Queen Anne style of the early 20th century was based on early 18th-century furniture from which it took its name. Instead of loosely borrowing from 18th-century architectural details, Edwardian 'Queen Anne' furniture frequently displayed a characteristic hoop back, with a simple straight or vase-shaped back splat and cabriole legs similar to real Queen Anne pieces. Although many traditional forms, such as the cabinet on stand, enjoyed a considerable revival in the form of top quality reproductions, several characteristics of this early 18th-century style were used in conjunction with new forms such as the elegant basin stand advertised by Shoolbred's in about 1910. This piece contained a large white porcelain sink, with plated fittings, supported on elegant cabriole legs ending in pad feet, the whole executed in American walnut. The Queen Anne style remained popular up to the outbreak of World War II. During the 1920's and 30's veneers in cabinet work were often strikingly marked and showed far richer configurations in woods such as walnut than normally would have been found on 18th-century work.

Other revival styles have continued to be made on large scale to the present day. 'Old oak' pieces in the Jacobean style formed another staple of mass production furniture from the beginning of the century up to the 1940's. It was particularly

Commercial producers of furniture between the wars favoured a continuation of the reliable-selling Jacobean styles such as this sideboard.

Armchair made by Liberty's in oak, with inlaid pewter and ebony decoration. *c* 1902.

suited to solid heavy dining room furniture. Sideboards of characteristically long, low form were supported on spiral twist legs, plain or twist-turned stretchers. Drawer and cupboard fronts were decorated with vaguely similiar mid-17th-century mouldings and applied split baluster columns, while occasionally pot board stretchers were fitted just above bun feet. Tables, many of the drawer leaf type and invariably treated in plain or stained oak, show variations of the bulbous cup-and-cover motifs beloved of Jacobean furniture designers.

The flowering of Art Nouveau

The original, highly distinctive, but short-lived Art Nouveau style developed in about 1890, peaked at the turn of the century and by the outbreak of the First World War in 1914 had passed. It had its origins in the preoccupations of the early English Arts and Crafts movement of the 1880's and 90's but was never fully explored in England, enjoying its greatest realisation through Continental – particularly French – designers. Ironically the very designer-craftsmen who were the first to use the forms and motifs characteristic of this style, including A. H. Macmurdo and Charles F. Voysey, were quick to reject the more extreme, sensuously curvilinear examples found in Continental Art Nouveau as a 'strange decorative disease'. But the style was quickly taken up by a number of commercial manufacturers, such as the large East End firm of J. S. Henry and the fashionable West End department store, Liberty & Co. The latter played a particularly important part in disseminating the style – so much so that it was also described as '*Le Stile Liberte*', as well as '*Le Stile Anglaise*' and '*Le Stile Moderne*'.

Inspiration for the Art Nouveau style came principally from abstracted organic forms derived from nature. Sensuous curvilinear shapes based on the female form (particularly the head in profile and details such as hands and hair), swirling plant forms, root and stem tendrils, flowers open and in bud (such as the tulip and the rose), and heart shapes were typical. In England, however, the style was markedly restrained and was used mainly in the application of more obvious motifs to pieces which owed their form to the symmetrical and rectilinear forms advocated by the Arts and Crafts Movement. It is not unusual also to find typical Art Nouveau patterns combined with the traditional forms of Edwardian furniture. Most of the decoration was in the form of inlaid work and applied metal mounts, particularly in the case of handles and hinges. Another characteristic, which derived from the Arts and Crafts movement and the work of Voysey, was the frequent use of long, tapering uprights finished with distinctive flat or rounded mushroom caps, often projecting, as they did in the examples most closely aligned to the Arts and Crafts influence. It was fashionable to add glazed leaded light doors to sideboards and display cabinets – perhaps showing a floral or whiplash Art Nouveau pattern in the stained glass.

The legacy of the Arts and Crafts Movement

By 1900 furniture inspired by the traditional Arts and Crafts style provided yet another type of design to enjoy widespread popularity, though many of its superficial forms were confusingly similar to those found on the more decadent Art Nouveau pieces. It was fired by a split within the Movement at the turn of the century, between those who elected to make original, beautiful, even luxurious pieces of hand-crafted furniture, and those who chose to design simple, rustic pieces on a commercial scale, which satisfied the early Morrisian tenets such as fitness for purpose and honest construction. While the former denied the role of machinery, the latter accepted it. The tradition established by small breakaway groups of the anti-technological persuasion – some of whom set themselves up in remote country villages, such as Gimson and the Barnsley Brothers in Sapperton in the Cotswolds – still thrives. But their methods resulted in a type of high craft making unique, but expensive, pieces of furniture which in the end denied a fundamental principle of the Arts and Crafts Movement: that it should be 'art made by the people and for the people'. Furniture was based on traditional forms and tended to be square or rectilinear in outline with very sparing use of ornament – usually only a simple, geometric, inlaid border. These almost functional-looking pieces in woods such as oak, ash, yew, walnut and the more exotic rosewood and ebony, anticipated the spare forms of later 20th-century English furniture.

While a few in the Arts and Crafts tradition chose to disassociate themselves completely from the commercial furniture world – especially the use of machinery for mass-produced lines – others, including C. F. Voysey, M. H. Baillie Scott and the young Ambrose Heal, did design for firms such as J. S. Henry, Liberty & Co and Heal and Co. Their work showed it was possible to ally good design with mass production techniques. In general pieces were made in plain oak with very little decorative detail. Fielded panels and inlaid patterns with geometric designs were typical, though Voysey was noted for his elaborate metalwork mounts.

There were several details which became trademarks of Art Nouveau furniture. The long, attenuated strap hinge, terminating in tulip motifs; the pierced heart cutouts which appeared so often on chair backs and uprights, as well as mother-of-pearl inlay, all made their way into the turn-of-the century repertoire. Much furniture continued to be based on traditional country forms and oak and rush seating on chairs became almost obligatory.

The new continental look

The exciting role which Britain had played in design since the middle of the 19th century came to an abrupt end with the advent of the World War I. After the war Britain never managed to recover the earlier lead which she had successfully established in the mid-19th century, and the greatest impetus for furniture design came from abroad, particularly from the German Bauhaus School. The new Teutonic approach to design was to have the greatest influence on international furniture and initiated the development of a truly modern style. The almost excessive

Writing desk made by commercial manufacturers but showing the influence of the Arts and Crafts Movement in the tall uprights and long hinges. *c* 1912.

Walnut sideboard designed by Christopher Heal in about 1935. Note the smooth, uncluttered surfaces and functional lines of furniture of this 'between the wars' style.

Walnut secretaire designed and made by Peter Waals, whose work continued the high standards of hand craftsmanship established by Gimson and the Barnsleys. *c* 1920.

ornament used in Continental Art Nouveau was abandoned in favour of clean, simple, functional lines and the use of machinery was stressed, even applauded. Gradually form became subservient to function though early examples of the post-war style were comprised principally of harsh geometric and rectangular shapes reminiscent of Cubism and the Dutch de Stijl movement. It was a member of this Dutch group, G. T. Rietveld, who produced a major pioneering work in his 'Red-Blue' chair in 1917. The uncompromising angular lines of the chair, painted in strong primary colours, was devastatingly radical and still seems so today. Similar ideas were expressed by designers across the western world, many of them architects by training: in America, Frank Lloyd Wright and le Corbusier in France. In keeping with the new age, modern materials like tubular steel and chrome plating were used along with improved laminating processes and plywood.

Many of these materials were used in the style which reached its peak during the 1920's and now is loosely labelled Art Deco. It derived its name from a famous exhibition held in Paris in 1925 – the Paris *Exposition Internationale des Arts Decoratifs et Industriels* – but it was not so much international (Germany for example was excluded) as a final expression of the French taste which had dominated European and American design since the 18th century. Furniture continued to reflect the feminine aspect of Art Nouveau

A modern Italian reproduction of the famous chair made in chrome metal and with leather seat and back designed by Le Corbusier in the late 1920's.

but without the decoration. Forms were more geometric and quite frequently achieved a theatricality not seen in the Bauhaus 'modern' style. Surface textures – particularly in the furniture designs of

The 'Barcelona' chair designed by Mies van der Rohe in 1929. Made in steel and with upholstered leather back and seat cushions, this Bauhaus classic changed the course of European design.

A two-tiered table in chrome and black lacquer designed and made during the 1930's. Similar furniture was already on view at the 1930 Ideal Home Exhibition.

Emile Jacques Ruhlmann and Eileen Gray – were rich, luxurious and often exotic. Oriental lacquer techniques and tropical woods such as macassar ebony were used in conjunction with mother-of-pearl inlay, silver and gilt metal finishes and chrome metal frames.

The Arts and Crafts traditions died hard in England and many aspects of that tradition survive today. The Continental modern style, already well-established and recognised internationally, was not accepted and promoted until the 1930's. In 1936 Marcel Breuer, a former leading member of the Bauhaus School (closed in 1933 by the Nazis who regarded the school as decadent), designed his 'long chair' for the firm of Isokon. The produc-

tion of this laminated plywood chair demonstrated a complete application of industrial processes. But English designers, such as Ambrose Heal and Gordon Russell, also exerted considerable influence between the wars. Both continued to work in the tradition of the Arts and Crafts Movement, indeed Ambrose Heal had been a member of the Art Worker's Guild since 1906. Much of their furniture is in the same style as pieces made by contemporary craftsmen such as Edward Barnsley. But, unlike Barnsley, neither felt that machinery necessarily precluded good design. 'The pieces herein described' states a Heal's catalogue of the 1920's 'are planned first of all for convenience and durability and secondly with an eye

Right: Mahogany bedside table designed and made by Betty Joel, a well known interior designer in the 1930's. Like several contemporary designers, such as Syrie Maugham and the Omega Workshop, her work is often exotic and luxurious.

Left: Elegant side cabinet designed by Emile Jacques Ruhlmann, who often emphasised the exotic qualities of a material, such as the amboyna and inlaid ivory details used here. c 1925.

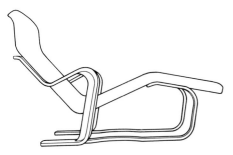

Long chair made of laminated wood and bent plywood by the London firm of Isokon to a design by Marcel Breuer. Furniture by designers such as Breuer, Aalto, and Mathsson are now collected and are, as yet, not expensive.

Ebonised, laminated wood chair, cut and shaped from a single rectangle of wood. Designed by Gerald Summers for 'the Makers of Simple Furniture'. *c* 1935.

An ottoman in the fashionable Art Deco style of the 20's and 30's. A tassel in the headrest is the handle to a drawer and the top opens for storage.

to good proportion and pleasant outline. The material used is sound and well seasoned; the construction is workman-like: much of it is necessarily handwork, but where the machine makes for econ-omy it has been used, frankly and straight-forwardly . . . and not as a shame-faced accomplice in the turning out of pseudo handwork'. Much of this underlines the strong feeling aroused by the poor quality, in both materials and workmanship, of cheap 'Jacobean' revival styles. Oak was the wood most consistently used, often left unpolished as 'sufficient proof of our confi-dence in its quality'. Other characteristics of this style – which while being essential-ly functional retained some appearance of the 'craft look' about it – was the use of plain, virtually undecorated surfaces and rectangular shapes. Traditional forms such as ladder backs were often used on chairs. But both firms began to introduce tubular steel into their work and in 1931 an employee of Russell's, confusingly called (R. D.) Russel, was designing revo-lutionary cabinets specifically for the radios made by the firm of Murphy. Thus the role which precision engineering was to have on 20th-century furniture design was emphatically underlined at an early point in the development of the tech-nological age.

Cherrywood cabinet-on-stand reminiscent of the writing cabinets popular during the second half of the 17th century. This example was designed by Gordon Russell in 1926.

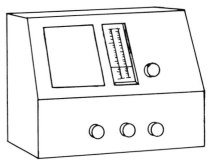

Radio cabinet designed by R. D. Russell for the communications firm of Murphy. *c* 1935.

Twentieth-Century Pottery and Porcelain

Earthenware

The opening years of the twentieth century continued the seemingly endless variety of pottery carried over from the previous century. In the main it was dominated by the type of 'art pottery' which had developed during the latter half of the 19th century. It had evolved out of a reaction to the belief that the creative ability of the individual was about to be swallowed up under the overwhelming weight of 19th-century industrialism. Though the original impetus had stemmed from the Arts and Crafts Movement and the ideas of individual thinkers such as William Morris and John Ruskin, it was not long before its appeal was appreciated by the larger commercial firms such as Doulton of Lambeth and Mintons, who were to establish their own Art Pottery Studio in 1870 with the intention of training prospective decorators. Unfortunately the studio burnt down some three years later and was never replaced.

The dominance of coloured glazes

While a number of potteries continued to produce wares which had been a staple product for some years – such as the De Morgan lustre pieces, a type of decoration taken up by the Pilkington Tile and Pottery Co Ltd – there was growing interest at the turn of the century for simple, well-potted shapes and straightforward 'unadorned glazes'. These high- and low-temperature metallic oxide glazes, which introduced a whole range of startling and beautiful colours many of which had hitherto been unknown in Europe, had already been of interest on the Continent during the last quarter of the previous century. But it was not until the first decade of the 20th century that any considerable success was stimulated by Continental discoveries. But in addition, during the closing years of the 19th century, there had also been an interest in finding a clear leadless glaze which would avoid the very real hazard of lead poisoning to which potters had been exposed. Early experiments in these simple monochrome glazed pots were produced at the Linthorpe pottery, which had from 1879 to 1883 been associated with the important industrial designer, Christopher Dresser. Dresser died in 1904, which sets him squarely in the 19th century, but his ideas and preoccupations were for the most part far in advance of his day. It was his keen interest in Japanese and Oriental art, already visible in the late 19th-century work of Linthorpe, that continued to be a pervasive influence throughout the first half of the present century.

The development of these high transmutation glazes was brought about by a number of remarkable potters who for the period 1900–1914, also largely became chemists, constantly experimenting and working on new possibilities. The newly-established Doulton factory at Burslem, Staffordshire, was only one of several firms to introduce ranges which grew from their interest in these highly-coloured glazes. The flambé wares developed in about 1904, the brilliant blues of Titanian were introduced in 1915, and the Sung Ware range shown in 1920 carried progress forward and mirrored the fascination which Oriental ceramics continued to have for Europeans.

But it was the deep crimson colour of the *sang de boeuf* glaze, developed by Bernard Moore and introduced for the

Vase made by De Morgan during the early Fulham period, 1888–97, showing the crane motif which he often used. It is in ruby lustre, a glaze which continued to be used through the early 20th century.

Coffee service designed and made by Susie Cooper at the Crown Works in about 1935. Each piece is coloured in pastel shades and many are marked and numbered.

first time in Europe, which captured public imagination. Despite its early Western début it was a glazing technique familiar in China since the 11th century. Moore worked with the Doulton studio for the first three years of the century but later went on to establish his own studio at Stoke. The pottery, which lasted from 1905–1915, produced earthenware and porcelain. Most examples were marked with Moore's monogram BM. Two other firms noted for their unusual pottery were William Moorcroft's Cobridge works and Pilkington and Co, who established their Lancastrian pottery near Manchester in 1891.

Earthenware dish by the Royal Lancastrian Pottery, decorated by William S. Mycock. Signed on the underside. c 1900–1910.

Moorcroft and Pilkington

William Moorcroft began by working for the Burslem pottery of James MacIntyre & Co. In 1898 his Florian ware was launched. Like the Aurelian ware which followed, the design was quite different to the rest of the firm's output. Florian ware and Moorcroft's other pottery was hand-thrown rather than cast (the more economical method normally used by most commercial potteries) and is distinguishable by its raised, stylised floral patterns, many of which reflected the somewhat commercialised Art Nouveau style then familiar in Britain. Each flower was raised and outlined in slipware decoration,

Earthenware bowl with 'Spanish' flower motif in yellow and red on a green ground made by the William Moorcroft as part of the Florian ware range sold through Liberty's. c 1911.

which also served to separate the colours during firing, thus preventing them from merging with one another. Background colours tended to be white and the flowers blue, pink, and red, with green foliage.

In 1913, Moorcroft established his own pottery at Burslem and continued to make 'art pottery' with lines such as his Powder Blue tableware, and monochrome-glaze pieces. From about 1920 he concentrated on flambé or high-transmutation glazes and worked on these until his death in 1946. Much of the work designed by Moorcroft carries either his signature or, from 1913 on, 'Moorcroft, Burslem', and is widely collected today. Some of the ranges continue to be produced but the colours do not compare well with the earlier pieces.

The art pottery of Pilkington's enjoyed particular success under the direction of William Burton, who joined the firm as artistic and technical director in 1892. Like many other potteries at the beginning of the century they were fascinated

Vase by Pilkington's Royal Lancastrian pottery with a mottled blue monochrome glaze. The firm produced some good examples of this type of ware, though their lustre pieces are probably better known. Early 20th century.

with the potential of developing new and exciting glazes. Pottery shapes were restrained, even simple, sometimes based on ancient forms such as Grecian Kylix or amphora forms. Of the new glazes discovered in the first decade, one was a brilliant ultramarine blue, then critically described as a 'queer poisonous blue' (later slightly modified and christened Kingfisher blue), and others included a brilliant orange and a scarlet resulting from the use of uranium. Such glazes were difficult to achieve. Colour and consistency varied from kiln to kiln and even from piece to piece.

As well as producing pottery decorated with these brilliant coloured glazes, Pil-

Stoneware vase with celadon (pale green-grey) coloured glaze by Charles Vyse, a studio potter inspired by Chinese porcelain and pottery. Marked CV, 1930.

Buff-coloured stoneware vase with brown fish-like motif by the studio potter Bernard Leach. c 1935.

Earthenware jar by the studio potter Michael Cardew, who was interested in slip-decorated peasant pottery of the 17th century. This example demonstrates his preoccupation. c 1937.

kington's also made pieces decorated with highly-stylised pictorial patterns. A typical motif was a sailing ship with a high prow ploughing through waves. These lustre pieces are similar to those used by De Morgan's pottery – an influence which may have been transmitted through Walter Crane, who produced some designs for Pilkington's. In 1934 Joseph Burton died and the factory never recovered from this loss. It closed finally in 1938. Other potteries which reflected a similar interest in the chemistry of potting and especially in glazes, included the Ruskin Pottery at Smethwick (regarded by some as among the finest although its output was relatively small).

Leach and the Studio Potters

From the beginning of the 20th century the role of the artist potter became more and more precise. He was no longer satisfied, as he had been in the 19th century, to be responsible for the artistic direction, leaving much of the actual potting to

craftsmen employed within the pottery. Instead the new men gradually took over the entire process. At the most extreme the studio potter – as he became called – even took to digging and refining his own clay ready for use prior to potting. This idea was best exemplified by the life and work of the 20th-century's most celebrated studio potter, Bernard Leach.

Leach was born in Hong Kong in 1887 and after attending the Slade School of Art in London, where he studied fine art, he returned to the East in 1908. But rather than going back to Hong Kong, he went instead to Japan where he intended to teach etching and drawing. Once exposed to the potter's wheel, however, his awakened interest led him to learn the craft under the famous potter, Ogata Kenzan. In many respects Leach's ideas echoed those of William Morris, who in a lecture given in October 1888 had spoken of trying 'to get the most out of your material, but always in such a way as honours it most'. This idea was, however,

already fundamental in Japanese pottery and is embodied in Leach's work.

Leach set up his own pottery in England in 1920, at St. Ives in Cornwall, following his return from the Far East. He had also spent some time studying the pottery of China and Korea and his pottery specialised in producing fine quality stone and earthenware which strongly reflected the influence of Chinese, Korean and Japanese 'raku' pottery. Leach also undertook to train a number of student potters, many of whom went on to become famous in their own right. Among these were Michael Cardew, known for his slip-trailed decoration in the manner of traditional English slipware, Katherine Playdell-Bouverie and Norah Braden. The work of these individuals epitomised some of the finest decorative pottery made by studio potters working between the wars.

'Industrial' art pottery

In addition to the studio potter there were also a number of artists who chose to

Small sugar, pepper and mustard pot showing the use of bold decoration and linear, geometric shapes favoured during the 1930's.

Propaganda teapot 'that right shall prevail', made for Dyson and Horsfall of Preston in 1939 to replace aluminium stocks taken over for arms production

work within the industrial ceramic world. Keith Murray, Clarice Cliff and Susie Cooper became well known for their inimitable styles. Clarice Cliff worked for A. J. Wilkinson and in the 1930's became Art Director. She stayed with the firm until 1939, during which time she developed a characteristic style of bold designs and strong bright colours. Motifs varied from abstract, geometric patterns to landscapes and stylised flower designs, particularly the crocus which appeared in colours varying from yellow and orange to purple and blue, generally on a cream ground. Her two best-known and much-collected patterns include Bizarre and Fantastique. Pieces carry her facsimile signature. Other famous artists employed by Wilkinson's to design patterns included Laura Knight, whose work often showed scenes from circus life, Duncan Grant, Frank Brangwyn and Graham Sutherland.

Keith Murray was a highly successful industrial designer during the interim between the world wars. In 1933 he began designing for Wedgwood, a firm which unlike many of its contemporaries was consistently progressive and modern in its outlook. His designs for glass and silver are both characterised by smooth lines, elegant shapes and plain, undecorated glazes often finished with a dull matt eggshell finish. Some of his pottery designs made use of lathe turning which gave them a clean, crisp, functional look well-suited to the modern era.

Porcelain

The Edwardian era saw the traditional grandeur of the Victorian period continue unabated until the shattering drama of the First World War 1914–18 brought about its abrupt demise. Ever since its introduction into Europe in the mid-18th century, porcelain – and latterly, the hybrid fine bone china wares peculiar only to the British – had represented the epogee of ceramic production. Many firms

Teapot designed by Clarice Cliff, who in the 1930's was art director for both the Newport and Royal Staffordshire potteries. It is one of her most familiar motifs: crocus in yellow, green, orange and purple.

Two Wemyss Ware pottery cats painted in pink and green on a white ground. They are in the style of Karl Nekola, an earlier decorator. c 1930–1950.

– Minton, Worcester, Coalport, Doulton (which became Royal Doulton in 1901), Copeland, Crown, Derby and Wedgwood – which had so successfully met the increasing demands of late-Victorian society, continued to do so. Their ability to produce large quantities of china was due primarily to the combination of cheap skilled labour and a very high degree of technical proficiency. This enabled virtually all sections of society to afford even inexpensive examples of English bone china from the outset of the 20th century.

Edwardian dinner ware

Like silver, the preponderance of production was given over to the manufacture of tableware, though large numbers of purely decorative pieces were also made. Dinner services and breakfast services poured out in large quantities, as even a modest Edwardian household was considerably larger than it is today. Much of the porcelain continued to repeat the styles of the late 19th century and the ubiquitous 18th-century shapes and patterns. Today many of these old services have been dismantled and dispersed. Single plates, meat dishes, sauce boats and tureens are collected principally for decorative purposes, which makes finding a complete dinner service of some one hundred pieces even more difficult. Patterns, as well as imitating both traditional English and French – particularly Sèvres – motifs, also covered themes such as hunting and sports. Game birds were frequently used to decorate the centre well of a quality dinner service, each plate portraying a different bird either individually painted or printed. Border patterns, sometimes reflecting the influence of Art Nouveau – which otherwise played only a small part in English porcelain, unlike its Continental counterpart – showed stylised floral designs or formal patterns suitable for mass production printing techniques. Other patterns, some of which are very similar to patterns still in use today, show the continued popularity of oriental motifs like the Indian Tree Pattern of Royal Worcester or the Imari pattern of Crown Derby.

Tea and coffee services

Tea and coffee sets were also made in considerable quantities. Many better-quality coffee services were sold in lavish silk-lined boxes, which sometimes included specifically-designed silver spoons. Other services, again of fine quality, were sold without either teapot or coffeepot, indicating that the purchaser was more likely to prefer the use of a silver pot instead of the cheaper porcelain one. Tea sets benefited by the frequent addition of tea plates. Patterns, generally based on earlier styles, were as varied as the range of shapes available. Birds – such as swans, peacocks, pheasants and partridges – were again popular themes for decoration. Some of the finest examples were those painted by the decorators James Stinton, Jack Stanley and C. Baldwyn. All worked for the Royal Worcester Porcelain Company, so styled since 1862, and in so doing continued the firm's long-standing tradition of employing fine decorators. Stinton (1856–1954) was also well known for his misty waterside scenes and particularly for his portrayals of Highland cattle.

Other patterns included rather densely portrayed fruit clusters – both traditional 'Billingsley'-type flower patterns and those inspired by oriental peony and prunus blossom motifs. Plain monochrome colours, which also enjoyed success on contemporary pottery, were in high demand. A particular favourite was Royal Worcester's powder blue reminiscent of an earlier 18th-century type.

Finest of the fine

The popularity of fine quality decorative porcelain continued long into the twentieth century. Parian ware, both glazed and unglazed, which had been developed by Copelands in the 1840's continued to be made by several firms including Minton, Royal Worcester and the Irish firm of Belleek. By the turn of the century Belleek had added 'Co Fermanagh, Ireland' to their mark just as English firms had added 'England' to theirs since 1890 in accordance with the importation laws of the United States of America. A further refinement was the phrase 'made in England' which became common practice after about 1910.

Vases, used more for display than as receptacles for flowers, and fanciful objects intended principally for the china cabinet, were among the numerous items which received lavish decorative treatment in the Edwardian period. *Pâte-sur-pâte*, which had been developed by M. L. Solon (d. 1913) for Minton, continued to be made during the first decade of the century but it was such an expensive medium that only the availability of very highly-skilled artist-craftsmen could justify its continuation.

Among other examples of very elaborate work produced at this time were the delicately pierced porcelain pieces made by George Owen for the Royal Worcester factory. His work, now avidly collected, was individually hand-pierced – often with an overall lattice pattern, giving it an instantly recognisable style. Tiny blobs of enamel, looking like pearl dots, give it a jewel-like appearance.

Gilding was a very evident addition on most Edwardian porcelain. In particular it was featured around rims and along the shoulder lines of virtually any item which could justify the use of this expensive medium. It was costly because the quality of the gold used was – and still is – of either 24 or 22 carat standard. Anything lower would distort in the firing and could possibly produce a completely different effect.

Post World War I styles

It became increasingly obvious after the First World War that many far-reaching changes were taking place. The lavish style which had characterised the pre-war house party had vanished; even the well-off found themselves moving into smaller houses and flats. Reaction to the cloying appearance of much Victorian and Edwardian art was strong. There was widespread acceptance for the dawn of this new age which ushered in schools of design such as the German Bauhaus. At the same time there was also a nostalgia for the whimsical fantasy world created in Wedgwood's fairyland lustre. These popular bone china pieces were decorated with designs by Daisy Makeig-Jones. In part they echoed the earlier interest in fairyland settings found in book illustrations of Edmund Dulac and Arthur Rackham. These printed pieces are heavily peopled with fairies and elfin-like figures cavorting in colourful but haunting landscapes. Colours are bright and clear against a typically blue ground which has a slightly iridescent finish.

But apart from limited ranges like the

Imperial punch bowl decorated with one of Daisy Mackeig-Jones' favourite motifs: the Woodland Bridge against a flambé background. Wedgwood, (D9½ in.)

fairyland lustre pieces, 20th-century English bone china decoration changed very little and the shapes even less so. Discussing Wedgwood production in a series of articles on Industrial Design, Nicholas Pevsner wrote that 'Wedgwood bodies are still to-day based on recipes going back to the age of the founder, and – which is more important from our point of view – their shapes also are quite often those conceived in Georgian days'. This continues to be true today, forty years after the article appeared in the Studio Magazine. One significant difference however between the 'bodies' was that they were no longer only made in earthenware (which the founder used) but were also made in bone china – a medium which had been re-introduced in 1878 after a lapse of just over a half a century.

The reticent use of decoration seen on much pottery production between the wars was just as visible in many ranges of the more expensive bone china. Porcelain was readily available, but true porcelain was largely imported from Continental factories such as the Royal Copenhagen Porcelain Co Ltd. Both Jackson and Gosling Co Ltd of Stoke, and Paragon China Ltd (formerly the Star China Co

1900–1920) made elegant coffee and tea services in plain white bone china, relieved only by simple gilding lines around foot, lip and handles. Other designs reflected the influence of naive peasant pottery, placing sprigs of flowers against an otherwise plain background. Simple white porcelain wares were made in the form of cheap souvenirs sold mainly at seaside resorts up and down the country. They were first produced by William Henry Goss in 1893 and were decorated with armorial devices of seaside towns and other places of interest. Goss died in 1906, but his firm continued until 1944 when the Cauldon Potteries took them over and the factory was renamed the Goss China Company.

Like the Art Nouveau style prominent at the turn of the century, the so-called Art Deco fashion of the 1920's and 1930's had considerably less impact on English porcelain manufacturers than it had on the Continent. Its most significant influence was in the modelling of Art Deco figurines, particularly those showing either a female nude or female figure transfixed in the middle of a dance. A few animals were also featured – the gazelle in leaping, standing and sleeping poses, all of which were very stylized, seems to be among the most characteristic.

Twentieth-Century Silver

There were a number of exciting developments in silverwork at the turn of the 20th century. Much of this excitement stemmed from the Arts and Crafts Movement, with the Guild of Handicrafts – established in 1888 by Charles Robert Ashbee – being especially to the fore. But the distinguished firm of Liberty and Co, despite their commercial stance, were also influential. Some of their lines such as the revived neo-Celtic, Cymric range provide a link between the acceptable aspect of commercialism and the principles of the craft movement.

The great family firms

But the vast majority of silver and silver plate was produced by manufacturing firms, many of which were also retailing outlets, such as Garrards, Elkington and Co, Mappin & Webb and James Deakin & Sons Ltd, who professed in their catalogue of 1889 'to show the Widest Variety of Design, the Lowest Consistent Price, the Highest Standard of Quality' in their work. Deakin's, like the vast bulk of the trade, were manufacturers of both silver and silver plate, using the electroplating technique, first developed by Elkington's in the 1840's. Objects in the same style were invariably available in both mediums though the plated example was usually about half the price. In 1930, for example, Elkington's advertised a 'Fluted Georgian Service', comprising a teapot, coffee pot, cream jug and sugar basin, decorated 'with gadroon mounts' in sterling silver at £44.8s.6d. Exactly the same service was available in electroplate for only £20.16s.6d. Furthermore it is an interesting reflection of the times that firms were sufficiently confident to publish prices of items in the catalogue, rather

than adopting the modern practice of including a separate price list to accommodate the swift rise in prices. Elkington's, who made some of the best quality silver throughout the period, marked their pieces with the words 'Elkington' or 'Elkington & Co', both of which were registered trade marks until 1963 when the firm became part of British Silverware Ltd.

In general manufacturers concentrated on producing an unending stream of domestic silver, though a few firms manufactured the more elaborate presentation pieces. These varied from small – often electroplated – cups, to the more expensive rose bowls based on the shape of the late 17th-century monteiths and early 18th-century punch bowls. Even the Warwick vase enjoyed another revival. Of the domestic silver, tableware was numerically the largest category, but some pieces made for individual use throw an interesting light on the habits that characterised life in the first quarter of the 20th century. The 'novelty' falls into the final category, and in many respects it provides the widest range of amusing knick-knacks and trivia available to today's collector.

Tableware and tea sets

By the early 20th century, tableware in virtually any pattern produced since the middle of the 15th century was available in both silver and plate. It covered everything necessary for the partaking of any meal, from complete dinner services, breakfast sets, tea and coffee services, cutlery – used in the modern sense to include knives, spoons and forks, though it is still common in the trade for spoons and forks to be described by the traditional

Two candlesticks in late 18th-century style. The right hand example is an actual specimen of 1788, filled with pitch and with a generous base. The left-hand example is modern, and costs about a tenth of the price of its antique inspiration.

Forks in the Albany design popular during the 19th century and Edwardian period. 1890–1908.

each service was described by the style of decoration and pattern with which it was treated. One of the most common was the so-called Queen Anne pattern, a name which was applied indiscriminately by virtually every manufacturer in the trade. Though the name of the pattern suggests that the early 20th-century version might reflect the bullet or pear-shaped examples typical of the early 18th-century Queen Anne period, many of these services bear more resemblance to late 18th-century and early 19th-century neo-classic shapes. The common 20th-century use of fluted body work is also more typical of a service made in the early 19th century. So although it is easy to recognise 20th-century 'revival' styles as such, it does not always imply that the 20th-century name bears any relation to the original style that the manufacturers claimed to be copying.

Cutlery patterns were a wonderfully fertile area. An abbreviated list might in-clude such names as York, Albany, Antique bead, Queen Anne (distinguished by its use of bright-cut border patterns), French-threaded, Empire, Versailles and Kings Pattern. The last was, in fact, usually fairly closely based on the early 19th-century original. Knife handles were frequently made of ivory, though xylonite had been available since the last quarter of the previous century and was still available in the Elkington catalogue of 1930. Small tea knives were also fitted with mother-of-pearl and green-coloured handles, a colour that met the approval of both the progressive firms such as Liberty's and of the Arts and Crafts Movement. The architect Edwin Lutyens had designed green-handled knives to contrast with dead white, undecorated Wedgwood plates at Barham Court in 1911. Tea stands in silver or plate were also popular and were capable of holding at least two or three plates, either in china or the more occasional metal.

word 'flatware' – decorative display pieces such as vases, centrepieces, epergnes (these last two were invariably made in silver rather than plate), and candelabra, to smaller items and special dishes in the form of entrée, vegetable, muffin and butter dishes and cruet stands. After World War I, accompanying the fashion for cocktails, came silver shakers – vase-shaped with tightly fitting lids – and hors d'oeuvres trays. These latter generally had a silver rectangular frame, fitted with loop or swing handles, into which four, six or sometimes eight glass dishes fitted.

Tea and coffee services – made up of a teapot and coffeepot, cream jug and sugar basin – were produced in both silver and electroplate. While basic body shapes were often very similar, if not identical,

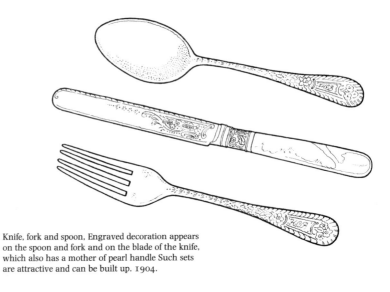

Knife, fork and spoon, Engraved decoration appears on the spoon and fork and on the blade of the knife, which also has a mother of pearl handle Such sets are attractive and can be built up. 1904.

Luxury and novelty silver

Personal items, especially the enormously varied dressing table sets, came in all sizes and patterns. They were usually so beautifully boxed that it seemed a shame

Three cut-glass and silver-mounted dressing table jars. Probably used to contain hair pins and ointment. They show the predaliction of the Edwardians for elaborate, deep cut glass.

to remove them from their silk or velvet-lined interiors and some are still in them. Others came in travelling cases made of leather, exotic woods such as ebony or tortoiseshell decorated with brass in the manner of *boulle*. These latter were a speciality of Asprey & Co of Bond Street, who early in the 20th century concentrated on such luxury items. In general the more elaborate examples showed the continued popularity of rich repoussé decoration though plain versions were also available. A full set would include a pair of fine silver-backed hair brushes and their own brush tray; a hanging mirror or hand mirror was also essential, as were clothes brushes and combs. Other optional extras could include variously-sized and shaped trinket trays and pin boxes,

powder boxes, glass eau-de-cologne bottles fitted with silver tops, bonnet whisks, button hooks both large and small, shoe horns, glove stretchers and even boxes for holding curling tongs, crimping irons and

a lamp for heating them. Similar sets also came in materials including tortoiseshell (which should properly be called turtleshell since it comes from the sea creature not the land tortoise), and the slightly more expensive enamel-coloured silver sets in reds, pink, pale greens, yellow, turquoise and various shades of blue. Some of the items were also sold singly or in small groups, a trend continued by today's collectors who frequently concentrate on one particular item such as button hooks, glove stretchers or scent bottles.

The novelty item had been popular among Victorian society before the middle of the 19th century and remained so throughout the 20th century up to the present time. While many novelties had no other function than to be fun, amusing and collectable – such as the hundreds of miniature pieces of silver furniture that were very popular from about 1890 to

1910 (and are still made today) – there was a growing preference towards the close of the 19th century for novelties which might also serve a purpose. The choice was overwhelming and catered for

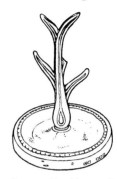

A charming dressing table addition in the form of a tree for hanging finger rings or other pieces of jewellery on. 1905

every requirement. An advertisement in their catalogue of 1905 put out by the Goldsmiths and Silversmiths Co Ltd claimed among hundreds of other items 'a large selection of Novelties for the writing table in stock'. These might include everything from elegant writing boxes – including one in the form of a late 18th-century knife box – to stamp containers, blotters, inkwells and pen trays. For the rich and sentimental it was possible to have inkwells made out of the hooves of a favourite horse or a blotter bound with the hide of a cherished pet. In Piccadilly a shop calling itself 'The Jungle' specialised in such memorabilia and advertised 'Hoofs of Animals Mounted in New & Original Designs'. It also sold similar items in horn, tortoiseshell and ivory. Miniature toys destined for the table were made in the form of salt and pepper pots masquerading as milk churns or miniature imitations of mid-18th-century farmyard animals fitted with velvet-lined panels to take pins. Geese and pigs were especially popular as pincushions and an example showing a trough fitted to the feeding pig provides an overspill for an excess of pins.

Miniature silver furniture was a vogue which was sometimes given an additional use. A chest of drawers and a grand piano might be opened to reveal a velvet- or silk-lined interior suitable for small pieces of jewellery. Other items that might be regarded as 'useful' novelties included a patent pickle fork, photograph frames whose myriad number cluttered the table tops of most early 20th-century interiors, vesta boxes and even an electric tea kettle. One of the first of these was brought out by the Regent Street emporium of Mappin Brothers.

The arrival of 'art' silver

But not everyone was satisfied with the general quality of trade silver. Charles Robert Ashbee, a doyen of the Arts and Crafts Movement and a founder of the Guild of Handicrafts in 1888, evidently suffered much frustration and distaste. It prompted him to write a short essay in 1909, in which he observed that 'the phenomenon evinced by the English Silversmiths Industry at the present moment is that of decrepitude and decay. This has been evident for the last twenty-five years. Judged by the qualitative not the quantitative standard, the work of such houses as Mappin & Webb, Elkington, the Goldsmith and Silversmiths' Alliance, and many others one could name, is of very little value.' For him, as indeed for all the followers of the Movement, the answer lay in a return to handcraftsmanship, based on the principles of a medieval guild system, and a rejection of machinery which was regarded as an interruption of the creative process. Ashbee himself did not totally refuse to use machinery – he accepted it for the purpose of casting, or for rolling plate but he regarded methods such as spinning silver, a technique developed during the 19th century as 'unregulated machine competition'. It really was a 'protest against the modern industrial system which has thrust the personal element further and further into the background until the production of ornament instead of growing out of organic necessities has become a marketable affair controlled by the salesman and the advertiser, and at the mercy of every passing fashion'. (The Studio, Vol II, p 3, 1893.) Inevitably the movement which had been initiated as a social, artistic and philosophical response to the overwhelming threat of a machine age quickly developed its own recognisable styles, almost in spite of the insistence of individual expression. The retention of the hammer marks which reflected and glorified the actual process of the craft was to become one of the most distinctive features. Ashbee, in particular, disliked the mechanical-looking finish of highly polished silver and encouraged the craftsmen working in the Guild of Handicrafts to adopt this method. Ironically the technique was not beyond the possibilities of the machine and it was not long before trade imitations began to appear. By 1905 the Goldsmiths and Silversmiths Co were advertising their own version in the form of 'a New Hammered Flower Vase ($7\frac{3}{4}$ in high)' at £2.16s.d.

But it was line which was all important – or as Walter Crane put it 'line determinative, line emphatic, line delicate, line expressive, line controlling and uniting'. Crane himself had been a founder of the Art Workers Guild, which four years after its inception in 1884 became the Arts and Crafts Exhibition Society and was thoroughly imbued with the ideals of the

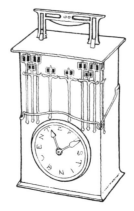

Silver clock with enamel decoration, by Liberty & Co, 1900. The straight lines and flat platform top have been influenced by the Arts and Crafts Movement.

Silver bowl with a wirework handle set with a cabuchon stone. Designed by C. R. Ashbee, it was made by the Guild of Handicrafts in 1905.

movement. Silver shapes were generally simple and took their inspiration from a number of sources including neo-Celtic, Gothic, Japanese art and natural forms. Ashbee, who was principally a designer and not really a practising silversmith, also based much of his work on neo-Gothic shapes. Many of his designs carried out by the Guild of Handicrafts were of simple pieces such as bowls, cups and dishes. By 1900 the sinuous lines which did so much to influence the more exaggerated, even decadent, forms of Art Nouveau were especially visible in the delicate wirework handles and feet of much of his work. But from the 1880's onwards it had also shown the influence of flower and plant forms such as embossed or chased leaves, tulips and hearts. Colour was also important in the silver work of craftsmen working in the Arts and Crafts idiom, and pieces were set with semi-precious stones and coloured enamels.

The Liberty style

The Continental Art Nouveau style, which had its origins in the Arts and Crafts Movement, was to a great extent taken up and popularised by the famous emporium, Liberty and Co, set up in 1875 by Arthur Lazenby Liberty. The success of the style was relatively short-lived and was at its peak from about 1890 to 1910 but Liberty's were still retailing examples in the style well into the 1920's. The firm showed that it was possible to promote artistic and well-designed silver and silver plate on a commercial scale without having to resort to the costly and drawn-out process of using handcrafting techniques. In doing this Liberty's employed a number of designers, many of whom were

Above top: Two-handled cup by George Connell, whose firm produced a wide range of domestic silverware influenced by both the Arts and Crafts Movement and Art Nouveau. 1904.

Above bottom: Teaspoons made and sold by Liberty and Co in 1929, showing the continued influence of late 19th- and early 20th-century styles.

familiar, if not closely linked, with the aspirations and ideas of the Guilds. Unfortunately few pieces can be attributed to particular designers, since it was not Liberty's policy to allow individual recognition for different designs. Among the best-known designers to work on the silver sold through the shop were Bernard Cuzrer (1879–1956), Rex Silver (1879–1965), Archibald Knox and Jessie King. Though the shop had originally been conceived as a specialist dealing in oriental goods, it registered a silver mark as early as 1894. Designs were not sold, however, until some four years later. Much of the work was carried out by the Birmingham-based manufacturer W. H. Haseler, and in 1899 the successful

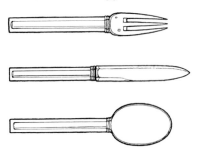

Knife, fork and spoon designed by the French silversmith Jean Puiforcat in the fashionable Art Deco style. The understated decoration is well-served by the streamlined shape. 1925.

Cymric range was brought out with its neo-Celtic look. Another firm to supply Liberty's with 'Art Nouveau' silver included Wm Hutton & Sons of Birmingham.

Surfaces often retained the soft hammer marks, already successfully used by several Guild craftsmen, and colour was added by the use of enamels and inset semi-precious stones. The firm did much to familiarise the general public with the

Arts and Crafts Movement, even though the high ideals of the group were probably not so easily transmitted. Natural forms, especially plant designs, whiplash tendrils, peacock feathers, the female nude and a use of asymmetrical shapes characterised the Art Nouveau style, which was synonymous in Italy with the *stile Liberté*. In England, Art Nouveau was always more restrained than contemporary Continental examples, despite the strenuous attempts by the Studio magazine, launched in 1893, to promote a more uninhibited European approach.

Following the initial flourish of Art Nouveau, many retailers returned to selling popular revival styles which had always found a ready market since the 19th century and continue to do so today. The revisionists included Liberty's, whose chairman had expressed himself as dismayed at the excesses and 'gross exaggerations of [Art Nouveau's] principles and aims'.

Functionalism and modernism

The next wave to hit an increasingly style-conscious public, whose startling cosmopolitanism had been brought about by the ease of worldwide communication, was perversely one which displayed a fascination for the machine, and a passion for the simplicity and logic of functionalism. An early influence on this most distinctive of 20th-century styles was the work of architect-designer C. R. Macintosh (1865–1933), who had himself been influenced by Arts and Crafts ideas.

Macintosh was a member of the famous 'Glasgow Four' particularly admired on the Continent. Though he was best known as an architect, probably his most famous building being the Glasgow

School of Art, he was also noted for his designs for furniture, tableware and metalwork. While much of his work displays an affinity with Art Nouveau, it also presaged the severely simple, often attenuated, lines of the modern style. His work, like that of another British designer, Christopher Dresser (d. 1904), was admired by members of the German Bauhaus School. The latter, under the direction of Walter Gropius, was to dominate international style, stressing the importance of machinery in production, function as the primary dictate of design and form, and the abandonment of ornament.

Art Deco, which sprang up in the 1920's and lasted through the 1930's, also sought to glorify and extend the new machine age. But it was an unashamedly luxurious and stylish fashion as well, promoted not by industrial designers but by the leaders of fashion – particularly those from the *haute couture* world of the Parisian demi-mondes. Favoured materials were expensive and aggressively modern, such as bakelite or chrome. With its stress on decorative quality, Art Deco was antithetical to the functional, modern 'Bauhaus' style, even though many of its forms were based on geometric arrangements. Other motifs typical of this fashion included formalised flowers (reminiscent of the designs of Macintosh), fountains, leaping gazelles, sunbursts and lightning streaks. These motifs became more fashionable during the 1930's, following the growing preference for more angular designs.

In Britain the modern style was slow in being taken up. A number of craftsmen, including Omar Ramsden and Allwyn Carr continued to work in the tradition of the Craft Movement. Much of Ramsden's

Art Deco silver tea and cofee service made by Viners Ltd of Sheffield, with ivory finials and handles. Each piece is stepped and flared in the distinctive design. 1934–39.

work between the wars shows a continued interest in early English Gothic and Tudor forms, although he increasingly made use of machinery and only occasionally were pieces hand-raised in his workshops. Ramsden was basically an entrepreneur who evolved a house style which provided precisely that blend of modernity and traditional craftsmanship demanded by a moneyed community beginning to react against the excesses of mechanisation.

This tradition was further fostered by the establishment of the Crafts Centre of Great Britain, though the centre has, since 1967, slightly altered its original role of accepting work from handcrafting studios. Today pieces must reflect a certain standard of design and execution. More recent craftsmen who, like Ramsden between the wars, run their own studios but sometimes work closely with industry, include Stuart Devlin (born 1931), Leslie Durbin, and Gerald Benney (born 1930). The latter has also contributed a number of designs for tableware in stainless steel, a metal commonly used in place of increasingly expensive silver.

Four-piece coffee set designed by Gerald Benney, showing the smooth and textured surface decoration which is typical of his work.

Twentieth-Century Glass

Turn-of-the-century wine glass by Stevens & Williams, exhibiting the intaglio work for which the firm was famous in the late 19th century. Intaglio work is deep wheel-cut engraving.

Following the stream of exciting techniques and developments which emerged in the glassmaking industry during the latter half of the 19th century, there seemed relatively little that was dramatically new in the Edwardian period. Several of the techniques – even new forms of glass – which had made an appearance only late in the Victorian era continued to find a steady market. But in general it was the traditional forms of English glass – cut lead glass now known as 'cut crystal' – that proved once again to be the staple of English glass production.

Ever-popular cut glass

Despite John Ruskin's pronouncement in the middle of the previous century that 'all cut glass is barbarous', it remained very popular into the Edwardian era. Traditional, deep, wheel-cut patterns, reminiscent of the early 19th-century Regency hobnail and diamond classics, were used for all sorts of table and ornamental glass ranging from silver-rimmed table salts, trays, bottles, boxes – the latter three all used for dressing table sets – to elaborate chandeliers. Other cut-glass pieces reflected the Edwardian preference for lighter styles. Firms such as Thomas Webb & Co, who had long been renowned 'for supremacy in diamond cutting', exemplified the standards demanded in this highly-skilled process. Their work at the beginning of the century was typical of the range then popular in both the heavy overall style of cutting and the lighter method. The Franco-British Exhibition held at White City in 1908 earned the firm a top award for their table and ornamental glass. The citation noted that 'quite the newest thing is the development of the Chippendale and Adams schemes in glass in order that harmony may be complete in rooms furnished in these styles'. Tall, thin-stemmed tazza-shaped champagne bowls displayed the shallow-faceted stems regarded as characteristic of mid-18th-century 'Chippendale' styles. Neo-classic Adam features, sometimes seen to be combined with the earlier style, were incorporated into appropriate festoons and flowers which were engraved or etched on to the sides of thin-walled, elegant Edwardian drinking glasses.

As well as the enjoyment of traditional cut glass there was also a fashion for very simple table glass. Usually left unadorned, it alternatively might be decorated with a mechanical-looking key pattern around the rim of a glass or the ovoid body of a decanter. Other motifs reflected the influence of the Art Nouveau style.

Art Nouveau glass

Art Nouveau was particularly suited to the subtle manipulative qualities inherent in glass. The origins of the style itself are complex but a number of its more immediate stylistic influences are patently visible. Principally concerned with nature – looking afresh at natural forms – it owed a debt to 'Gothic' and Japanese art. Both had played a significant part in European art since the middle of the 19th century. But it was above all a style which, through its use of free-flowing, asymmetrical lines, rejected the historic weight of classical antiquity which had so persistently imbued conservative academic taste for the last 400 years. Art Nouveau reached its peak during the twenty-year period from about 1890 to 1910, but was never fully taken up by English glasshouses as it had been on the Continent – particularly France – and in

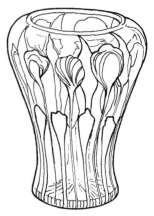

Rare paperweight vase made by Tiffany, using a technique similar to *millefiori* decoration, incorporating long thin rods into the glass. Here it is used to imitate the crocus. *c* 1900.

Turn-of-the-century vase in the irridescent 'aurene glass' made by the Steuben Glass Works of America. Such glass found an international market and is now collected. *c* 1900.

Large cameo glass vase by Emile Gallé, a leading French glass maker. Although his work is characteristic of Continental Art Nouveau, it was available in London, New York and Paris.

America. Famous names such as René Lalique, Emile Gallé and Daum in the former country, and Tiffany in the latter, produced innumerable masterpieces in the style. It was also an early example of truly international expression in an age when world communication and transport had improved dramatically and examples from renowned glasshouses were as readily available in London as they were in Paris or New York.

In England the style was appreciated by commercial firms principally because of the possibilities it opened for applied decoration. But the glass-makers Stevens and Williams did produce a type of 'art' glass called 'Silveria', whose fluid forms bore some similarity to contemporary

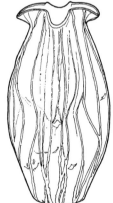

Silveria glass vase made by Stevens and Williams in the early 1900's. The technique was developed by John Northwood II. Pieces are often marked with an S or a W.

Continental work. Its silvery colouring was due to a layer of silver foil trapped between two layers of clear or slightly tinted glass which were subjected to extremely high temperature conditions and

made to crizzel into tiny pieces. The firm was also known for making other types of art glass which, like art pottery, were intended more for decoration rather than for use. One range was called Alexandrite – a treatment also effected by Thomas Webb and Sons who patented their method in 1903. Although the results of both companies – an opaque-coloured glass shading from blue to pink to yellow – were almost identical, the processes involved differed substantially. Webb's method involved continual reheating of areas of glass, causing it to change under the high temperatures, while that used by Williams & Stevens relied on the use of a clear amber-coloured glass cased with a layer of pink and another of blue. These

Alexandrite wine glass with patterned surface. Plain examples of this glass, which shades from yellow to pink to blue, are more common.

then were cut through to reveal the colours beneath.

Cased and cameo techniques

The revival in the 19th century of cased

glass had been one of the great achievements of the period. With it were resurrected a number of techniques, including cameo carving. This highly-skilled process had been developed in England by John Northwood (1836–1902), following the successful completion of his own version of the so-called Portland Vase (also known as the Barberini vase) in 1876. Similar developments were undertaken in France by the famous glass-maker Emile Gallé, who was particularly interested in the methods used earlier by Japanese glass-makers. Northwood died in 1902 but this technique, dormant in Europe since antiquity, was carried on by his son John Northwood II (1870–1960), and a dedicated handful of craftsmen working principally in the Stourbridge area. Output was slow and relatively little was made, each piece commanding prices greatly in excess of the average glass-maker's weekly wage.

Both Northwoods worked for the Stourbridge firm of Stevens and Williams, but the other leading firm, Thomas Webb & Sons, was fortunate in employing the equally-talented Woodall brothers, Thomas (1849–1926) and George (1850–1925). Subject matter for pieces decorated in the costly cameo technique differed considerably as taste at the beginning of the century varied. The older Northwood favoured classical themes reminiscent of the Portland vase, or his equally well-known engraved version of the Elgin vase. The other decorators depicted themes based on flower motifs influenced, on the one hand by oriental – especially Japanese – work, and on the other by fashionable Art Nouveau styles. But although the cameo carving carried out by English craftsmen generally showed greater technical facility, their work is often regarded as showing less artistic and imaginary verve than carving carried out on the Continent by glass-makers such as Emile Gallé.

Free-blown art glass

As well as traditional cut glass and the more elaborate decorated type of art glass produced at the beginning of the century there were a few designers and glass-makers who favoured a return to blown and manipulated glass in place of labor-ious cut glass. Instead of carefully con-trolled – even forced – shapes elaborately formed and decorated, simple, free-blown forms became their forte. Very early ex-amples of this simple, unadorned glass were made by the firm of James Powell and Sons of the London-based Whitefriars glasshouse, to the designs of Philip Webb. Powell's were also noted for making stained-glass windows for the firm of Morris & Co in the later years of the 19th

century. Another house famous for making similar, organically-inspired art glass was the Scottish firm of James Couper & Sons of Glasgow. The range was called Clutha glass and had originally been designed by the eminent Victorian industrial designer, Christopher Dresser, already noted for his contributions to both silver and pottery. Later designs were made by George Walton.

Modern 'industrial' design

The 20th century set the seal of approval on the important role of the industrial designer. In 1915 the first Design and Industries Association was established and was followed up the next year with a department based at Sheffield University for 'Glass Technology'. But during the war, many firms found that, like every other industry not involved directly in the war effort, production was greatly re-duced and concentrated principally on making plain table glass. Some, like

Webb's, turned to making electric light bulbs. The immediate aftermath of the war proved to be little better for several firms who in the depression lost many skilled glass-makers and decorators.

The taste for simple forms, principally subordinated to function, became the main consideration of glass design in the period between the wars. Early examples of this modern style came from the in-fluential Swedish glass firm of Orrefors, established in 1898. In England com-parable work could be seen in both the pottery and glass designs of Keith Murray, who worked for the firm of Stevens and Williams from 1932–1939, but who nevertheless successfully managed to retain a distinctly English appearance in much of his work. Other designers in-cluded Barnaby Powell and Tom Hill, both working for James Powell & Sons (Whitefriars) Ltd, which moved from their original site near St Paul's Cathedral in London to Harrow. This occurred in 1923

The simple solid lines of this green glass vase, designed by Barnaby Powell and Tom Hill of the Whitefriars Glass Works, are typical of 20th-century functionalist design.

Glass and gilt metal wall light, holding three electric light bulbs which shine through the pale yellow, blue and pink glass petals. An unusual and attractive addition to the home. c 1930.

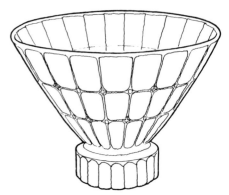

Flared vase with wide facet-cut decoration, designed by Keith Murray for Stevens & Williams in 1939. Glass examples of Keith Murray's designs are comparatively rare.

Another example of Keith Murray's talents as a designer. Glass vase with geometric motifs characteristic of the 1930's.

when, as their catalogue states, the works took 'larger premises at Wealdstone and a brazier of live fuel was brought in a lorry from the old Works to light the first furnace at the New Works. So it can be said that the fires of Whitefriars have been alight continuously from its original founding until the present day.'

In spite of the impact of the new styles the cutter still played an important part in English glass design, initiating the use of bold clean lines in his work and the trend for freer and simpler cutting. Sculptural shapes in the form of trailed ribbon decoration and internal bubbly patterns were other innovations. Engraved decoration turned toward simple abstract patterns and plants which had only become familiar in the 20th century, such as the prickly cactus.

Mary Gregory type of glass vase with a figure painted in white enamel colour on a blue glass background. The blue is less common than green, clear and pink glass. c 1900.

Art Deco figures

Small, elegantly-poised figures, frozen forever in stylised poses, were very popular among the fashionable during the 1920's and 30's. Many of these attractive sculptures were purely decorative, to be placed in niches or on shelves or cabinet tops. But some were given a *raison d'etre*, pressed into service as table lamps or fruit stands.

Among the finest examples were unique sculpted works, some in limited editions, by famous modellers such as F. D. Preiss, D. H. Chiparus and Jacob Epstein. Less familiar but highly-regarded names include George Otto Poertzal (whose name was for a time also thought to be a pseudonym for Preiss) and Marcel Bouraine. The majority of these sculptors – as their names suggest – were of Continental origin. Many worked in Paris which, with the Austrian capital Vienna, was the main centre of manufacture.

The materials used by leading makers of these elegant statuettes were principally bronze and ivory, though porcelain – generally from a well-known factory – was also used. Ivory was readily available in Europe from the Belgian Congo, following the takeover of the vast central African state by the Belgian government in 1908. It was used mainly for limbs and heads, its creamy white texture providing the ideal surface for finely carved details such as hands and faces. In those figures which combine ivory with bronze – known generically as 'elephantine bronzes' – the metal is generally used for the clothing. Frequently bronze alone was used. Colour was added in the form of painted decoration applied when the bronze was cold. Painted hair and face details were also added to ivory heads

although with time these have often worn away. Bases were generally of marble, though onyx was favoured by D. Chiparus, who was particularly noted for his fanciful, sexy designs which sometimes incorporated geometric patterns inlaid in coloured marbles.

Cheaper imitations of these unique examples were made for a much wider mass market and large numbers of these inferior figures still exist today. The standard is reflected in their price; such pieces can be found for a fraction of the amount demanded for a high-quality signed work by a well-known maker. Cheaper materials used include ivorine, a type of plastic that when new resembled ivory but which with time becomes yellow and lifeless. Spelter, a white-coloured metal, is actually a zinc compound. Even when patinated to look like bronze this metal is much softer and lacks the crisp casting qualities typical of the harder metal.

Motifs were predominantly feminine. Sveldt women, caught in theatrical and stylized dance poses, were especially favoured, and reflected contemporary interest in exotic themes also appearing in cinema. Other stylishly modern themes depicted the 'new' liberated woman of the 20's and 30's. She was envisaged as an elegantly chic society woman with her dogs (usually greyhounds) and cigarettes, or as the energetic but no less stylish sportswoman with her golf clubs and rackets. Others appear in contemporary flapper 'gear'.

Children were another popular subject, often naturalistically sculpted in 'sweet' finger-sucking poses.

Tin Toys

The manufacture of tin toys began early

The 'Torch Dancer' by F. Preiss in cold painted bronze and ivory on an onyx base. A number of different bases were used for this model, of both stone and metal.

A bronze sculpture of a 'Girl in a Hoop' by Gilbert Bayes. English contributions to sculpture in the Art Deco style are relatively few. 1916.

in the 19th century. The increase in toy
production was largely aided by the impact of the Industrial Revolution which
not only created the base of the industry
but ensured a solid and growing market
in the rapidly expanding middle classes.
Throughout the 19th century the production of tin toys was dominated by
American manufacturers. Classic firms
were Steven and Brown, and Francis,
Field and Francis, but by the opening
years of the 20th century their pre-
eminence was unseated by the German
toy-making firms of Lehmann, Gebruder
Bing, Schoenner and Marklin. These
firms, many based in and around Nurem-
burg, continued to rule the tin toy industry up to the Second World War, when
the Japanese and Chinese outstripped that
of both European and American manufacturers.

Tin plate, which superseded the more
expensive porcelain and wax materials
used in the early 19th century, made
production much more economic. Full-
scale mechanisation enabled the hundreds
of tiny bits necessary for the production of
the toys to be stamped out with precision
from sheets of tin plate, the bulk of which
came from South Wales. Decoration was
usually painted by hand but the introduction of off-set lithography around 1875
ensured a faster, cheaper method of
decoration on tin plate, which earlier had
successfully resisted direct printing.
Simple clockwork mechanisms, which
like the tin toy itself were surprisingly
robust, added movement – however jerky
– to the magic world of toys and continued

Popeye, made in tinplate, clad only in a barrel. This
tin-plate version of Popeye was made by the firm of
A. J. Chein of America. It is stamped 'King Features
Syndicate Inc, copyright'.

the tradition of automata which had begun in the early 18th century. Other methods included rack and lever actions, pulling a piece of string which set a small flywheel into motion, a more sophisticated steam engine or, later still, the twisted elastic band which acted as a 20th-century catapult.

The range of tin toys made during the first half of the 20th century closely imitated the events of the day. The era which preceded the First World War in 1914 was one in which 'gunboat' diplomacy on the high seas became miniaturised into a whole range of impressive iron clads and other warships. Boats in general were top of the popularity poll, and they represented all walks of life, from elegant leisure yachts to simple but gaily coloured barges and paddle boats. Trains, cars, carriages and even rickshaws (at a time when the Boxer Rebellion of c 1900 was on everyone's lips) were made by the thousand from the beginning of the century and faithfully recorded the changing fashions.

Novelty figures and animals were also common. Some reflected the jokey fairground tradition, others a more everyday note. Clowns, circus figures on tightropes, magicians and performing animals come within the former category, while dancing couples, clockwork laying chickens, bald-headed men at the barber's, parlour maids chasing larger than life mice, and two-inch long beetles – to set into action under the furniture or outside in the grass – fall into the second. The beetles – a special favourite of naughty schoolboys – were made by Lehmann's from about 1900 to 1930.

Up to about 1920 many of the tin toys had been designed to appeal as much to adults as to children. Generally heavy and robust, these little figures were decorated in a life-like way. After about 1920, however, there was an increasing tendency among toy makers to take the requirements of children more seriously, and often features were incorporated that suggest an educational purpose. This concern mirrored the theories of educationalists such as Dr Maria Montessori and Ernest Froebel. Other toys were based on comic strip characters. The most endearing of these figures to emerge were the cartoon figures of Mickey Mouse and Donald Duck.

Enamelled advertising signs

From about 1880 to the outbreak of World War II brightly-coloured enamel street signs were a common sight along the streets and pathways of urban Britain. They were the characteristic medium of advertising in a period of stability and of slowly changing social tastes, an unaggressive form of advertising unimaginable in the mad rush of the later 20th century. By their very nature these signs – selling everything from fashionable department stores (among them Maples and Harrods), the newly-invented gramophone records, and confectionery to cureralls and animal feed – were designed as permanent fixtures and many quickly became recognisable landmarks.

The process of enamelling on to cast sheet iron was developed early in the 19th century. Among its early large-scale uses was the production of some 100,000 enamelled railway station signposts for the fast-developing railway lines springing up all over the country. These early examples, which reached their peak during the 1914–18 war, are characterised by clear translucent enamel colours over the soft mid-grey colour of the sheet iron, which is clearly visible on the back of these plaques. Since the early 1920's iron has gradually been replaced by steel. The latter is instantly recognisable by its darker blue-black hue and the cleaner finish of the enamel colours which were latterly sprayed on. Early signs were decorated by the stencil process, a slow labour-intensive method now superseded by screen printing.

Unlike today's huge hoardings, capable of displaying vast expanses of photographic posters, the largest enamel signs rarely exceeded seven or eight feet in height. Three or four feet was the average, though the smallest used for display on locations such as stair risers – on the stairs of trams, trolley buses, and the underground – were only a few inches high.

The products displayed on these colourful plaques are a humorous and telling indication of social customs in years past. It is evident, for example, from the number of brands advertised, that in the early years of this century tea drinking was more prevalent than coffee, with 'Camp Coffee' alone representing the latter beverage. Tea was sold by a multitude of firms, only some of which survive today. Other products added a humorous touch to their ads – one for 'Burma Sauce' depicted a young freshfaced lad saying gleefully, 'The only *Sauce* I dare give Father'.

Tobacco and cigarette advertising, much of which would not be acceptable by today's standards, were equally widespread. Popular brands included Black Cat, Belga, Players Drumhead, Wild Woodbine, Will's Flag and Gold Flake Cigarettes, and Players 'Airman' Tobacco.

Twentieth-Century Antiques
What To Look For

Viewing and Buying

Dealers, local auction rooms, junk shops, street markets, jumble sales and skips.

Furniture

20th-century furniture has long been unfashionable, but there are signs that this is changing. As most is still very cheap it is advisable to go for good quality in design, timber and manufacture. Not all furniture is held in such low regard, however and some 20th-century pieces, such as C. R. Macintosh's chairs, fetch as much as £90,000.

Marquetry decoration varies considerably in quality on Edwardian 'Sheraton' style furniture. Also check the need to restore.

Single cottage or kitchen-type chairs are very numerous and cheap making it possible to build up a matched set for less than the cost of most modern furniture.

Other items which are often cheaper, more decorative and better made than much furniture made since 1950, include large wardrobes, beds and wooden bed boards. Wardrobes are not as numerous as they once were, as many have been broken up (during the fashion for built-in wardrobes), converted and exported.

Points to Watch

There was a tendency during the early 20th century to skimp on wood, especially on chair and table legs. These are liable to breakage. Avoid broken legs and any other broken main structural member such as a chair back upright as these will never be strong despite restoration.

Stamped and labelled furniture by well-known firms or designers may well be of interest.

Pottery and Porcelain

Large quantities of all types of both pottery and porcelain-bodied wares make these pieces a competitive alternative to buying ceramics fresh from the factory.

Some names including Susie Cooper are well known and marked pieces becoming more expensive as are the examples attributed to particular factories. These include Shelley ware and Wedgwood's fairyland lustre, the latter which is now well established amongst collectors. Examples are beyond the means of all but the most serious collectors.

Silver

Much 20th-century silver is only worth its 'melt down' value. So for those who enjoy using silver and seeing it on their sideboards and tables, second hand pieces can be found surprisingly cheaply.

Glass

Many 20th-century firms making quantities of fine quality lead crystal in traditional cut-glass styles provide an opportunity to buy complete sets of good quality glass – particularly drinking glasses of all varieties – at a fraction of the cost of buying new glass, often in the same or similar patterns.

Because of its cheapness there appears to have been little or no attempt to imitate 20th-century glass.

Certain types of glass are becoming sought after including 'art glass' attributable to certain designers and variously-coloured 'cloud glass' made by George Davidson & Company during the 1920's and 30's.

Bibliography

General Background/Social/Architecture

ANSCOMBE, I. and GERE, C., *Arts and Crafts in Britain and America* Academy Editions, London, 1978

CALDER, J., *The Victorian Home* Batsford, London, 1977

COOK, O., *The English Country House. An art and a way of life.* Thames and Hudson, London, 1974

EASTLAKE C. L., *Hints on Household Taste* London, 1868

EDWARDS, R., (*ed*), RAMSEY, L. G. (*ed*), *The Connoisseur Period Guides* The Connoisseur, London, 1958
The Stuart Period 1603–1714
The Early Georgian Period 1714–1760
The Late Georgian Period 1760–1810
The Regency Period 1810–1830
The Early Victorian Period 1830–1860

GARNER, P. (*ed*), *Phaidon Encyclopaedia of Decorative Arts 1890–1940* Phaidon, Oxford, 1978

GIROUARD, M., *Life in the English Country House. A Social and Architectural History* Yale University Press, New Haven and London, 1978

JOURDAIN, M., *English Interior Decoration 1500–1830* Batsford, London 1950

NAYLOR, G., *The Arts and Crafts Movement* Studio Vista, London 1971

PEVSNER, N., *Pioneers of Modern Design* Penguin, London, 1968

Priestly, J. B., *The Edwardians* Heinemann, London, 1970

READER, W. J., *Victorian England* Batsford, London, 1974

SAVAGE, G., *Dictionary of 19th century Antiques and later Objets d'Arts* Barrie & Jenkins, London, 1978

SUMMERSON, Sir J., *Architecture in Britain 1530–1830* Pelican, London, 1977

TAYLOR, A. J. P., *English History 1914–1945* Oxford University Press, Oxford, 1966

WATERSON, M., *The Servant's Hall. A domestic History of Erddig*, London and Henley, Routledge & Kegan Paul, 1980

PUBLICATIONS
The Studio Yearbooks, 1897–1950 The Studio Magazine (Studio International), London.

Furniture

AGIUS, P., *British Furniture 1880–1914* Antique Collectors' Club, Woodbridge, 1978

ASLIN, E., *19th-Century English Furniture* Faber, London, 1962

COMINO, M., *Gimson and the Barnsleys* Evans Brothers, London, 1980

EDWARDS, R., *Shorter Dictionary of English Furniture* Country Life Books, London, 1964

GARNER, P., *Twentieth Century Furniture* Phaidon Press, Oxford, 1980

GILBERT, C., *The Life and Work of Thomas Chippendale* Studio Vista/Christies, London, 1978

HAYWARD, H., *World Furniture* Hamlyn, London, 1972

HEAL & SONS, LTD., *Reasonable Furniture and Furniture for Small Cottages and Flats* Catalogue, 1925

JONES, O., *The Grammar of Ornament* London, 1856

JOY, E., *The Connoisseur Illustrated Guide to Furniture* The Connoisseur, London, 1972

JOY, E. T., *English Furniture 1800–1851* Ward Lock/Sotheby's, London, 1977

JOY, E. T., *Pictorial Dictionary of British 19th century Furniture Designs* Antique Collectors' Club, Woodbridge, 1980

Ceramics

BARNARD, J., *Victorian Ceramic Tiles* Studio Vista, London, 1972

CHARLESTON, R. J. (ed), *World Ceramics* Hamlyn, London, 1968

CUSHION, J. P., *Connoisseur Illustrated Guides: Pottery and Porcelain* Connoisseur, London, 1972

GODDEN, G., *Encyclopaedia of British Pottery and Porcelain Marks* Barrie & Jenkins, London, 1964

GODDEN, G., *Victorian Porcelain* Barrie & Jenkins, London, 1961

HONEY, W. B., *English Pottery and Porcelain* A & C Black, London, 1962

JEWITT, L., *Ceramic Art of Great Britain* Revised Barrie & Jenkins, London, 1972

WATNEY, B., *English Blue and White Porcelain of the 18th century* Faber, London, 1973

Wills, G., *English Pottery and Porcelain* Guinness, London, 1969

Silver

ASHBEE, C. R., *Modern English Silverwork* London, 1909

BARR, E., *George Wickes: Royal Goldsmith 1698–1761* Studio Vista, London, 1980

Birmingham City Museum and Art Gallery, *Omar Ramsden, 1873–1939: Centenary Exhibition of Silver Catalogue*, 1930

BURY, S., *Victorian Electroplate* Country Life Collectors Guides, London, 1971

CULME, J., *Nineteenth Century Silver* Country Life Books, London, 1977

DEAKIN, JAMES & SONS LTD., *Catalogue of Silver*, 1899

ELKINGTON & SONS LTD., *Catalogue*, 1930

The Goldsmith and Silversmiths Company, *Catalogue*, 1906

GRIMWADE, A., *Rococo Silver 1727–1765* Faber, London, 1974

HUGHES, G., *Modern Silver throughout the World 1880–1967* Studio Vista, London, 1968

OMAN, C., *English Domestic Silver* A & C Black, London, 1965

OMAN, C., *Caroline Silver 1625–1688* Faber, London, 1971

ROWE, R., *Adam Silver 1765–1795* Faber, London, 1965

TAYLOR, G., *Silver* Penguin Books, Middlesex, 1970

WARDLE, P., *Victorian Silver and Silver Plate* Herbert Jenkins, London, 1963

Glass

BARRINGTON HAYNES, E., *Glass Through the Ages* Penguin Books, Middlesex 1970

BEARD, G., *Modern Glass* Barrie & Jenkins, London, 1968

HURST VOSE, R., *The Connoisseur Illustrated Guides: Glass* The Connoisseur, London, 1975

NEWMAN, H., *Illustrated Dictionary of Glass* Thames and Hudson, London, 1977

POWELL, JAMES & SONS *Catalogue* Whitefriars, 1938

WILLS, G., *Antique Glass: For Pleasure and Investment* John Gifford, London, 1971

WILLS, G., *Victorian Glass* G., Bell, London, 1976

WOODWARD, H. W., *Art, Feat and Mystery: The Story of Thomas Webb & Sons* Antique Collectors' Club, Stourbridge, 1978

Glossary

Acanthus

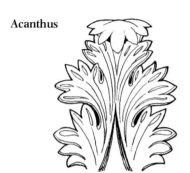

Classical motif based on deeply serrated, curling leaf of the acanthus and widely used in all European decorative art. Scrolling acanthus form often used in profile.

Anthemion

Flower motif based on the honeysuckle. Though much used throughout Europe and America during the neo-classical revival of the 18th century, it originated in ancient Greek and Roman architecture.

Apron piece
Shaped ornamental section directly under table top, chair seat, dresser, chest of drawers or stand. Sometimes joins legs at the junction of the rail.

Arabesque
Pattern derived from Roman, Arabian and Persian art. It consists of highly stylised leaves and scrolling lines elaborately interlaced.

Arm pad
Padded arm section on chair.

Backstool
Term used to describe single chair in 17th and 18th century. It was characterised by a square, upholstered back, with large gap between the back and the seat.

Baluster
Columnar member that is shaped or turned. Much used in furniture and for the stems of drinking glasses between about 1685 and 1760. Balusters assumed a variety of different forms including twisted, inverted, tapered or vase-shaped, and were sometimes combined with cushion, annulated, mushroom or acorn knops.

Basalt
Black, unglazed stoneware body developed by Wedgwood in late 18th century, who described it as having 'nearly the same properties with the natural stone'. Much used for vases, medallions, busts and useful domestic wares. Also called Egyptian black.

Beading
Applied ornamental moulding in the form of a row of beads. Much used on furniture, silver, glassware and ceramics in late 18th and early 19th century.

Bellarmine
Round-bodied, narrow-necked stoneware jug characterised by a mask of a bearded man said to resemble Cardinal Bellarmino (1542–1621). Used mainly to import Rhenish wines into England in late 16th and 17th century, it was later copied in this country throughout the 18th century.

Bin label
Large pottery label hung beside wine bins. Early examples date from the late 17th century and were probably made at one of the Lambeth potteries. Later examples were made in Staffordshire.

Biscuit
A term describing fired but unglazed pottery or porcelain. Its use was particularly common in porcelain, mainly in imitation of marble. Notable examples include Derby biscuit porcelain used in figure modelling and Parian ware.

Blanc de Chine
Type of Chinese porcelain developed under the Ming Dynasty (1368–1644), in Fukien province. It was noted for its highly translucent body and lustrous glaze and was exported to Europe during the 17th and 18th century.

Bombé
Term used to describe curved bulging shape characteristic of mid-18th-century silver and furniture, such as commodes.

Bone china
English type of porcelain first developed by Josiah Spode c 1800. Made up of china clay and stone strengthened and whitened by bone ash.

Bright-cut engraving
See engraving.

Cameo glass
A piece composed of several layers of glass in which the top layer is relief-cut to form the design. Technique similar to that used on shells or gems to produce cameos. Perfected by the Romans and later used in Europe during the 19th century.

Canted
Bevelled or chamfered surface which has been cut away from a square.

Cased glass
Two or more layers of blown glass, often white between two coloured layers.

Chasing
See flat chasing.

Cream ware
See Queen's Ware.

Cristallo/crystal
Type of clear, colourless glass developed in Venice during the 15th century and noted for its resemblance to rock crystal. Also known as *façon de Venise* when made in countries other than Venice, though it was usually under the direction of Venetian glassmakers.

Crizzle
Disease brought about by an imbalance of ingredients during the glass making process resulting in cloudiness and a fine network of cracks. Often causes the glass to crumble.

C-scroll
Shape in the form of a C. Often used as form of handle.

Cullett
Broken, discarded glass, re-used to make new glass. Its use helped to improve fusion and quality of new metal. Also used as a frit in the manufacture of early soft-paste porcelain.

Cushion frieze
A convex or cushion-shaped form commonly used on cornices and on friezes decorating late 17th-century case furniture. Also used for mirror or pier glass frames from Restoration to the end of the 17th century.

Cut glass

Glass, usually lead glass, ornamented by shallow- or deepcut facets.

Date letter
Assay mark used on all English silver since 1478 to denote the year of hall-marking. Each assay office has its own cycle and forms of lettering but only single letters of the alphabet are used.

Demi-parure
Small matching set of jewellery, usually comprising necklace and earrings, and often a brooch or bracelet.

Dentil moulding
Type of moulding carved to resemble small rectangular blocks or teeth.

Diaper pattern
Allover trellis pattern formed by inter-secting diagonal lines. Used on silver, porcelain, and in marquetry on furniture, often as a background motif.

Distressing
Method of damaging furniture in order to simulate age by staining, marking, bruising etc.

Drawn Stem
Wine glass with stem drawn out from the base of the bowl rather than being stuck on.

Duty mark
Mark found on English silver between 1784 and 1890. It took the form of the sovereign's head, indicating that duty on gold and silver had been paid.

Ebonised wood
Wood, often beech, stained black in imitation of ebony.

Egg-and-dart

Ornament of Greek origin used on mouldings. It consists of raised ovolo or egg-shaped motifs alternating with darts or anchors. Used in Europe on furniture and silver since the 16th century.

Embossing
Like repoussé, a way of ornamenting metalwork by hammering on the reverse side to produce a design in relief. The term is often used to mean any decorative method resulting in relief patterns. The embossed surface is often finished with chasing.

Enamel colours
Also called low-temperature or over-glaze colours. Used to decorate porcelain and glass.

Engine turning
Mechanical method of decorating silver and ceramics on a lathe to produce a regular pattern of hatched, diced, fluted or other geometric forms.

Engraving
Technique of incising the surface of a metal object with a cutting tool, either for decorative purposes or to produce an image prior to printing. Bright-cut engraving was a popular form of decorating silverware at the end of the 18th century. It removed the metal with a bevelled cutting tool giving a glittering effect.

Escutcheon
Ornamental metal surround of a keyhole. Also an armorial shield used as a decorative device on 18th-century furniture.

Faience
French term for tin-glazed earthenware.

Fairings
Small ceramic figures sold at fairs during the 19th century. They usually illustrated famous people, topical events and situations connected with family or married life.

Fall-front
Sloping, hinged flap on bureau which, when lowered, is supported beneath by sliding rails, also called lopers.

Felspar china
China containing felspathic rock developed by Josiah Spode the Younger in about 1820. Marked 'Felspar Porcelain' within a wreath beneath the name SPODE.

Festoon
Ornamental garland of flowers, fruit, leaves, and draped folds of cloth popular since the Renaissance. Sometimes called a swag.

Fillet
Thin, narrow strip of wood often used between mouldings.

Final
Crowning ornamental knob, often in the shape of a classical urn or vase, pineapple, or sometimes the human

form. Used principally on furniture pediments and lids of silver items.

Firing glass
18th-century toasting glass. Characterised by its drawn bowl, thick stem and stout heavy foot. The latter when banged on the table made a sound resembling musket fire. Also called hammering glass.

Flambé glazes
High-temperature, coloured glazes developed in China in which kiln conditions produced variegated colour effects. Technique copied by 19th-century artist potters in both Europe and America.

Flashed glass
Thin outer layer of glass, usually of a different colour, on a glass object. Made by dipping cooled glass object into molten glass. The surface is sometimes decorated by cutting and etching, but the result always lacks depth.

Flat chasing
Technique of decorating metal surfaces with low relief patterns by working the metal from the front without removing any metal. Often used in conjunction with embossed decoration (worked from behind). It is sometimes used for filing off roughnesses caused in casting metal.

Flatware
Traditional term used to describe flat metal articles such as spoons, and forks.

Flint glass
Early term for lead glass.

Frigger
Frivolous glassware made by glass makers in spare time in forms such as rollingpins, hats, walking sticks, bells and model ships.

Fluting

Shallow concave grooves found on classical columns. Much used on furniture, silver and glass as a decorative motif, often as a border ornament. Opposite to reeded decoration.

French polish
Transparent gum-based surface coating applied to furniture, noted for its hard, very shiny finish. Introduced in England in the late 18th century, though it did not become widespread until the 19th century.

Frit
Ground-up ingredients used in glass-making prior to melting in a crucible.

Fretwork
Popular geometric, abstract patterns either carved and applied to furniture or pierced and left as open decoration. Appears in styles mainy inspired by Chinese or Gothic taste.

Gadrooning
Decorative pattern used principally as border motif. It consists of radiating convex lobes of either curved or straight form, and is usually found on silver and furniture.

Gaffer
Principal glass maker in a glass-house.

Gallery
Raised ornamental border or rail round the edge of a table, tray or shelf.

Garniture
Matching set, usually consisting of five ornaments, designed for the mantelpiece in ceramic and silver. Common elements are a vase, candlesticks, tray and clock. Also called a *garniture de cheminée*.

Gather
A blob of molten metal (glass) gathered onto the end of the glass-blower's blowpipe ready for blowing.

Gesso
Foundation of chalk and parchment size, bound in water and glue, used on furniture as a medium prior to carving and gilding. Often found on table tops, mirror frames and stands from the late 17th century onwards.

Gilding
Technique of applying thin coat of gold to glass, ceramics, silver or wood. Various methods used include honey, oil, water and acid gilding. Woodwork was coated with gesso before gilding.

Girandole
Carved and gilt sconce, or wall light, which by the mid-18th century often enclosed a mirror plate.

Glaze
Thin glassy non-porous material used to coat pottery, stoneware and porcelain. Lead glaze was most common type used on all ceramics up to end of 19th century except for hard-paste porcelain and salt-glazed stoneware, though leadless glazes were developed during the 19th century.

Greasepan
Small, circular dish situated just below the nozzle of a candlestick into which the molten grease from candle dripped. Also called drip pan.

Greek key pattern
See key pattern.

Ground colours
Background colours used on porcelain or enamels over which decoration is sometimes added or applied within reserved panels.

Guilloche

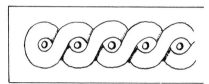

Classical ornament consisting of interlaced circles, sometimes enclosing foliate rosettes. Much used on neoclassical-style furniture and silverware during the 18th century.

Herringbone banding
Decorative border pattern much used on furniture in the late 17th and early 18th century. Composed of strips of veneer set diagonally. Sometimes called feather banding.

Hollow ware
Any vessel designed to hold liquids.

Honeysuckle motif
Another name for anthemion.

Inlay
Ornamental surface decoration achieved by inserting different coloured materials flush into a background panel, usually wood. Materials varied from wood, ivory, mother-of-pearl, and tortoiseshell to a variety of metals.

Japanning
English term used to describe lacquer made in imitation of Oriental lacquer. Also used in the 18th century as a general term to describe much painted furniture. Common colours were black, scarlet and green, which were applied to a wide range of furniture including bureaus, screens, mirrors, seat furniture, cabinets and clock cases.

Jasperware
Dense, hard, fine-grained stoneware developed by Josiah Wedgwood over a long period of time. Differed from jasper dip by being coloured throughout in shades of blue, lavender, green, lilac, yellow (rare) and black. It was usually decorated with contrasting applied white jasper ornament in the neo-classic style and is still made today. Jasper dip was the name given to a white jasper body covered with a surface colour wash.

Kakiemon style
Distinctive Japanese style of decoration used on porcelain and much copied in 18th century by European porcelain factories. In England Bow, Worcester and Chelsea Kakiemon pieces are characterised by asymmetrical designs.

Kaolin
Chinese name for china clay; a white-bodied, refractory clay commonly found in Cornwall.

Key pattern

Also called Greek key or Greek fret. It is commonly used on friezes and borders, and is a geometric, repetitive design made up of straight lines joined at right angles at alternate ends.

Kick
Dent beneath a glass object made so that the pontil mark, a rough, uneven scar, did not impede stability. Mainly found on pre-1760 bottles, bowls and decanters.

Kiln waster
A ceramic item, either pottery or porcelain, spoilt in the firing and discarded.

Knop

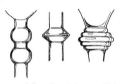

An ornamental knob, either solid or hollow, occurring especially on 18th-century drinking glass stems.

Knurling
Ornamental ridge of irregular line mainly used as silver decoration in 18th century. Also used to describe the curled-under foot in furniture.

Krater
Two-handled Greek vase with a wide mouth.

Kylix
Two-handled Greek vase with narrow mouth, standing on a foot.

Lacquer
Type of variously coloured varnish prepared from a resin. The recipe is of Oriental origin. The varnish is applied in number of layers to form a hard surface on wood, leather or other materials. The term is often used interchangeably with japanning.

Latten
Metal alloy of copper zinc, lead and tin; formerly used for making church articles such as bells.

Latticino
Interlaced opaque white threads used to decorate clear or coloured glass, much used to decorate mid-18th-century drinking glass stems. Developed in Venice in mid-16th century, but popular elsewhere in Europe.

Lead crystal
Type of glass, developed by George Ravenscroft by 1675, containing lead oxide. Differed from soda glass by being

heavier, more glyptic and having the ability to refract light, making it suitable for cutting.

Leer
Carefully controlled, heated chamber or tunnel in which glass was toughened by cooling slowly by annealing.

Lemon-squeezer foot
Type of moulded foot found on glass objects in the late 18th and early 19th century. The domed foot was embellished with radial ribs on the underside resembling a lemon squeezer.

Lotus ornament
Ornamental motif based on the water lily of the Nile which appeared in ancient Egyptian decoration. Commonly used during the early 19th century.

Lunette ornament
Commonly found on furniture in first half of 17th century. Composed of formal semi-circles, either carved, inlaid or painted, and often embellished.

Lyre ornament

Motif favoured by Robert Adam in the late 18th century and much used on furniture, particularly chair backs and sofa table supports. Its inspiration is the Grecian lyre.

Marlborough leg
Straight, square leg, sometimes tapering and often on a square plinth. An English term, but much used to refer to American furniture of the mid-18th century.

Marquetry
Decorative veneer of different-coloured materials, mainly of wood but also mother-of-pearl, tortoiseshell or ivory, cut into delicate patterns and applied to the carcase of a piece of furniture.

Marver
Marble or iron slab on which the lump of molten metal (a paraison) is rolled and smoothed into shape.

Matting
Popular decoration used in silver, effected by punching small dots onto the surface, creating a dull, roughened background texture.

Metal
Term used for glass material, either in molten or cold state.

Millefiori glass
Type of glass decorated with coloured canes embedded in clear glass forming flower-like designs.

Monopodium
Support used mainly for tables in the form of single leg and foot, often with an animal's head – like a lion's – at the top.

Monteith
Large silver bowl with scalloped or indented rim designed to support the bases or feet of drinking glasses while the bowls were cooled in cold water or ice. Used from the late 17th century onwards.

Mortice-and-tenon joint
Type of joint used in furniture making where the mortice is a rectangular- or square-shaped cavity into which the tenon fits exactly.

Mould-blown glass
Glass made by blowing a gather of metal (molten glass) into a mould. Used industrially from early 19th century, following the development of the two-piece, open-and-shut, mould.

Mould-pressed glass
Glass made by pouring a gather of metal into a mould and pressing it into shape either by hand or mechanically.

Nozzle
Socket in which candle is held in place in a candlestick, wall sconce, candelabra or chandelier.

Ogee moulding

Decorative moulding shaped as a double curve, the lower part being concave and the upper convex. Appears S-shaped in side view.

Opaque glass
Glass made opaque by the addition of tin oxide or calcined bones.

Ormolu
English term to describe decorative objects and furniture mounts of cast or gilt metal, usually bronze or brass.

Ovolo mouldings

Convex moulding that is quarter circle in section. Sometimes used with egg-and-dart enrichment.

Oyster veneer
Surface decoration composed of veneers cut from small branches. The resultant moulded pattern resembles an oyster shell.

Palmette
Classical ornament popular in 18th century, composed of stylised palm leaf, also resembling a spread fan.

Pap boat
Also called pap dish and commonly made in silver from early 18th century onwards. Used for feeding babies, it had a small, shallow, oval bowl with a tapering lip or spout at one end.

Paraison
Lump of inflated but unformed molten glass on end of a blowing iron.

Parcel-gilt
Part or partially gilt.

Parian ware
Type of unglazed porcelain developed by Copeland about 1845 resembling fine white statuary marble.

Parquetry
Form of veneer, composed of geometric patterns.

Patchmarks
Unglazed marks left on underside of ceramic objects caused by clay pads used to support pieces during firing. Commonly found on 18th century Derby figures.

Patera

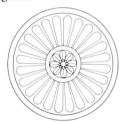

Classical ornament much used in late 18th century composed of round or oval decoration.

Pâte sur pâte
Slow and costly method of decorating parian ware by the careful application of a design in white slip. Each layer was painted on individually, carved and fired.

Pier wall
Section of wall between two windows.

Pinchbeck
Metal alloy consisting of copper and zinc invented by Christopher Pinchbeck in early 18th century. Much used for making small trinkets, snuff boxes, jewellery and watch cases in 18th century, it was often gilded.

Plate
Generic term applied to wrought silver or gold and later applied to imitative wares such as Sheffield plate, nickel plate, and electroplate.

Pontil or **ponty mark**
Rough scar left on glass objects where the pontil rod was broken away.

Pontil rod
Iron rod used to hold glass object for finishing manufacture after removal from the blowing iron.

Pouncing
Method of decorating metal surfaces, such as silver, to obtain a powdered or dimpled effect.

Prunt

Applied blob of tooled or moulded glass used mainly to decorate the bowls and stems of glass drinking vessels. It often resembled a strawberry in shape.

Quaich
Shallow, circular, two-handled, Scottish drinking bowl of medieval origin. Commonly made in silver from 17th century onwards.

Quartetto tables
Term used by Sheraton in early 19th century to describe nest of four tables.

Queensware
Fine creamy-white coloured earthenware covered with transparent lead glaze. It was developed by Josiah Wedgwood in second half of the 18th century. Queen Charlotte patronised this type of ware and allowed it to be called Queensware. Also known simply as creamware.

Rails
Furniture term used to describe horizontal members.

Reeding
Opposite to fluting. Type of pattern consisting of convex moulding resembling a series of reeds.

Registry mark
Appeared on English decorative wares, such as ceramics, in two cycles from 1842 to 67 and from 1868 to 83. Consisted of a lozenge showing a series of numbers and letters assigned by the Registration of Design Office, indicating classification and date of manufacture.

Relief decoration
Ornament that is raised above the surface of the surrounding ground. Can be high relief, when decoration stands out boldly, or low relief (sometimes called bas relief) when decoration stands out only slightly.

Repoussé
French term for embossing. Technique used to raise a design in relief in metalwork from behind.

Rose-engine-turning
Engine lathe-turned patterns on pottery and porcelain, resembling basketwork weave patterns.

Rummer
Drinking glass popular in late 18th and early 19th century derived from a German romer. Early example are characterised by a short-stemmed glass with capacious, thinly-blown bowl and small foot. Later examples have heavier, straight sides and often stand on square feet.

Sabre leg

Shape based on heavy, curved, single-edged sword. Much used in early 19th-century furniture.

Salt-glazed stoneware
Stoneware in which the glaze is formed by throwing salt into the kiln at about 1300°C. The salt decomposes and forms a thin coating of glaze, often causing a slightly pitted surface. Made in England from the 18th century, especially by Staffordshire potters.

Scagliola
Composition of marble chips, glue and plaster used to imitate marble.

Serpentine
Undulating form consisting of a convex shape flanked by concave curves.

Sgraffito
Technique of decorating pottery by incising or scratching through a coating of slip to show the colour of the body underneath.

Shell
Ornamental motif resembling a scallop shell, much used during first three quarters of the 18th century.

Silesian stem
Type of moulded stem popular in England from the early 18th century to about 1750. Composed of high-shouldered, faceted, tapering, sometimes ribbed stem (early examples were 4-sided, later 6 or 8), commonly found on drinking vessels but later also used on sweetmeat dishes and candlesticks.

Slip
Creamy mixture of clay and water used for decorating pottery, either by dipping the object into it and covering it all over or by applying it in lines and dots.

Soda glass
Early type of glass made with soda, improved in 19th century and still made today, particularly in Venice. Superceded in England at end of the 17th century by the development of lead glass.

Splat
Vertical section between the uprights of a chair back, either solid or pierced.

Spur marks
Small, unglazed mark left by the support, or spur, on which ceramic ware rests during firing.

Stoppers
Used mainly in decanters from the 17th century onwards. They take various shapes such as bull's-eye, mushroom and spire.

Stringing
Inlay of thin lines of wood – occasionally other materials such as bone, ivory or metal – usually in furniture.

Tear
Single air bubble trapped in glass and tear-shaped. Found in the stems of wine glasses, in the base of bowls or in knops.

Tester
Canopy, commonly found above bedsteads.

Tine
Prong of a fork.

Tin glaze
Opaque white glaze made with the addition of tin oxide and applied to earthenware. It unfortunaty chips easily. Variously described as Maiolica (Italy), Faience (France), Delft (Holland) and delftware (England), when decorated with enamel colours. Superceded in popularity in England by creamware in the middle of the 18th century.

Top-rail
Highest member of a chair back.

Trefoil
Triple-lobed ornament resembling a leaf.

Trifid

Motif found in late 17th- and early 18th-century silver and furniture, consisting of a lobed outline split by two deep notches, and resembling a cleft hoof. Sometimes called *pied de biche*.

Underglaze decoration
Printed or painted decoration applied to ceramics before the application of the glaze. The colours are permanent.

Uprights
The outer members of a chair back running vertically from the seat rail to the top rail.

Veneer
Very thin sheet of wood, often of a figured or exotic kind, glued to the carcase of furniture for decorative effect. Introduced into England in second half of 17th century. Early examples were hand cut, now most are machine cut.

Vitruvian scrolling
Also called wave pattern. Classical border decoration composed of a band of convoluted scrolls.

Volute
Deep spiral scroll, often associated with architectural decoration. The Ionic capital is composed of two volutes in profile, placed back to back.

Wine funnel
Silver object used for decanting wine. The tapering funnel has a detachable strainer.

Wine glass cooler
Straight-sided bowl with one or two lips in the rim. It resembles a finger bowl but is used for cooling glasses.

Wrigglework
Type of zigzag engraved decoration used on silver and pewter and popular in the late 17th century.

Wrythening
Swirled or diagonally-twisted ribbing or fluting used to decorate bowls and stems of glass objects.

Yoke
Term used for the top rail of a chair which extends beyond the uprights, thus resembling a yoke for carrying pails. Common in the early 19th century.

Index